THE WORLD AND THE INDIVIDUAL

THE WORLD AND THE INDIVIDUAL

JOSIAH ROYCE

Second Series

Nature, Man, and the Moral Order

DOVER PUBLICATIONS, INC.

NEW YORK

Published simultaneously in Canada by McClelland & Stewart, Ltd.

This new Dover edition of *The World and the Individual, Second Series,* first published in 1959, is an unabridged and unaltered republication of the First Edition.

Library of Congress Catalog Card Number: 59-14226

Manufactured in the United States of America

Dover Publications, Inc.
180 Varick Street
New York 14, N. Y.

PREFACE

The discussions upon which the present volume is based formed the second and concluding series of my Gifford Lectures on "The World and the Individual." They were delivered before the University of Aberdeen in January, 1900. The delay in publishing them is largely due to the revision to which I have subjected the original manuscript. This revision amounts, in a portion of the lectures, to a rewriting, and has also come to include statements and arguments that I had not previously put into shape at all. These additions have caused me, in some cases, more trouble than I had anticipated, and more, as I hope, than the text will directly make manifest to the reader.

The general need for such changes did not spring, I am sure, from any lack of effort on my part to adapt the lectures, actually read at Aberdeen, to their announced purpose. The variety and the complexity of the topics of the present volume require the printed book to contain much that could not have been adequately stated in any oral discussion; while these same characters of my subject-matter led, at some points, to a diffuseness in the original lectures which I found it possible to abbreviate in preparing the volume for publication. In the public lecture-room the hearer has no time to meditate, and the speaker too little opportunity to be either concise or exhaustive. While some of the same general grounds for a change from the originally prepared text existed in case of the revision of my former series of these lectures, they proved to be less effective than here, since, in that series, the single problem of the Conception of Being dominated the entire discussion, while here the relations of the Theory of Being to various problems of empirical research, and to the demands of our ethical consciousness, have complicated the undertaking.

The scope of this closing volume includes a sketch of an idealistic Theory of Human Knowledge, an outline of a Philosophy of Nature, a doctrine about the Self, a discussion of the origin and destiny of the Human Individual, a summary consideration of the world as a Moral Order, a study of the Problem of Evil, and, finally, an estimate of all these views in the light of what seem to me to be the interests of Natural Religion. This is a large and manifold programme. It was required of me by my interpretation of my task as Gifford lecturer. I well know how inadequate the consideration of each topic has necessarily proved to be.

As to the first of these topics, — the idealistic Theory of Knowledge, — what I here have to say is founded upon studies which I began as a student at the Johns Hopkins University in 1876–1878. The first formulation of these studies I made in my thesis for the Doctorate at that University. A further stage of my inquiry was published in 1881, in a paper on Kant's *Relation to Modern Philosophical Progress*, printed in the *Journal of Speculative Philosophy* of that year. The interpretation of our knowledge of finite facts as largely due to an active "acknowledgment," whose significance is ethical, rather than to a mere passive acceptance of "given" contents of present experience, was insisted upon in the concluding section of that paper. When, in preparing my *Religious Aspect of Philosophy* (published in 1885), I had definitely passed over from my earlier sceptical position to the constructive Idealism that I have ever since endeavored to work out, I attempted at once to take up this former view of our finite knowledge into what was then, in my own personal growth, a new doctrine as to the nature of the Absolute. In 1892, in my *Spirit of Modern Philosophy*, I essayed a still further development of this theory regarding human knowledge, in the lecture entitled *The World of Description and the World of Appreciation.* Since then, in the paper called *Self-consciousness, Social Consciousness, and Nature*, published as one of my *Studies of Good and Evil* (1898), as well as in other essays, I have attempted to apply the same essential view to the explanation of the bases and characteristics of our human knowledge of the physical world. In recent years I have been much interested in comparing my views about this matter with those of my colleague and friend, Professor Münsterberg, who has independently reached a somewhat similar doctrine regarding the twofold nature and basis of what he also consents to call our "descriptive" and our "appreciative" knowledge. This topic, as well as the ethically significant character of our "acknowledgment" of facts, has been discussed summarily in Professor Münsterberg's book, entitled *Psychology and Life*, and, more exhaustively, in his important *Grundzüge der Psychologie* (Vol. I, 1900). In giving final form to my present statement, I have undoubtedly felt the influence both of these expressed opinions of Professor Münsterberg, and of the admirable monograph by Professor Rickert entitled *Der Gegenstand der Erkenntniss*, — a work to which Professor Münsterberg first called my attention, shortly after its publication in 1892.

In my own former accounts, so far as they bore upon this doctrine, the contrast between these two types of human knowledge, the "descriptive" and the "appreciative," has been made to depend solely upon the difference between the "social" and the "individual" points of view. I still defend, and, in the fourth lecture of this volume I expound afresh, the thesis that the contrast between our "descriptive" knowledge of the *physical world* and our "appreciative" knowledge of the facts of finite life, is determined precisely by this difference between our social consciousness of what is "valid for all individuals" and our personal consciousness of what is valid for the Self. But it is true that one must still seek *within* the consciousness of the individual Self for the motives that make it logically possible for this Self to regard the abstraction called "a view valid for all individuals" as a possible abstraction. We must show how the Self can make such a view the object of its own contemplation in any sense whatever. For the human Self, although (as I have shown in the course of these lectures) it comes to be aware of itself in terms of its social contrast with other Selves, still (in so far as it has become self-conscious at all) acknowledges its objects as valid, in the first place, from *its own* point of view, and not from the point of view of another Self. How comes it, then, to interpret its world of facts as such that *another* Self could find *these same facts*, or some aspect of them, to be also its own facts? The power to make this abstraction, however much social intercourse is needed to give it definition, must have its logical roots in the consciousness of the Individual. Accordingly, in the second lecture, I have here presented a theory of how far the general contrast between the World of Description and the World of Appreciation can be logically (not psychologically) defined, apart from explicitly social experiences, on the basis of a certain contrast that arises between two aspects of the inner personal consciousness of any intelligent individual whose relations to the world are such as are our human relations. This logical deduction of the primal contrast between the "descriptive" and the "appreciative" points of view does not set aside my still emphasized doctrine that both the psychological development and the *concrete* logical application of the categories of the World of Description are possible *only under essentially social conditions.* For, as I point out on p. 96, *sqq.*, of the text, the World of Description is essentially a world of abstractions, valid for the Self only in so far as it conceives itself as at present unable to find *how* the facts express its own conscious purpose, and, consequently, valid for the Self only in so far as the Self, in its submissiveness, conceives these facts as also valid for an indefinite number of *other* points of view, which it has not yet made its own. Thus, *within* the individual consciousness, I point out one of the roots from which the more abstract interpretation of the world that is "valid for all" the members of a society grows. My present account of the logical basis of the "descriptive" view of things is therefore a supplement to my former discussions. This present account contains, moreover, a good many elements which are to me, as I think that they will be to others, decidedly new, so that the resulting view of the theory of our finite knowledge is at any rate not the conventional one. The views here expressed, so far as they are new, have been, in my own mind, the outcome of an effort to study some of the recent literature of the Logic of Mathematics, — a region in which the Supplementary Essay of the former volume of these lectures sought for light. The second lecture of the present volume carries still further the train of thought of which that Supplementary Essay was a part. Whatever my success or failure, I am convinced that such study of the Logic of Mathematics is a region where the philosophical student of to-day ought to work. I call special attention here to the doctrine of the two forms of Serial Order, and to their respective relations to the "descriptive" and "appreciative" points of view.

The Theory of Time and Eternity which follows, in my third lecture, was briefly outlined in one passage of the former volume, but is here developed at length. It is of central importance for all the problems of the later lectures.

The cosmological discussions which follow, in the fourth and fifth lectures, constitute a deliberate effort to mediate between Idealism and our human experience of Nature. I have tried to show that an idealist is not obliged either to ignore or to make light of physical facts in order to maintain his theory of the Absolute. That the latter theory is, in the only reasonable sense, itself an empirical doctrine, I have set forth in the former series of these lectures. Here I attempt to point out what links connect our general idealistic interpretation of *all* experience with our special interpretation of our experience of Nature. Hypotheses are, in such an undertaking, unavoidable. I pretend only to provisional views regarding all the details of the discussion. But that one has a right to such hypotheses, at the present stage of our knowledge, I have tried to make plain so far as my space has permitted.

In these first five lectures of the present series, I have come nearest to the ground which was covered by the much more thorough and closely reasoned lectures of my predecessor in the Gifford Lectureship at Aberdeen, Dr. James Ward. I had intended to find room in the text for some discussion of the volumes entitled *Naturalism and Agnosticism*, in which these lectures appeared. But discovering that I could not adequately deal with Dr. Ward's volumes under the present conditions, I have preferred to leave until a future opportunity a treatment of the relations between his views and mine. Apart from such usually minor differences of opinion as exist between us, I feel that the two lines of argument are complementary to each other. Dr. Ward has approached the problem of our knowledge of Nature from the side of a criticism of special doctrines that have been held, and of special problems of science. I have made the topic one to which my previously stated general theory of Being is to be applied. At certain points, as I have been rejoiced to find, we have independently reached the same special statements both of our questions and of our solutions, although by very different roads. Dr. Ward's account, in his second volume, of the unity of the universal and the individual experience, his treatment of the dualism which has come to make the two seem divided, his consequent criticism of the mechanical conception of Nature, — all these are matters with which I find myself in close agreement. I shall be glad indeed if my own much more superficial discussion of this portion of my task can be of any service to the readers of his work.

From Nature these lectures pass to the Human Self. Characteristic of this part of the argument, and of previous statements of my own upon the same topic, are: my entire willingness to lay aside all assertion of the existence of a substantial Soul; my unreserved acceptance of the empirical evidence regarding the dependence of the Human Self, for its temporal origin, for its development, and for its preservation in its present form of life, upon physical and social conditions; and my insistence that various Selves can possess, in the whole or in a part of their lives, identically the *same* experiences, so that one Self can originate, or can develope *within* another Self, and so that the lives of various Selves can be interwoven in the most complex ways. The known empirical facts of "multiple personality" possess nothing surprising for such a doctrine. The individual Human Self appears, in my account, as a part of the Selfhood of the race. Social intercommunication amongst Selves is explained as a phenomenal indication that they share in a common larger Selfhood. The phenomenal dependence of Mind upon Matter is interpreted as another sort of evidence whereby our personal participation in the various forms and stages of Selfhood that are present in Nature is indicated. No facts upon which Materialism has ever based its arguments need be either overlooked or belittled by such a view. Death, for my theory, no longer appears as a "sundering of soul and body." Dualism in the interpretation of the relations of the Self and its environment is wholly laid aside. And yet, as I undertake to show, no spiritual possession of the true Self is endangered, no aspect of its ethical dignity is belittled, no sense in which it is near to God is called in question by this very doctrine of the temporal origin, and of the social, physical, and divine relations of the Self. The reconciliation of our natural knowledge about the Self with our Idealism and with our fundamental religious interests, is indicated, in these discussions, in a fashion that I believe to be, to a considerable extent, new. If my views have any coherence, the importance of the subject ought to insure for them a serious hearing. They are, again, not the conventional views about the Human Self.

As to the problem of Immortality, it is one that I long deliberately declined, as a student of philosophy, to discuss in any formal way, because, for years after I published, in my *Religious Aspect of Philosophy*, my first statement of that general idealistic view of Being which I have ever since maintained, I was not clear as to *how* the general doctrine ought to apply to the case of the finite Individual. The problem of Individuality, as I have since more clearly seen, and, in the first series of these lectures, have explained at length, is the most central and important one in the idealistic Theory of Being.

I felt this fact, although with less clearness, from the first. I was of course sure, from the time of the first statement of my doctrine, that I attributed conscious individuality to the Absolute; and I plainly insisted, in my *Religious Aspect of Philosophy*, that, in the Absolute, all finite individual lives, wills, meanings are consciously recognized, fulfilled, and justly expressed, precisely as they deserve to be. But I was not clear as to what consequences were involved in this thesis when one applied it to the question as to the continued existence of *this man*, as he at present conceives himself. Now a philosophical student waits for light; and does not teach a doctrine until he finds light about that doctrine; and is careless what *other* people think of the practical value of his teachings, so long as he is conscious that he is sincerely looking for truth. I can at all events say that my own little contribution to the doctrine of Immortality, such as it is, has been no product either of a feverish desire for the endurance of my private consciousness, or of a similar longing regarding any friend of mine, or of any wish to conform to the traditional lore upon the subject. In my discussion with Professor Howison (published in the book called *The Conception of God*), in my more recent Ingersoll Lecture on *The Conception of Immortality* (published at Boston in 1900), and, finally, in the present volume, I have simply reported the results to which meditation on the nature of the Ethical Self and on the place of Individuality in the Theory of Being have led me. To make clearer my personal equation, I may add that, since childhood, I have never had any faith about the problem of Immortality except in so far as I have seemed to myself to see philosophical reasons for such faith, and that I regard the whole issue as one for reason, in precisely the sense in which the properties of prime numbers and the kinetic theory of gases are matters for exact investigation. That all our beliefs about truth of any grade and that all theories have a practical meaning, I do indeed explicitly teach. That, in fact, as my reader will see, is my whole philosophy. But the process of coming to consciousness as to what we can rationally desire, mean, and believe, as the fulfilment of our highest purposes, is a process in which private desires must be subordinated. We must obey in order to triumph. And such obedience, for the student of philosophy, takes the form of a cool reflection and a patient wandering in the wilderness of ignorance until he sees the road home. That has been my own method in dealing with the problem of Immortality.

My treatment of the Problem of Evil, in the eighth and ninth lectures of the present volume, is inevitably, in the main, a restatement of what I have elsewhere repeatedly discussed. Yet I have tried to bring to light several new aspects of this issue, in particular its relation to the theory of the Temporal and the Eternal. The doctrine of Freedom and of the Moral Order, as presented in my later lectures, touches upon several matters that I have not before formally discussed. The discussion of the Union of God and Man, in the closing lecture, will also, as I hope, appeal to some theologically minded fellow-students as containing some relatively novel suggestions.

In sum, these lectures have tried to be not a perfunctory defence of the faith, and not a mere repetition of the common tradition of modern Idealism, but the expression of an individual experience of the problems at issue. I do not want to make mere disciples; but I hope that I have helped some fellow-students toward a clearer knowledge of God and of themselves. Such knowledge, however, they can never get by merely accepting my views. They must use their own labor.

My further acknowledgments are still due to many helpers. First, I must here remember my own pupils, whose criticisms have frequently aided me,—in particular, my friend, Dr. Richard Cabot, who for years has stood by me with counsel, encouragement, and criticism, even while, from time to time, he has found room, amidst the duties of his own medical profession, for some continuance of his philosophical studies in connection with my Seminary at Harvard; and Mr. Reginald Robbins, who, while also an occasional member of my Seminary, has written several closely reasoned criticisms of my work, by which I have profited more than he knows. My indebtedness to the influence of Mr. Charles Peirce continues in the present volume, remote as my views often are from his. And in closing the task that for two years gave me an official relation to the University of Aberdeen, I must especially acknowledge my indebtedness to my colleagues there, and to colleagues in the other Scottish Universities with whom I came in contact during my two visits. In particular, Professors W. R. Sorley (now of Cambridge, England) and W. L. Davidson, not only brightened my stay by their kindness, but aided me, by their counsel, in adapting especially this second course of lectures to its academic purpose. To the Senatus of the University of Aberdeen I offer, as my last word, not only my thanks for the opportunity which that body gave me to put into this form my philosophical studies, and for the kind hospitality shown to me personally, but my cordial recognition of the interest thus expressed in closer relations between Scottish and American University life and work. May we learn still further the arts of coöperation with our brethren.

CAMBRIDGE, MASSACHUSETTS,
September 29, 1901.

CONTENTS

LECTURE IX

LECTURE X

LECTURE I

THE WORLD AND THE INDIVIDUAL

SECOND SERIES: *NATURE, MAN, AND THE MORAL ORDER*

LECTURE I

INTRODUCTION: THE RECOGNITION OF FACTS

WITH no question is the student of Philosophy more familiar than with the inquiry: Of what bearing upon life are the studies in which you are engaged? This challenge, when uttered by one not engaged in the study of philosophy, comes home with especial force to the investigator of the fundamental problems of metaphysics. For such problems are, upon their face, of the most universal character. It would seem as if their significance for the whole business of every man ought to be immediately obvious, unless indeed the philosopher who expounds them has failed in his task. What concerns any man more than his place in the world, and the meaning of the world in which he is to find this place?

But when the layman listens to the actual teachings of students of philosophy, as they discourse concerning knowledge and being, concerning truth and duty, and when, after listening, such a layman then asks afresh, "What is it that I have learned about *my* life, and *my* duty, and *my* world of daily business?" — the answer of many a listener is too well known: "I have learned," such an one will often say, "not at all what I hoped to learn. I have learned that problems are intricate, and that truth is far away. I have learned how little the wise men see, and so I am fain to turn back again to life, that I may there find how much the good men do. The philosophers do not help me as they promised. Action is more enlightening than speculation. I will work while it is called the day, but I will not try, like the philosophers, to look with naked eyes upon the sun of truth. Such researches only hinder me."

Both this confession of too many listeners to philosophical discourses, and the resulting question to which I have just referred, are to nobody more familiar, I have said, than to the student of philosophy himself. Nobody, in fact, ought to know better than he does the limitations of mere speculation. Does he not often feel them bitterly himself? Is not the imperfection of what he would like to call his wisdom, brought home to him at every moment when he has his own practical problems to solve? But a confession of weakness is not a cry of despair. Part of the business of life, and no small part of it, is to learn to live with our inevitable defects, and to make the best of them. The inevitable defects of philosophical study are to nobody clearer than to one who, sincerely loving philosophy, devotes his life, as best he can, to seeking clearness of thought and a soul-stirring vision of the truth. The way of reflection is long. The forest of our common human ignorance is dark and tangled. Happy indeed are those who are content to live and to work only in regions where the practical labors of civilization have cleared the land, and where the task of life is to till the fertile fields and to walk in the established ways. The philosopher, in the world of thought, is by destiny forever a frontiersman. To others he must often seem the mere wanderer. He knows best himself how far he wanders, and how often he seems to be discovering only new barrenness in the lonely wilderness.

Yet if such defects are to be freely confessed, and if the philosopher even glories in them, because they are for him a part of the search for truth, the practical good sense of mankind is to be respected when it demands that the solitary labors of the seeker for truth shall in the end be submitted, not only to those theoretical tests which philosophy recognizes as, in its own domain, the only decisive ones, but also to the social and ethical judgment of practical men. The truth of a philosophy is indeed a matter for reason alone; but the justification of the pursuit of philosophy as one of the tasks to which a man's life may honestly be devoted, requires a recognition of the common interests of all men. The frontiersman may wander; but he must some day win what shall belong to the united empire of human truth. Those are wrong who ask him merely to stay at home. He wanders because he must; and God is to be found also in the wildernesses and in the solitary places of thought. But those are right who ask that the student of philosophy shall find, if he succeeds at all, a living truth; and that the God of the wilderness, if indeed he be the true God, shall show himself also as the keeper of the city.

Now, in the former series of these lectures, appealing as a student of philosophy to fellow-students, I undertook what was, from the start, and confessedly, a wandering into the most problematic regions of theory. And in the present course, especially in the earlier lectures, I shall still be busy with highly theoretical issues, and I shall still appeal, above all, to my fellow-students. But we have now won the philosophical right, and have become subject to the practical obligation, not only thus to follow out our theoretical interests, but also to show how the philosophy set forth in our earlier lectures stands related to the more immediate problems of life. I shall devote the present lectures, in the main, to considerations that, however abstract they may seem, are meant to help us towards an interpretation of Man's place in the universe; and I shall be guided by a determination to attempt, before I am done, a definition of man's nature, duty, and destiny. The former lectures emphasized the World; the present course shall be directed towards an understanding of the Human Individual. The previous discussion dealt with the Theory of Being; the aim of what is to come shall be a doctrine about Life. This doctrine will still belong to philosophy; but its outcome shall have to do with the practical interests of Religion.

The order which has so far been followed is, indeed, as I must hold, the only order for a student of philosophy. Therein, if you please, is just where lies the practical defect of philosophy, — viz. in that it can only reach the civilized realm of our daily business by the way of the wilderness of solitary reflection; that it must first, to use Emerson's word, meet God in the bush, so that only later, and painfully, it learns to find him in the mart and the crowded street. I confess the defect. I want to show also some of the excellencies of the very way which this defect has required me to follow. Faith has its glories; but the hard toil of critical reflection brings its own rewards. None prize the home-coming more than those who wander farthest.

I

My first task, in the present lecture, is to indicate in what spirit the Theory of Being, to whose definition and defence the first series of these lectures was devoted, is hereafter to be applied to the treatment of the more special problems of experience and of life. Our Theory of Being had especially this character, namely that it did not undertake to demonstrate *a priori* what particular facts we should meet with anywhere in the world, but that it did undertake to show us a certain method whereby we ought to proceed in attempting to estimate those facts, to interpret them, to find what rank they held in the realm of Being. People come with false expectations to philosophy when they expect it to furnish them any substitute for special science, any peculiar power to anticipate the particular results of experience, any intuitive capacity to see in the finite world facts that other methods of inquiry have not made evident. For the primary purpose of a Theory of Being is not thus to discover what special finite beings are real, but to interpret the sense in which any fact whatever can be real. Its application, therefore, does not come in advance of experience. On the contrary, it is a critical study of the meaning of experience, which it therefore presupposes. And we are now to endeavor to find of what nature such applied Philosophy may be.

For just in such application lies, as we shall come to see, the peculiarly intimate relation between what is deepest in philosophy, and what is truest and most abiding in religion. Some people have expected the philosopher to construct for them, *a priori*, a precise scheme of all things in heaven and in earth. But just so other people have looked to their religious faith to tell them, in advance, their private fortune, to assure them that their days would be long, their flocks prosperous, and their health abounding. And just as too enthusiastic students have thus anticipated from philosophy a certain magical insight regarding the detailed structure of nature and of man, so an unenlightened generation has asked its religious teachers for signs and wonders, and has held that the true faith must manifest itself through special Providences. But the one hope is as little founded in the deeper spirit of reasonableness as is the other; and the demand for a direct sign from heaven is not the abiding expression, either of the religious or of the philosophical consciousness.

Applied philosophy is like practical religion. It illumines life, but it gives no power to use the arts of the medicine man. What religion practically gives to the faithful is not the means for predicting what is about to happen to themselves, but the strength to endure hardness as good soldiers. Religious faith involves no direct access to the special counsels of God; but it inspires the believer with assurance that all things work together for good, and endows him with readiness to serve in his station the God who is All in all. Such religion is not, then, the power to work miracles, but it is the wisdom to find in all things, however obscure, or fragmentary, the expressions, however mysterious, of the Divine Love. The faith of the devout does not forewarn them as to the future, nor does it annul the value of worldly prudence; but it makes them glad to suffer, and willing to wait, and sure that however far off God seems, he actually is near. Now what faith accomplishes in the daily practice of the devout, a Theory of Being must also undertake, in so far as it is successful, to provide for us in our efforts to understand Nature and Man.

What we men call Nature comes to us as a matter of our extremely finite common experience. In dealing with nature, we feel our way; we pass from fact to fact; we collect fragments. When our special sciences succeed in joining these fragments into some sort of empirical unity, the procedure is distinctly human, and the result is always provisional. Now no philosophy can predetermine in this realm, either what special facts shall be observed, or what particular hypotheses as to their connection shall first be attempted, or what provisional theories shall prove best adapted to the purpose of any special science. Philosophy is powerless to act as a substitute for special science, precisely as it is powerless to add to the products of the industrial arts. It is as unable to formulate a thesis in the realms properly belonging to physics or to biology as it is to build a steam engine.

And in the same way, when we deal with Man, — with the concrete issues of his daily life, — with the problems of private passion or of public policy, we have to do, primarily, with human nature as it is, and with all the unconquerable naïveté of our desires, of our imperfections, and even of our virtues. Philosophy does not create men, but reflectively considers their life. And man is as full of mystery as is the rest of nature, and is known to our experience as a mere fragment of a whole whose inmost unity is far beyond the reach of our present form of consciousness. Psychology, viewed as one of the special sciences, studies man; and so also do all the human branches of inquiry, — political science, economics, anthropology. Philosophy cannot predetermine the course and the outcome of any of these sciences. The Theory of Being is not based upon our knowledge of any such special regions of experience, but is due to a thoroughgoing reflection upon the presuppositions of all experience. In its turn the Theory of Being teaches us neither anthropology nor psychology, neither economics nor politics. Into such regions the philosopher, as philosopher, enters like any other layman, to learn the facts if he desires to know them, but not as one endowed with any magic power of divination.

And yet, just as the devout are required by their religious faith to see God's hand in whatever happens, and to view their life as his constant revelation of his will, although they can work no miracles, and cannot tell what a day shall bring forth; just so our philosophy, if indeed our former Theory of Being was sound, has its strength in the general interpretation of the facts, when once they have been found. The Theory of Being requires us to view every fact of nature, and of man's life, as a fragmentary glimpse of the Absolute life, as a revelation, however mysterious and to us men now in detail illegible, of the unity of the perfect Whole. Why we hold this to be a true theory, we have set forth at length in the foregoing series of lectures; and the detailed proof of the general thesis concerns us here no longer. But the spirit in which we are to apply our doctrine to the theory of our knowledge of particular facts, and to the interpretation of such facts, interests us here in much the same way in which practical religion is interested in the spirit that the faithful ought to preserve amidst the cares and sorrows of daily life. What is it to believe, as the faithful do, that God is in all their fortunes? What is it to maintain, as our Theory of Being does, that, amidst all the complexities of Nature and man's life, we are dealing with fragmentary glimpses of an Absolute Unity, of the type depicted in our foregoing series of lectures? The two problems, in many respects, resemble each other. What you already know of the solution of one problem goes far to prepare you for the other.

II

The scope and the proposed order of the present series of lectures may be more precisely indicated as follows: —

I shall begin our inquiry by a preliminary study of some of the conditions that are characteristic of our human type of knowledge. Knowledge, such as we have of particular facts, is only one special case of what we can and do conceive as the range of the possible forms of knowledge. Not only theology and philosophy, but also, as we shall see, the empirical sciences themselves depend upon conceiving of higher types of knowledge, higher "forms of consciousness," than our human type, as at least possible. By contrast with such ideally definable higher types of insight we constantly become aware of our own limitations as human seekers for truth. We shall, accordingly, try to characterize in general terms some of the most marked limitations and powers of man's intellect. As we do so we shall be led to state the first principles of a theory of the Organization of Human Experience. Kant's problem of the Categories, which determine in what way we conceive the objects of human knowledge, and which also, in giving form to our experience, define the unity that we ascribe to Nature and to our own life, is one that we can only touch upon very briefly. But so far as our time permits, we must outline our view as to the essential forms in terms of which we conceive concrete facts and their connections. Upon the basis of the general theory of human knowledge thus broadly sketched, we shall next pass to a study of the questions offered to our scrutiny by Nature, when viewed in its relation to Man. Here our main purpose shall be to apply our general idealistic doctrine, concerning what is meant by Reality in general, to the problem as to the sense in which Nature and Man are real.

In case of Nature we have to deal with a realm whose material seeming, whose unchanging laws, and whose apparent indifference to all individual interests, and to all ethical ideals, constitute a formidable obstacle in the way of every interpretation of Reality in the interest of the religious consciousness. It will be our task to scrutinize the reasons that make Nature wear, to our vision, this forbidding aspect. Hereby we shall be led especially to consider the centrally important place that Man, when viewed as a product of Nature, occupies in our ordinary views about the cosmos. And so the development of our Metaphysics of Nature will enable us, before we are done, to sketch an hypothesis as to the meaning of the processes known to us men, at present, under the now favorite name Evolution. The sense in which Nature is a realm of fixed law will also engage our attention; and in the same connection we shall prepare the way for our theory of the Freedom of the Will. Passing over, after we have studied these problems, to what is properly called the Moral World, we shall, in our closing lectures, apply our general interpretation of Being to a study of the Human Self, of its Place in Being, and of the Moral Order, to a consideration of the problem of Evil, and finally to a statement of what seem to us to be the results of Idealism regarding the final relations of the Absolute and the human Individual, or in ordinary speech, of God and Man. In this connection we shall be led to state briefly our own thesis regarding Immortality. Herewith the task of these lectures will be completed.

III

I pass to the promised general considerations regarding the limitations of our human type of knowledge, and regarding the organization of experience.

All knowledge is of matters of experience, — this principle we ourselves have maintained as part of our Idealism. But what does this proposition mean when applied to the case of human knowledge? *Whose* experience is in question when we speak of truth?

By any man's private experience, taken in the narrowest sense of the words, we mean what a man *now* has present to his consciousness. As I speak, I am conscious that these words are now uttered. This is present experience. You have a corresponding present experience as you listen. One's whole present consciousness of his meaning, *i.e.* of what we before called the Internal Meaning of his ideas, is, in a similarly limited sense, empirical. But the term experience, as customarily employed when our human science is said to be founded upon experience, is used in a much broader sense. The term, as thus applied, refers to a wide range of facts which are said to have been experienced by various men at various times. But, as we had occasion to point out in the Eighth Lecture of our former series,[1] it cannot be asserted that *any* human experience (taking that word in the narrowest sense) ever makes present to any man the fact that various men besides himself have their various experiences present to them. The broader conception of what is called "human experience" is a conception that thus obviously transcends every particular present human experience. The very existence of the body of facts called "man's experience" has never been verified by any man.

Now this perfectly simple observation gets a serious importance so soon as we consider its bearing upon the question: What shall constitute, for an empirical theory of knowledge, the test of an "accredited fact"? When and how is any fact known to be a "fact of human experience"?

[1] See First Series, p. 364, *sq.*

We often say that the results of scientific observation and experiment, or the contents of the world of common sense, as known to men in their daily life, are typical examples of "empirically accredited facts." These, as we add, belong to the "accessible realm." These we cannot deny without "running counter to actual observation." On the other hand, the contents of any religious faith, — assertions about God, about Immortality, or about the "Unseen World" in general, — these are typical examples of what we frequently regard as lying "beyond the range of human experience." These, then, are "inaccessible" matters. What is in such regions fact "nobody amongst men can verify." Equally, of course, a philosopher's assertions about the Absolute, — as, for instance, an idealist's Theory of Being,—are concerned with what "lies beyond all human experience"; and such theories attempt to "transcend the range of verifiable fact." This contrast between the "empirical" and the "metempirical" realm is very familiar. It is apparently a fairly definite contrast. And to be sure, if you first define arbitrarily the limits of the collective whole called "human experience," you may, with equal arbitrariness, define a realm of what is to be called "transcendent" or "inaccessible" fact, lying beyond this whole.

But what now concerns us is not an arbitrary classification of conceived ranges of knowledge, but a closer consideration of a very obvious and natural distinction between the two conceptions: (1) Of that which any man at any time experiences as present; and (2) Of the totality of the several facts that are, or that have been experienced by the various men. The question is:

Does *any* man experience the fact that there *exists* any collective whole to be called the totality of human experience? Does any man experience the fact that any other man has experience? Surely, the astronomer does not observe in his world of presentations the fact that the physician observes the phenomena of disease, or that the carpenter observes the making of houses. But if the carpenter, the physician, and the astronomer believe, as they do, each one, that the others have experience of facts, then each believes in an existence, viz. in the existence of the totality formed of their three orders of experience, although this totality is "inaccessible" to the personal experience of any of them. And still more, when the astronomer or the physician or the carpenter appeals, as a man of science or of common sense, to the "general experience of mankind," or to the experience of any selected company of experts, as the guarantee of the truth of any of his beliefs, each of them appeals to a body of fact which, as such a body of fact, has never been present to the experience of any man at any time.

It is plain, then, that if we say: "That only is to constitute 'accredited fact' which some individual man has verified for himself through its presence in his experience," our doctrine can be interpreted in either one of two ways. The first and in fact the usual way of interpreting the thesis is as follows: "There does exist the body of accredited facts, *a*, *b*, *c*, etc., such that any fact belonging to this body of facts — as, for instance, *a* — has been verified by the experience of some man, let us say by A, while some other man, as B, may have experienced as present to himself the fact *b*, and so on, — some of the various facts having been observed indeed by the same man (as a Galileo or a Faraday observed, each for himself, various physical facts), while different facts, in many cases, have been severally presented in the experience of different men. Now only such facts as belong to this body of 'facts of experience' are to be regarded as duly 'accredited.'" The thesis thus stated, with various added provisos regarding the sorts of experience, or the types of observers whose facts are of enough importance or exactitude to count as sufficiently verified, represents a frequent interpretation of the meaning of the doctrine called empiricism. But it is obvious that, in this formulation, familiar though it be, the thesis simply contradicts itself. For it expressly asserts the *existence* of the various facts, *a*, *b*, *c*, etc., while referring them, in general, to the experience of various observers, A, B, etc., whose existence is also regarded as "accredited." But since A, by hypothesis, has never had present to his experience the experience of B, nor any observer the observations of another observer, it is plain that there is no one man who has personally experienced either the existence of all the several observers, A, B, etc., or the presence of their various facts, *a*, *b*, *c*. Yet these existences and these various facts are, according to the thesis, "accredited facts," in case the thesis itself is to be an accredited truth. And, nevertheless, according to the same thesis, no facts were to be regarded as "accredited" unless some man, A, or B, or some other, had verified them in his experience. The thesis, as stated, consequently asserts the existence of an indefinitely vast range of fact that it also declares to be not "accredited fact." To become consistent our thesis would have to be amended thus: "No fact is 'accredited' unless it belongs to the system above defined, *except*, to be sure, *the fact that* this system, together with its various observers, exists. *That* fact, indeed, is present to no human observer's experience. And yet, although it thus transcends every man's observation and verification, it is an 'accredited' fact." But the thesis, as thus amended, is no longer even a relatively pure empiricism. It is a synthesis of an appeal to human experience with an admission of principles that, whatever they are, or however they are grounded, transcend every man's experience. This is a simple, but a curiously neglected, consideration.

The second form in which the thesis may be held is this: "No fact is 'accredited fact' except in so far as it is verified by the present momentary experience of myself, here and now, to whom it thus becomes accredited fact." So stated, the thesis is indeed remote enough from common sense, since it excludes me from recognizing, not only your experience, but my own experiences of an hour since, or of yesterday, or of last year, as "accredited fact," and so excludes me from regarding as "accredited fact" either the observations of experts, or the experience of mankind in general, or the results of my own observations during the course of my brief life, as far as that life lies beyond the limits (whatever they are) of what I call the present. We are not concerned with examining here all of the metaphysical implications of this form of the thesis now in question. The result of such an analysis, if thoroughgoing, would involve, as we indicated in the passage just cited from the Eighth Lecture of our First Series, the same dialectic process by which we were led through the series of the concepts of Being from Realism to Idealism. For we should have to ask: What form of Being have the facts that are at present so verified by me as to constitute a realm, however apparently insignificant, of "accredited facts"? And the answer to the question would lead us to observe that these facts, in so far as they have true Being at all, are neither wholly independent, nor wholly immediate, nor merely valid, but are what they are by virtue of their place in a self-determined system of facts, whose totality is simply our idealistic Absolute.

Meanwhile, however, although it concerns us not here to go again over the ground of our whole metaphysic, it will be of service to us to recall so much thereof as to let us see that the thesis, in this second form, is, as it stands, quite as self-contradictory as it was in its first form, unless, indeed, it means to assert that at the present instant I can verify an infinity of facts.

A moment's reflection serves to show me, for the first, that I do not clearly know what constitutes the whole, the totality of fact, that I can and do just now verify in my present experience. Nor can I clearly distinguish between what is now verifiable and what is not now verifiable. I may say that I verify the fact of my present speaking of these words, so that thus much, at least, is, in the sense of my thesis, "accredited fact." But what is it to *speak these words?* What is it that I verify in observing my own speech? Nothing is harder than to say how, at any one instant, taken, so far as possible, by itself, my words are present as facts in my own consciousness. Nor can I easily verify how far I just then realize what I mean by them, or how far their sound, their connection, or the act of uttering them is emphasized or obscured in consciousness by my concern that you should hear me, or by my chance consciousness of how the light of yonder window falls upon this paper, or by my muscular sensations as I turn the leaves of my manuscript. Ask me, then, to tell *what* is now present to my consciousness, and the notorious difficulty of every introspective problem reminds me that by what now *is* actually present to my consciousness, I mean much more than I can be said, in every sense, now consciously to verify. Even my verification itself occurs in degrees. I may verify without being clearly conscious that or what I verify.

And thus the present moment has about it all the mystery that everywhere clouds finite facts. I am conscious just now, but I am not wholly conscious of my consciousness. If I were, I should be capable of verifying an infinity of facts; for, as the Supplementary Essay, published with the former series of these lectures, has shown at length, to be self-conscious, in any complete sense, would be to be aware of the completion of an infinite series of presented facts. But if, as is true, I am not completely self-conscious, then I never completely verify *what* it is that I am just now verifying.

"But," you may insist, "surely I can now verify *some* present fact of experience, the sound of *this* word, the presence of *this* feeling of discomfort, or of this intellectual inquiry." Yes, I answer, — the present moment may answer, and does answer up to a certain point, although never completely, certain specific questions that have been submitted to it, by my former processes of inquiry, for its definite verification. If I have asked a specific question: "Does some word now sound?" "Is this definite hypothesis now verified?" — then a present, although always a fragmentary and unsatisfactory answer, may be possible. But my consciousness, even now, has its background as well as its foreground, its obscurity as well as its clearness, its presented questions as to its own constitution as well as its presented answers to definite questions. And nobody amongst us human beings, as now we are, can verify precisely the whole of what it is that the present moment furnishes to his experience. In other words, the present experience itself, or even the verification of the facts of this present experience, has more Being than I am able now to observe. It *is* more than it at present shows; it *means* infinitely more than it brings to the light of passing human consciousness. Just this aspect of the present moment was the one that we emphasized when we defined our Fourth Conception, and our relation to the "Other" which a finite consciousness always seeks as its own fulfilment.

Whatever, then, it is that I now verify, and whatever sense or degree of verification I count as sufficient, still, the very fact known to me through verification may be also known, through an indirect demonstration, to contain more Being than I verify. Thus let us suppose again that I verify the fact of my present utterance of words. If I do so, then *the fact that I verify* my utterance of words is as much a fact as is the fact verified, viz. the utterance itself. For the *whole* fact defined is, by hypothesis, the fact of my verification of my utterance of words. But to be conscious of my consciousness involves something more than merely to be conscious without such self-consciousness. In general, unless a philosophical argument calls my attention to the matter, I shall verify the fact of my utterance of the words without verifying, *i.e.* without consciously observing the first verification itself. That is, I shall verify without being aware that I do so. Now not only is this the case, but to deny that our verifications, whatever they are, always are facts that in their turn contain more Being than we at present verify, would be to assert that at present we consciously verify an infinity of facts. For to verify the fact that we make verifications, and to verify again this verification, and so on, all at the present moment, would indeed involve a present and completed infinite complexity of consciousness. Whoever asserts the thesis, however, that no fact is "accredited" from my point of view unless I now verify it, asserts a fact, viz. the fact of my verification of facts, while not meaning to attribute to me the infinite present knowledge that would be implied in declaring that my verification itself is reflectively and exhaustively verified.

Moreover, whoever asserts this same thesis defines as real the fact that "I" experience. "I," then, am a fact. But at this moment, unless I have completely solved the problem of self-consciousness, I am in some respects, yes, obviously in nearly all respects, ignorant of who I really am, or of what the true nature of the Ego is. What deeper human mystery is there than the Ego? On the other hand, if I have completely solved the problem of self-consciousness, and if I am aware at this instant of the solution, so as to verify all that, as a fact, I am, then, for the same reason as the one before cited, I have present to myself an infinity of contents of consciousness. The maintainer of our thesis does not intend to assert that the Ego of this instant, of whom he speaks, does at present consciously verify this infinity of facts. It is clear to me just now that I do not do so. But the only alternative for the defender of our thesis is the assertion of a fact, viz. the Ego, — a fact whose Being is not wholly verified at present, although it is indirectly known as a fact, and as a fact possessed of this verified wealth of reality. And thus the thesis is indeed reduced to a self-contradiction. For the result is that there are "accredited facts," implied in the very acceptance of the thesis, which are still not facts now verified by me.

IV

It is quite impossible, then, to assert that there are no "accredited facts" in the world, as known to us men, except those which have been verified, or which are verified in the experience of some individual man, or in the several experiences of various men. Human experience is logically and inseparably bound up with elements which remain for us men, in our present form of consciousness, metempirical. The assertion that we know the world only in so far as individual human experience has verified the facts of the world cannot be consistently stated, and is never consistently applied, even by the most ardent and most sceptical empiricists. While then philosophy is unable to predict *a priori* the special contents of human experience, it is forced to insist that by the term "human experience" we always mean more than the facts that are verified by individual men.

It remains perfectly true, of course, that the empiristic thesis which has just been examined is not without its deep significance, and that what empiricism has intended to emphasize is, when its statement has been properly modified, a truth, and one of the first importance. In the former series of lectures,[1] we had occasion, when discussing the Third Conception of Being, to point out the sense in which, even in pure mathematics, "experience is the only guide to concrete results." As we there indicated, all our transcending of experience is in a perfectly definite sense based upon our experience. When we reason about the unseen, as, for instance, about the "infinite assemblages" of recent mathematical theory, or about our idealistic Absolute, still, in all our investigations, "actual experience guides," "presented facts sustain" us, just as, in the passage cited, we set forth. Yet there is no inconsistency between observing this truth, and still rejecting the thesis of the empiricist in the form in which it has often been stated. Our whole argument in our transition to the Fourth Conception of Being illustrated how it is of the very nature of our human experience of our Internal Meaning to point *beyond* what is presented, for the sake of defining the very fulfilment which our presented meanings demand, and without which they have neither truth nor Being. It is true that every exact and demonstrative

[1] See p. 253 of that series.

proposition which does transcend the presented and verified data of our experience is capable, for us men, only of an indirect demonstration, such as we in fact gave for our conception of the Absolute in the Eighth Lecture of the foregoing course, and such as we have just given for our assertion that every human experience is inseparably bound up with elements which remain, for us men, metempirical. Yet an indirect demonstration involves precisely an appeal to present experience (namely to the present experience of an incongruity in the form in which given ideas now present themselves to us), for our warrant and guide in an undertaking whereby we transcend present experience. *In fact, then, our presented experience is indeed our only guide; but it always guides us by pointing beyond itself to that without which it becomes self-contradictory. We know of no metempirical truth except by means of presentations. But our presentations, in our present form of consciousness, get their whole sense from their reference to what, for us, remains metempirical truth. No fact gets "accredited" unless our experience gives it credit. But experience, when rationally interpreted, in the light of our indirect demonstrations, never gives credit to any facts except to those which, in some aspect, transcend our presentations.*

The most manifest lesson of memory, of our social consciousness, and of our reasonings about mathematical and physical truth, is that, for us men, the office of what is given to us, as presented fact, is to point beyond itself to what is not presented. Common sense generally makes this transition too easily, on grounds of mere habit, of prejudice, or of traditional faith. Philosophy has to criticise the grounds of the transition, and does so, hoping to learn to distinguish prejudice from rational insight, and well-grounded assurance from uncertainty. But while we live in presentations, and think in terms of them, we all constantly use them, whether rationally or irrationally, only to transcend them. What is given is indeed our guide; but what is not now given, namely, the whole true Being of things, is our goal.

In still another respect, as we also saw in our former course, the assertion of empiricism conveys a deep truth in an inadequate expression. The term "metempirical," which we have just used, is only a relative term. We have here employed it with express reference to the transcending of the narrow limits of human experience. But of course such transcending, so far as we get our indirectly demonstrable right to the assertion that facts lie beyond these narrow limits, is not a transcending of *all* experience. What lies beyond *our* presentations is still, in so far as it has true Being, presentation. For the world of fact exists in so far as it is presented in unity to the Absolute Experience. That we have asserted throughout. In so far as a consistent empiricism is opposed to Realism, our own argument has fully accepted the theses involved in such opposition. Every question about Being is also a question about the organization of experience, that is, about the organization of the true, the final experience, of which our own is always a fragment.

V

The characteristic *limitation* of human experience is, then, that it grasps, within the narrow limits of *this* or of *this* instant, fragments of a meaning which can only be conceived with consistency by regarding it as embodied in an experience of wider scope, of determinate constitution, and of united significance. That this is true, our general Theory of Being undertook to show. How in the concrete it takes place, in what special ways our consciousness is at once transcended, and included in a wider experience, it is the purpose of our whole present series of discussions to make clearer; and not until the end of the undertaking can one judge the degree of our success.

We proceed next to the characterization of certain more special principles that consciously determine us, at any moment, to acknowledge as real one rather than another fact or system of concrete facts, such as the existence of our fellows, or of Nature, or our own past lives. Herewith we enter upon the promised study of some of the fundamental Categories of human experience. We care not to write out or to defend any table of such Categories. We make no attempt to be exhaustive or systematic. But some specification of our general theory, in such wise as to show its application to our special type of human knowledge, is indeed a necessary preliminary to our study of Nature and of Man.

As in our general discussion of Being, so here, we must take our starting-point from the fact that our knowledge always involves deeds. In so far as I now consciously mean anything, I am acting. But, as I find, I am acting at present under a *twofold* limitation. I neither know the whole of *what it is that I mean to do;* nor do I know more than the most insignificant fragment of *the facts that express my will.* In consequence, the problem of philosophy, as of life, is twofold: (1) A practical problem, viz. the problem, What am I seeking? What is the Self whose purpose is mine, and whose life is the world? — and (2) A theoretical problem, viz. How is this purpose expressed in the facts? Now our discussion will throughout undertake, so far as that is possible, to treat these two problems in close connection. But they will tend, at various points, to fall apart in the argument. In the present lecture, in dealing with the most fundamental Category of Experience, we shall indeed be able to show very explicitly that our acknowledgment of facts as real is determined by definite, and philosophically justified, practical motives. But when we pass on, in the next lecture, to more special categories, we shall be led to make a provisional sundering of the two points of view, viz. (1) that of our *appreciative* or more explicitly volitional consciousness, and (2) that of our *descriptive* or more theoretical, consciousness. We shall know indeed that the sundering is provisional; but under our human limitations, it will prove, in its own place, inevitable. It will be by means of a further definition of just these contrasted points of view that we shall be able to explain the relation between our belief in the physical world, and our belief in the minds of our fellow-men. We shall express the opposition of the two points of view by calling the realm of Being as our more abstractly theoretical consciousness defines it, the World of Description; while the world as otherwise interpreted is the world of Life, — the World of Appreciation.[1] We shall show that, while the two points of view are contrasted, they arise in our minds in close connection with each other. The only justification for the more abstractly theoretical conception of the World of Description is its value as a means of organizing our conduct, and our conception of what the will seeks. On the other hand, without such a definite conception as the World of Description furnishes, the finite will is left only to vague longings. The two points of view will first be considered (in the next lecture) as they appear in the individual consciousness of any one of us. Then they will be discussed in their social aspects in the lecture on our conceptions of Man and of Nature.

For the moment, however, we begin not with the sundering of the two points of view, but with their unity. When I know, I am acting. My theoretical life is also practical. But, from my own conscious point of view, my acting is also a *re*acting. I am acting in what I often call "the given situation." And the word *given* here means, not only what is strictly the given, that is, not only the situation as now presently verified by myself, but also the whole situation which I acknowledge as real. I am conscious that I can mean something only by presupposing something; that I can seek an end only by acknowledging a starting-point and a goal; that I can create only on the basis of a recognition of what I am

[1] I made use of this terminology for expressing the contrast between the two aspects of Reality in 1892, in my *Spirit of Modern Philosophy*, Lecture XII. The choice of the term Description in that work was determined by the known usage of Kirchhoff, Mach, and others, in defining the purpose of natural science as the exact "description" (as opposed to "explanation") of facts.

not now seeking to create ; — in brief, that the fulfilment of my will through my present search logically depends upon my accepting a foundation on the basis of which I will, and an environment in which I work. Now what I thus presuppose as the hidden ground of my meaning, what I acknowledge either as the starting-point or as the goal of my seeking, what I thus recognize, not as my momentary creation, but as the condition of my activity, — this — the foundation of my present will — constitutes for me that concrete reality in which, at any moment, I believe as my special "world of facts."

A fact, then, is at once that which my present will implies and presupposes, and that which, for this very reason, is in some aspect Other than what I find myself here and now producing, accomplishing, attaining. Because of that aspect of a fact which the word Other very properly emphasizes, we are prone to insist that it is of the essence of facts to be "stubborn," to be "foreign to the will," to be, as facts, "beyond our power," "necessary," "forced upon us." But it is equally important, from our idealistic point of view, to remember that, in so far as I purpose, intend, pursue, or find myself accomplishing, it is of the very essence of my will to demand its own Other, to set its fulfilment beyond its present, and so to define its own very life as now in some sense also not its own, or as in some wise now foreign. Our rational purpose in living as we human beings now do, is essentially and always the wanderer's purpose. We seek our home, our city out of sight, our lost truth. But in the very search itself lies the partial embodiment of what we ourselves will.

It is, then, not *merely* our fate that makes our home far off, or the truth a lost truth. It is we ourselves who demand our object as the Beyond; and we are pilgrims and strangers in a world of seemingly foreign facts, not only because the facts, as such, *are* stubbornly foreign, but also because *we* insist that ours shall be the wanderer's portion. The very attitude of any questioner illustrates this truth. To question is to be active, to express an interest; and so it is to seek, as the relative fulfilment of one present purpose, a state of mind which also involves the dissatisfaction and instability of viewing something as still unknown and foreign. Nor can we here say that it is the compulsion of the foreign facts which is the sole awakener of our questions. Even a child's questions often illustrate the free play of a consciousness that restlessly longs to inquire, and that seems to us deliberately to create its own recognition of mystery, in order that it may have wherewith to concern itself. Still more, however, does the theoretical work of pure science illustrate this nature of the will to inquire. What foreign "compulsion" of facts is solely responsible for the astronomer's inquiries into the classification of stellar spectra, or for the modern theory of algebraic equations? Yet our whole modern conception of Nature and of Man has been the product of just such a free activity of asking questions.

Facts, then, are never *merely* Other, or "stubborn," or "compulsory." My will is never compelled merely by what is foreign to itself. It always coöperates in its own compulsion. The disappointed lover is such, not merely because his mistress rejects him, but because he wills to love her. If he did not so will, she could not reject him, and would lose her "compelling" character altogether. She controls his will by his own connivance. All this we saw in general in our former consideration of the concept of Being. It follows, however, that no account of the categories of experience, which founds our consciousness of facts solely upon our experience of their compulsory or foreign character, can be just to the nature of knowledge. What we experience is, in one aspect, always *our own will to be compelled by facts.*

The most universal character, belonging to all the various types of concrete facts that we recognize, is accordingly a synthesis of their so-called "stubborn" or "foreign" character, with their equally genuine character as expressions of our own purpose. A fact is for me, at any moment, *that which I ought to recognize* as determining or as limiting what I am here consciously to do or to attempt. For a particular fact I recognize, at any moment, only in connection with a particular attempt at action. This is the obverse aspect of what is defined, in Psychology, as the principle that all our cognitive processes accompany "responses to our environment." In explaining, for psychological purposes, the natural history of cognition, one presupposes an environment whose facts already have a recognized form of existence. One supposes also a conscious process as an existent fact, whose development is to be described. The basis of one's description is then the principle that the external facts, which are supposed directly or indirectly to determine the conscious process, arouse responses in the organism of the being whose consciousness is in question; and that the conscious states which constitute cognition accompany these responses of the organism to the environment. But our own theory of the categories of experience cannot thus base itself upon the assumption that the objective world, first existing, produces a series of corresponding responses in an organism, and consequently in the cognitive life which accompanies the processes of this organism. On the contrary, our purpose, in such a theory of the categories of experience, is to point out the principles that lead us, from within, *i.e.* from our own conscious point of view, to make any particular assertions whatever about the objective world. For us, therefore, in this theory, the objective world is not first known as prior to the cognitive responses, but is viewed as it is because the conscious process regards itself as meaning a response to a situation. The world of "accredited facts" is known to us to exist, because we know it to be acknowledged as existing. And it is thus acknowledged *because the purpose of any instant of rational consciousness is fulfilled better by recognizing it as thus and thus existent than by viewing it otherwise.* This assertion is the application of our general Theory of Being to the case of our concrete knowledge of any special fact or range of facts.

I acknowledge a particular fact, then, in connection with a particular attempt at action. My particular action is willed by me under certain limitations. These limitations are given to me, at the moment, in the form of my sense of incompleteness, of dissatisfaction, of imperfect expression of my present will. But they are not merely thus *given* to me as immediate contents of consciousness. They are defined for me by my consciousness that such and such further determination of my present actions would mean a completer expression of my will. The correlative of such completer action would be, as I hold, the experience of such and such, more or less completely defined, further contents of experience. And these further contents of experience constitute the facts that I acknowledge as real.

When I say to myself, "Such and such deeds, not now done by me, would more fully express my will," my practical consciousness is the one which is summoned up by further saying, "Then I *ought* to tend, even now, towards such acts." And the theoretical *Ought* of our judgments about facts, like the practical *Ought* of Ethics, is after all definable only in terms of what Kant called the Autonomy of the Will. I *ought* to do that which I even now, by implication, *mean to do*. My Ought is my own will more rationally expressed than, at the instant of a capricious activity, I as yet consciously recognize. The consciousness of the more rational purpose,—of a purpose looming up, as it were, in the distance, beyond my present impulses, and yet even now seen as their own culmination, like a mountain crowning the ascent from the foothills,—the consciousness, I say, of such a purpose, is what we mean in Ethics by the Ought. This Ought may appear foreign, but yet it is never at once the Ought and still something wholly foreign to my own will. Constraint, as such, is never moral obligation. The Ought is another will than my impulse, yet it is one with my own meaning; and it expresses more fully and rationally what my impulse even now implies. But if the practical Ought of Ethics is thus the fuller determination of my own will, viewed at once as mine and yet as superior to my present capricious and imperfect expression of my purpose, the theoretical Ought of our present discussion of the categories of Experience is similarly related to the theoretical aspect of my present conscious activity. The expression of my Internal Meaning, as I now embody my purpose, has contents and a structure, has characters and relations within itself, and so is not only a "mere Idea," but also has the correlative character of being, as we have all along seen, a fragment of Reality. The fuller expression of my will, defined by the Ought, has, in the same way, its own correlative embodiment in the Real. *This embodiment constitutes my world of recognized facts.* In recognizing the Ought on its practical side, as that to which I should even now conform my deed, I inevitably recognize the embodiment of this Ought, in the world of my completed will, as a fact. The present deed should be, then, at once a conformity to the Ought, viewed as a mode of action, and an adjustment or response to the facts, as the Ought, which is embodied in them, requires me to recognize them. The facts, as real, are embodiments of my purpose, yet not of my purpose as just now it transiently seems, but *as it ought to be viewed.* In recognizing them, I limit my present expression of myself through deeds, by virtue of my reference to these facts themselves. That *shall be* now (namely, in my deed), which conforms to the whole system that I mean, viz. to the world of the facts. *To view my present act thus is to recognize the facts as such.*

The extremely manifold and subtle implications of this

view of our consciousness of the realm of concrete facts can here only be indicated. Our later discussions of Nature and of Man must supply the details. It is plain, at once, that, according to our view, every concrete fact in the universe becomes for us, just in so far as it is acknowledged, the expression of a purpose, and so is never a *mere* datum of anybody's present experience, and is never a mere constraining power, that from without simply forces our assent. A fact may be acknowledged while yet many aspects of it remain mysterious. In so far it remains a "foreign" fact. But it is also our thesis that no purpose in the universe either is, or can now be rationally viewed by me, as wholly foreign to my own; while facts, so far as I understand them, become *ipso facto* expressions of ideas, and so of purposes. All purposes seek the expression that even now I am consciously seeking. Thus I myself am real, and I regard nothing real as *a me alienum*.

But, on the other hand, facts unquestionably limit me, and now seem to possess, at this passing instant, their often overwhelmingly foreign aspect. Why? In so far as I remain in suffering unreasonableness, no answer is apparent to such a question. But then, suffering unreasonableness, — a merely fragmentary mood of finite life, — if taken by itself, asks no very definite questions. For definite questions are reasonable, and imply successful inner deeds. But the mood of the unreasoning sufferer is lost in its mere failure to act successfully. It expresses its purpose only in so far as it is now conscious of its suffering. The rest of the universe it finds merely as something negative. Its word is, "True Being is not here." Whoever, on the other hand, not only suffers, but also asserts: "These and these *are the objective facts:* my disease is this or this — my enemy has won against me thus or thus — cruel Nature, indifferent to my will, has such and such a constitution" — any such more rational sufferer lays himself open to the question, "How do you know these ideas of yours about those foreign facts to be true?" If the answer is, "Such is the verdict of human experience in general," — then we already know that this very conception involves what we called relatively metempirical elements. No man of us has ever experienced what the general verdict of human experience really is. But if one answers, "This is what I myself now experience," — then we reply, "But you do *not* now experience the constitution of those external facts which you yourself characterize as foreign to you. You now only experience that you are not now succeeding." But if the sufferer goes on to say, "It would be, in view of my experience, simple folly, mere unreasonableness, to admit the doubt that the foreign facts really are such and such" — then his position, as far as his comprehension of the facts enables him to go, is at once substantially identical with ours. He recognizes that he reasonably *ought* to view certain facts as in particular ways external to the internal meanings of his own ideas. But a world where that is real which now ought to be regarded as real, is a world where explicitly at least a certain aspect of one's Internal Meaning is already recognized as expressed by the facts. For the Ought, as such, is never merely foreign to my own will. To recognize the whole fact-world as the final embodiment of Internal Meaning is merely to carry out to the end this same procedure.

Yet, as one may still insist, the question is not answered, Why do the facts often seem as foreign as they do? Why is their explicit conformity to our purpose, as defined by the Ought, joined with aspects of such hostility to all our purposes? In part this question is simply the problem of Evil, which will concern us later in another connection. In part our further discussion of the categories of experience, in our next lecture, will suggest its answer. In order to express the whole will which comes to our present consciousness in this so fragmentary human form, the facts, as we shall soon see, have to involve aspects that must now seem to us infinitely remote, and consequently, beyond our detailed comprehension at this instant. Thus, as we shall see, even the foreign aspect of the facts fulfils a purpose.

VI

It should be sufficiently plain by this time that in regarding our acknowledgment of facts as an expression of the Will, we do *not* assert that the will acknowledges facts in any merely capricious way. The will, whose relative satisfaction in this or in that present belief, or undertaking, or act of acknowledgment, or acceptance of the Ought, we have been observing, is known to us at any moment as by no means an altogether free or unconstrained will. Of the relative freedom of the finite will we shall speak hereafter. But for the present, when we say, "It is our own will which expresses itself in our interpretation of the real world," we are not to be answered by such a retort as, for example, the following: "Surely, you cannot *help* believing as you now do in these physical and social facts, in these rocks and hills, in these fellow-men, and in the rest of your well-known world. Therefore, it is not of your own will that you thus acknowledge their presence. If it were, you could cease, at pleasure, to believe in their existence. For if it is your will that causes your belief, your will could, if it chose, cause a change of belief, and at pleasure you could instead acknowledge the truth of the Arabian Nights tales, and believe yourself a dweller in Sirius. As a fact, you *must* believe in the facts of common sense, whether you will or no."

I reply to such an objection, first, that I do not call our will the *cause* of our present recognition of an external reality, and so still less the wholly *free* cause of this recognition, as if the will were a power that could now of a sudden change all our beliefs. What I say is that our present recognition of the concrete things in which we all believe is not a mere acceptance of any content of sense, but does include an intention to act, and *does* fulfil, as far as it goes, a purpose, and our own conscious purpose. How we came to get this purpose I do not here in the least care to explain by the hypothesis of any natural or supernatural causal process. Still less do I care now what psychological conditions enable the purpose to get itself expressed in our special beliefs. I report the observable inner facts, as the singer observes his own singing. It is so. I care not now what causes made it so. All our doctrines about causes, and about causation, whatever they are, are *instances* of just such expressions of rational purposes, — not means of explaining the fundamental fact that rational purposes get expressed in our conscious life. The so-called axiom of causation, or even the more generally stated "principle of sufficient reason," is only one of the forms in which the Idea gets partially embodied in our thought about things. And the only warrant for believing in such a principle at all is the Ought, whose deepest basis lies in our fundamental assurance that all reality embodies purpose. So I do not base my view on the assertion that the will causes our beliefs and is free to change them. I point out simply that to believe as we do about men and things seems just now more reasonable to us than does any other belief which we chance to have in mind as an alternative. But seeming reasonable means seeming to fulfil a purpose. And I prove my doctrine not only by this appeal to consciousness, but, indirectly, by letting my opponent try to refute me. If he does so, it soon appears that he rejects my account as something that seems to him unreasonable, *i.e.* as something that *ought not to be held*, just as our realist, in our former discussion, was found appealing to the "sanity" of his beliefs, to their usefulness for practical human purposes, as part of his warrant for maintaining that the reality is independent of all purposes. One thus refutes our doctrine of the Ought only by appealing to it. All logical discussion is, in fact, appeal to a norm, and a norm is a teleological standard.

Meanwhile, to say that my will is just now expressed in a given way, is by no means equivalent to denying that, in large measure, I *must* just now will thus. For that *must be* whose denial conflicts with what is already recognized as actual. If I *am* this way of willing, then one can express the fact in terms of a *must*. In one aspect my will may indeed possess freedom. In another aspect I am obviously as much under "constraint" in willing as in any other aspect of my conscious life. Only the constraint is not wholly external. It is my own. If I were to find my hand too near the fire, I should will to withdraw it, and should express my will in struggles if another man constrained me. But my willing itself, my determination to struggle for my freedom, would here be as clear a case of something that I just then *must* will, from the very internal nature of my will, as the act of my enemy who held my hand towards the fire would be the case of a condition externally forced upon my attention. In such a case I will, but to say that I also *must* will thus, is to express an aspect of what my will actually and consciously includes. So, too, it is in case of our disappointed lover, whose will gives his mistress power over him. His love is his will, but just now he *must* love. So our acknowledgment of the Ought is an act of will, but there may be a *must* bound up with this acknowledgment. Will is not mere wavering. It has a determinate nature. And whatever has a definite character, is such that you can express certain aspects of this character in terms of what you then call necessity.

VII

The category of the Ought thus has two aspects, and implies their unity. The aspects are those which, in our general Theory of Being, we defined as the External and Internal Meaning of Ideas. Only, in that general discussion, we were considering our relation to the universe as a whole. Here we are concerned to point out how our relations to the particular objects of experience result from those involved in our general theory of reality. When we define any particular object as real, we are indeed momentarily conscious of the aspect of external necessity, foreign constraint, compulsion; and this aspect, as a rule, is, in our present life, predominant. But when we were inquiring into the general metaphysical issues, our whole attitude was deliberately reflective, self-conscious, observant of the demands that our ideas consciously make. Hence the bridge that leads over from an idealistic metaphysic to a theory of our knowledge of Nature and of Man is always difficult to find. The reader of idealistic theory accordingly often says, "All this seems plausible, but what has it to do with hard facts?" Now we have pointed out that the "hardness" of particular facts depends upon their having a more or less determinate structure. We human beings, however, never verify at any one moment this structure in so far as it is "hard," *i.e.* stubborn, enduring, valid for all men, and real beyond the range of our momentary wishes and purposes. We can at any moment verify the fact that just then we do or do not find present what we seek. And we always do verify the fact in *some* respect, what we seek *is* present, since our seeking is already an act, and our act is already an expression of an idea. We also always verify the fact that, in some respect, what we seek is *not* present, since we are always dissatisfied. But the "objective facts," in Nature or in the life of Man, are not thus ever to be verified, at any one instant of our lives. They are real for us, but they are real as the acknowledged objects whose structure transcends what is now given to us. Our question in the present discussion being this, "What determines us to acknowledge as real one rather than another system of particular facts?"—we have here pointed out that the first determining principle, namely, the Ought, requires us to acknowledge at each moment as real certain particular facts which, even while they are conceived as limiting, constraining, and so determining our acts, *are also conceived as thereby enabling us even now to accomplish our will better than we could if we did not acknowledge these facts.* The "constraint" to which we here refer is meanwhile not first known as due to a cause, but comes to us in the form of the fact that our will is not now wholly expressed.

The Category of the Ought may thus be defined as implying three subordinate Categories: first, that of the Objectivity of all particular facts; secondly, that of the Subjectivity of the grounds for our acknowledgment of every particular fact; thirdly, that of the universal Teleology which, from our point of view, constitutes the essence of all facts. *Objective* are the facts that our experience suggests to us, because they are always, in some respect, *other than* what we now consciously find presented to us, as the relative fulfilment of our purposes, *within* our momentary experience. In this aspect they appear foreign to our will, and they so appear in various degrees, so that many writers have maintained that our "sense of resistance" is the fundamental warrant for our belief in facts external to ourselves. Such a view is inadequate, because it makes use of the category of causation as a primitive and irreducible conception. But unquestionably the facts *do* resist our momentary desires. *Subjective*, however, are all the grounds for our present acknowledgment of the facts. For in recognizing that our present wills are limited and controlled, we also recognize that only through such control can they win their determinate embodiment. And so it is our own will to acknowledge these foreign and objective limitations of our will. And thus no fact can furnish to us, wholly from without, the evidence that it exists. Nature embodies my will even in appearing foreign to my will; and thus only can I know that Nature exists as a system of facts defined by my ideas, but beyond my presentation. And, finally, the synthesis of these two characters appears in the essential *Teleological* constitution of the realm of facts, — a constitution which we shall soon have occasion to point out in the region where it seems least plausible, namely, in the so-called "mechanical," or better, in the seemingly non-teleological realm of natural law.

Such, then, is the beginning of our account of the Organization of Experience as human wit conceives that organization.

LECTURE II

LECTURE II

THE LINKAGE OF FACTS

THAT all our acknowledgment of facts is a conscious submission to an Ought, is a principle which still leaves numerous aspects of our world of human experience very ill-defined. We turn to a study of some of these aspects, and of their corresponding most fundamental Categories.

Let us give at once a list of the features of our experience which are here in question. First, then, the world of Facts is a world of Likenesses and Differences. These characters we find interwoven in our world with a most baffling complexity. We endeavor to deal with them, in an elementary way, by discriminating and classifying facts. But secondly, as we proceed to classify our world, we discover, for reasons which this lecture will have to study somewhat minutely, that the acknowledged facts appear as forming Ordered Series, and so as more or less obviously grouped into Systems, and subject to Laws. These laws, which have come to characterize all our modern views of Nature, appear to us to be universal in what I have called the World of Description. A decidedly new deduction of the most fundamental categories of this World of Description will be presented in this lecture. But thirdly, the very structure of this World of Description proves, upon closer analysis, that it cannot be the final expression of the inmost nature of things. We are led, then, in a way that profoundly concerns the interests of religion, to view the true world in another light. The genuine Facts of the universe are the facts of Life; and this, the necessary result of our general idealistic doctrine, will get a special expression in consequence of our present way of stating the contrast between the World of Description and the World of Will or of Appreciation. The one aspect of reality we shall later find embodied in the conception that *nature's laws are invariable.* The other aspect will receive embodiment in our Social Consciousness. The two aspects will be reconciled in subsequent lectures, by means of our Interpretation of Nature. We shall maintain that all special physical laws are only *relatively* invariable, and that our deepest relations to Nature are social.

To the consideration of the foregoing Categories in general, as leading up to our later study of Nature and of Man, the present lecture is to be devoted.

I

And first as to the Likenesses and Differences of Facts. The logic of the relations of likeness and difference first came to our notice when we were dealing with the problem of Realism in our former series of lectures.[1] We became better acquainted with the bearing of the general concept of Being upon these relations in the course of the Ninth and Tenth lectures of that series. Here we have to deal with the topic still more at close range. Every student of these problems knows that likeness and difference are two aspects of the world that simply cannot be

[1] First Series, p. 129, *sqq.*

sundered even by the utmost efforts of abstraction. In a sense, any two objects that you recognize as real, or as possible, have points of resemblance. In a sense, also, any two objects, however nearly alike, have differences. Moreover, if you detect a difference between two objects and are asked in what respect the two differ, or are asked for what is often called the "point of difference," a moment's reflection shows you that what you name in your answer is not only a point of difference, but also a point of agreement or resemblance between the two objects. Two artists differ in style or in degree of skill. That is, they also agree in both possessing style or skill. Two solids differ in contour. That is, they both have contour, and in so far are alike. No skill of abstraction ever enables you to sunder the likenesses and the unlikenesses of facts, so as to place the two aspects of the world apart in your conception. Each depends upon the other. Where you estimate degrees of likeness and difference, and call objects "more" or "less" different, you get further illustrations of the same principle. For two objects do not grow appreciably "more" different, for your usual fashion of estimate, merely by losing points of agreement. What you may often call a "very wide," or even the "widest possible" difference, comes to your consciousness in connection with contrasted or opposed objects, such as complementary colors, violent emotional changes, conflicts of will, and the like. But in such cases the difference is recognized as resting upon similarity. The complementary colors are more obviously contrasted than a color and an odor would be. Joy and grief, rage and gentleness, love and hate, are alike in being emotions, and the contrasted emotions of each pair resemble each other in being of the same more special types. Wills can differ or conflict by virtue of their relation to the *same* objects. On the other hand, where points of difference between objects multiply until we no longer recognize the correlative agreements, the objects in question become disparate for our consciousness. And disparity means at once the possession of so many differences that we can no longer recognize what they are, and a kind of secondary appearance of vague likenesses; since all objects whose relations we cannot clearly make out tend to lapse into a sort of blur in the background of our consciousness. There are countless differences amongst the miscellaneous objects that one sees in a crowded market-place, in case he himself is not seeking for the wares, or caring for the buyers and sellers. One observes that these differences are in one sense endless. One also observes that all this seems much alike to him; because it all means crowd and confusion, and leaves him "indifferent."

Herewith, however, we come to a point in the theory of our consciousness of likeness and difference which is, in my opinion, of critical importance for our whole doctrine about the particular facts of the world, and for our final interpretation of the problem of the individual. The likenesses and differences that we observe in facts are not merely thrust upon us without our consent or connivance. They are the objects of our attentive Interest. And they obviously vary with this interest. Nowhere more clearly than in case of our consciousness of likeness and difference do we see how significant the will is in determining what we shall regard as actual.

To attend, namely, is to take note of differences (and consequently of resemblances) which, were we inattentive, we should ignore. To turn our attention from certain facts, is to disregard differences of which we were before taking account. Now we are here speaking of attention, not as of a causally efficacious psychological process (for cause and effect concern us not yet), but as of one aspect of that relative fulfilment of purpose in present consciousness of which I have all along spoken. That to which we attend interests us. In attending to a sound, to a color, to an abstract conception, we find our purpose in some degree fulfilled by the ignoring or observing of some specific likenesses and differences. And the correlated likenesses and differences which appear before us in the observed facts are such as the direction of our attentive interest in some measure favors.

The world of facts is thus not merely *given* as like or different; it is at any moment *regarded* as possessing the correlative likenesses and differences to which we then and there attend. In fact, that reaction to our world, of which at the last time we spoke, is in great part an attentive attitude of the will, and is in so far a regarding of that to which we attend as more definitely different from the background of consciousness than it otherwise would be. It is perfectly true that we are not conscious of creating, *i.e.* of finding our purpose presently fulfilled in, more than a very subordinate aspect of the differences and correlative likenesses that we at any moment observe in the facts of our world. That is because of that relatively "foreign" character of the facts of which we spoke in defining the Ought. But it is also true that the more closely I observe, and the more carefully I submit myself to the requirement "to see the facts as they are," the more surely it is the case that the attitude of my attention in all this process of observation does, in its own degree, determine *what* differences amongst facts shall come to my observation. Careful measurement, for instance, that most characteristic of the processes upon which exact empirical science is based, involves a typically objective, "self-surrendering," submissive attitude of attention. Yet, on the other hand, we must insist that just this attitude, observant as it is of certain small differences which our less exact activities ignore, *finds what it seeks*, and what otherwise gets forced by outer nature upon *nobody's* observation, viz. precisely these small differences themselves, which meet our intent to be exact. What experience shows us as to the quantitative aspect of the world is, not that such differences exist wholly apart from our own or anybody's attention, but that the attentive will to measure does find a successful expression of its purposes in experience, so that a consciousness of small differences in lengths, times, masses, etc., comes to be recognized, where untrained and careless attention had ignored every such difference. Here, too, then, the fact observed is the fulfilment of our intent to observe that kind of fact.

In general, we may say: Likenesses and differences are not recognized by us as aspects of the world existent wholly apart from any of our specific purposes, but as correlative to certain tendencies of our will, *i.e.* to certain interests, which are fulfilled in recognizing these specific sorts of likenesses and differences which we come to observe. In the concrete, then, we must say, our intelligent experience involves at every step *an interest in regarding facts as like or as different.* This interest wins its way; and herein consists one aspect of the expression of purpose in fact which is characteristic of our own view of Being.

Most clearly this correlation of fact and purpose appears in all our Classifications. To classify is to regard certain facts as different (just because we find that to us certain differences are important), and certain objects as in a specific sense alike (because our interest in their likeness predominates over our interest in making certain possible sunderings). *What* classes your acknowledged world of fact contains, your own interest in classification obviously coöperates in determining. Hence the possibility of the well-known and endless disputes over whether our classifications in science stand for the truth of things, over whether our general ideas represent "external realities," and over the other historically significant problems of the theory of Universals. From our own point of view, these controversies get a very simple solution. Of course all classification is relative to the point of view, varies with that point of view, and has value only as fulfilling the purpose of whoever classifies. And, nevertheless, the question, *How ought I to classify?* has an objective meaning in precisely the sense in which any question about the facts of the world has meaning. Just now, when I classify mankind into two groups, you who hear me, and the rest of humanity, the classification fulfils a purpose of mine. It involves emphasizing certain presented or conceived differences, and regarding as equivalent certain facts that, from another point of view, could be subdivided or contrasted. The question whether this classification expresses anything "objective," anything bearing on the "true nature of things," is simply the question, How far is my momentary purpose in classifying thus an explicit and conscious expression of a certain infinitely wealthy purpose? This larger purpose comes to my present consciousness in the form of the assurance that *I ought to acknowledge* humanity and the universe, together with all that infinite wealth of meaning which my present thought of these objects even now hints to me, — and hints to me as that complete expression of my will which at every moment I am seeking.

The true problem about the objective validity of my classification is then the problem of the Ought, only here considered with reference to the question, What ought to be regarded as different or distinct, and what as equivalent, and in what respect? This is a teleological problem. It is to be solved, if at all, upon the ground of a consideration of the relation of this moment's passing purpose to the whole world-purpose of which it is a hint and a fragment. God distinguishes what it pleases him to distinguish. The logical as well as the moral problem is, Does my will accord with God's will?

So much, then, for Likeness, Difference, and Classification in general. The sum is so far this: Likeness and Difference are inseparable aspects of the world. Their recognition, and their very existence, are correlated with the interests which they fulfil. We express our own interests in them by means of our classifications, whose objective truth depends upon the significance of the will that makes them.

II

I pass next to an important special instance of likeness and difference, whose consideration will lead us over to the other categories of our list.

The most "subjective" of our classifications, that is, the one most expressive of the point of view of a particular consciousness, is founded on the distinction which any one of us finds himself making between the facts that he *just now* observes, acknowledges, thinks about, and the "rest of the universe." We not only recognize in the concrete the facts that we chance to be making the objects of our present and conscious consideration, but we all acknowledge a realm of truth beyond, whose reality we accept, but whose detail is unknown to us. London is real to us when we think of it; but our acknowledgment of its reality is far from being a concrete recognition of the wealth and variety of facts, social and physical, that we regard as being contained in what is meant by the name. It is so with all those distant facts which we found Realism using, at one stage of our discussion of that doctrine, as examples of independent facts that "make no difference" to a given knower, in a certain state of his knowledge. The unseen meteors of interplanetary space, the waves in the far-off seas, the craters in the moon, the ballads and legends of ancient Tartar tribes, the copper mines of Montana,—all such facts, and an infinity of others, equally varied, are lost, at any moment of our human consciousness wherein we do not concretely acknowledge their reality, in the nebulous blur of what we call "the rest of the world."

And so, what we seem to know, at any instant, consists of *two* regions, whose contrast is of more importance, in many ways, than is the one upon which we insisted at the opening of our former lecture. There we laid stress upon the difference between what is *presented*, at any instant of our consciousness, and what is then *recognized* or *acknowledged* as the expression of the theoretical Ought which controls our thinking. Here we draw the line of our classification at another place. We distinguish what either is presented or else is in some detail the object of belief, from what is acknowledged only as a whole and undifferentiated. Think of Asia, and think of some definite belief of yours regarding Asia, and what you think of is an object that, as you believe in it, is indeed not now presented to your observation. But it is present to your thought. The idea of it, as an Internal Meaning, is something of which you are definitely conscious. Yet, in addition to believing this or that about Asia, you unquestionably do recognize, however vaguely, even at the moment, that Asia is but a part of the universe whose reality you also acknowledge. Now this universe in its wholeness is real for you, at the moment, over and above Asia, because, as we have insisted, your idea of Asia is by itself unsatisfying, and so is inevitably viewed as something that cannot be expressed alone. It is felt to be essentially a fragment; and this feeling constantly tends to lead you to further thoughts, which still remain for your consciousness latent, — thoughts of the relation of Asia to the rest of the Eastern Continent, or of the relation of the Asiatic peoples to the British Empire, or to the world's history. But in what more concrete sense this idea of Asia needs and gets supplement through other realities, you are not conscious, so long as you fix attention upon the assertions about Asia alone.

Every concrete act of knowledge, in our conscious life, includes, then, a more or less deliberate abstraction from the background of recognized reality which we conceive as the world, for the sake of a clearer attention to certain special objects of our present acknowledgment. There results a contrast between this foreground and background of knowledge, the one containing the consciously distinguished objects of our present beliefs, the other containing only what is acknowledged in the lump, as the single and undifferentiated whole called "the rest of the universe."

Now this classification at once arouses a question as to its own basis and meaning. The question takes the form of the inquiry, What is the true relation of those various real objects of which at any moment we do not think in the concrete, to the whole state of our knowledge at that moment?

Realistic theories of knowledge, and in fact most of the popularly familiar philosophical views, even where they are only in part under the influence of technical Realism, reply to this question simply: "The objects now thought of by us are not present to our knowledge at all. They are absent objects, which do not now affect the mind. In some other state of our consciousness they may acquire a meaning for us. Then they become our objects. But when they are not thought of as these and these objects they are not thought of at all." This theory seems simple. It appeals to natural prejudices. But it is wholly opposed to our own analysis of the relation of Internal to External Meaning. We can entertain it no longer. It lapses with the realistic conception of Being.

For if nothing that exists exists independently of anything else, if the nature of everything is inevitably bound up with the nature of all other things, then knowledge, in facing reality at all, faces in *some* wise the whole of it at once, and the only question is how this at any instant takes place. The abstractness of our momentary knowledge, the vastness of our momentary ignorance of all concrete facts, no theory of knowledge recognizes more sincerely than does our own. But that all differences rest upon an underlying unity, — this is the very thesis which, in our present series of discussions, we are trying to make more concrete. For us, if you say, "The objects, other than Asia, which the world contains while I think, with conscious definiteness, only of Asia, must be objects of other acts of knowledge, and are in no sense present to this act," then it is necessary to reply: But the other acts of knowledge cannot, in their own Being, be *wholly* other than this one. For were they wholly other, they would have nothing really in common with this act. And if so, they would not be acts of knowledge at all. For two acts of knowledge have in common the real character of being knowledge. And this is a single character. If common to two facts, it gives them share in one Being. Just so, if the other objects besides Asia were *wholly* other than Asia itself, there would again be no community; and if Asia has Being, these other objects could have no Being. And so, in knowing Asia, I, in *some* sense, already know these other objects. And my knowledge, too, is in *some* sense one with the knowledge that more concretely possesses them. They are not, then, wholly absent objects. Even now, I, in *some* sense, mean them all.

Whoever denies this, after all, by implication, affirms it. For he asserts that there exist various objects, and various states of knowledge. He implies in his very assertion that his own present idea of these existences, his present meaning, is expressed in the existence of these same facts. This assertion, if true, implies a genuine unity, including, and by its nature differentiated into, the variety, not only of his sundered facts, but of these facts and his own knowledge of them.

And therefore, whoever knows *any* concrete object, knows in a sense *all* objects. In what sense is he then ignorant of any? This is for us the truly important problem.

We reply at once: The objects now concretely acknowledged are related to the objects not now concretely known, in precisely the same general sense as is that in which, at any instant of our conscious life, *the objects which our attention focusses are related to what, although present, is lost in the background of consciousness. Ignorance always means inattention to details.* In our momentary conscious life, such ignorance, so far as it relates to the presented contents of sense, is often due to a direction of attention which we can then and there alter by an instantaneous and voluntary shifting of our point of view. In such cases we speak of voluntary inattention, as when, in order to listen better, we neglect the facts of vision, or, in order to think better, disregard a bodily discomfort. But even within the limits of our momentary consciousness, our attention and inattention, although expressions of our will, are not always just then alterable at will. And even so, our inattention to the countless real facts, which at any moment of our human existence we altogether fail concretely to acknowledge, is due to conditions of our attention and of our inattention which we cannot at present alter except by the infinitely numerous small steps that together make up what we call the process of experience. This process of experience itself, of which empiricism justly makes much, is not, however, something determined wholly from without, by the mere coming of the facts to us. It is determined also from within, by our going to meet the facts, as we actually and restlessly do whenever we inquire, observe, or reflect. And every least shifting of our conscious momentary attention is one of these small steps whereby we continually undertake to make good the original sin, as it were, with which our form of consciousness is beset. On the other hand, this narrowness of our actual attention, this limitation to a few concrete facts, and this ignoring of the infinite detail of a world that, at any moment, we acknowledge as real only in its vague wholeness, is a condition fixed for us, not by a power wholly external to our own will, but by the very Will of which our every act of attention is the passing expression, namely, by the Will whose embodiment is the whole world of facts. And this very narrowness itself therefore constitutes, not indeed a present momentary act, but a *state* of our own will, a character of our present interest in the universe. This character is that we attend to only a few facts at a time, while the rest is the vague background of the world. Just as the disappointed lover of our former illustration is defeated, not without the connivance of his own will, although against his main conscious wish, so here, too, it is a present constitution of our own will that is in a genuine sense expressed in our very failure to know the detail of the universe, despite our conscious wish to know more than we do. For this inner conflict of the World Will with itself, this tragedy of satisfaction through the establishment and the overcoming of endless dissatisfaction, is a character of the universal purpose which we shall learn hereafter to appreciate, even as here we meet with an instance of it in the most elementary phenomena of the knowing process.

Our finitude means, then, an actual inattention, — a lack of successful interest, at this conscious instant, in more than a very few of the details of the universe. But the infinitely numerous other details are in no wise wholly absent from our knowledge, even now. They do "make a difference to us." Consciously we know them all at once, but know them abstractly, in the form of our acknowledgment of the "rest of the world" as real, over and above the few things we now recognize in detail. And since we are even at this instant, ourselves, in one aspect, a resultant of the meaning of all the "rest of the world," it is true, even now, that were the facts which we fail to know in detail, other than they are, our appreciation of what we do concretely know, our present attentive attitude, would be other than it is.

This is the general expression, in terms of our own theory, of the source of the present imperfections of our knowledge. Observe that we do not explain these matters by first assuming the existence of a certain being, called a finite knowing Subject, an entity amongst others, by next pointing out how knowledge gets impressed upon him from without, say through his sense-organs, and by then finally referring his ignorance to his lack of impressions. All such views, in so far as they are defensible at all, belong either to psychological theory, or, at best, to the developed metaphysical theory of the many individual Selves, and not to the general Theory of Knowledge. But Psychology, as a special science, is one result only of a particular human interest in the natural world which we shall come to know a little better in our fourth lecture. That special interest concerns us not as yet. Nor can we here presuppose that theory of the many individual Selves which we shall hereafter develope. In our general theory of finite knowledge we have to do only with the fact that a certain state of inattention exists at a certain moment of time. We know here, as yet, nothing of soul-substances, or even of metaphysical individual Subjects, such as, acted upon from without, come to build up their knowledge upon the basis of their impressions. Nor are there, from this point of view, separate series of "mental states," correlated to physical processes called brain states, and capable of being studied as to the laws of association which determine their sequence. All such conceptions can be viewed either as relatively valid, or as metaphysically final, only upon the basis to be established by a general theory of what constitutes our own type of knowledge. And for such a theory, — our whole present concern, — experience and reality alike contain only fulfilment of purpose, complete or incomplete, conditions of interest and attention, expressed or partially expressed in present consciousness, — acknowledgments of facts, and ignorance of facts, — beliefs, and truths related to beliefs. And of these only does the world of our considerations in this lecture consist. Hence we say, While the world in its entirety is the embodiment of our whole will, the fragment of that will, which this passing moment of human consciousness embodies, is a fragment that so far gets expressed in an attention to a few only of the world's real facts, and in such an inattention to the countless others as lets them all lapse into the vague background of acknowledged reality as "the rest of the world." Expressing the matter wholly in teleological, not at all in causal terms, we can therefore answer the question, "Why do we not now consciously and explicitly know all things, since the Being of all things is involved in our present meaning?" by saying simply, Because, as we are, we do not *attend* to all things, but only to a few. Or, again, Because *we are not duly and sufficiently interested* in the "rest of things," so that they fade into the background of knowledge, as the forests upon distant hills are lost in the contour of the rocky masses and become one with the whole. Thus simple, and in seeming no doubt paradoxical, is our formula for what is to be finite.

III

But the simplicity of the formula will prove endlessly fruitful. For this theory of our relations, as finite knowers, to the real world, predetermines what Form we ascribe to the system of facts whose reality we acknowledge.

We dealt at some length, in our study of the Third Concept of Being, with the definition of both physical and mathematical things as "objects of possible experience." But from the point of view which we have reached at the present stage of the inquiry, the facts that we acknowledge as real are for us, at any one conscious instant, Objects of Possible Attention. That is indeed not their whole Being. But it is one valid aspect of their Being. In the undifferentiated background of our present consciousness of "the rest of the world," all those real facts are even now present, but not as distinct objects. Any one of them could now be known, if only we were able to attend to its actual presence. Hence its real relationships are such as to permit, upon occasion, its discrimination from other facts in the way in which conscious attention discriminates.

Here, however, we meet, in its most elementary form, with that abstract way of viewing the world which expresses itself in the categories of the World of Description. The situation, at the moment, is this: A certain attitude of will, just now unchangeable by us, has determined each of us to a stubborn present inattention to the vast totality which we just called, in our discussion, "the rest of the world." To undertake to define the concrete facts of that world by a direct application of our general concept of Being is prevented, at the outset, by the consideration that the inattention in question hides from us not only the particular facts themselves, but the reflective knowledge of what it is that we ourselves will. For of all our human ignorance, our reflective ignorance as to the Self seems most stubborn. It is just this limitation of ours which requires us from moment to moment to view the facts in terms of the category of the Ought. We must submit in order to succeed, and must be conscious of subordinating ourselves before we can hope to find ourselves expressed. Or, to state the matter in other terms, we are in a position where we can only hope to view the world as, in the concrete, the expression of our will, in case we first can learn definitely to act; while, on the other hand, we can view our action, at the present stage, only as a *re*action. We have to presuppose our facts in order to make concrete our purposes, while we can define our facts, if at all, only in terms of our purposes. This is the fatal circle of our finitude, from which we can indeed escape, as we do in some measure, at every instant, by acting, — more or less blindly, — more or less at haphazard, — seeking in the process of experience both our own purpose, and the means of executing it, both our dream, and the interpretation thereof.

But when we still try to give our undertaking the clearest definition possible at this stage, the only way is to repeat, deliberately, a process which, in a still blinder form, one sees in the early life of any being that is destined to win intelligence. Not knowing what it craves, the young creature first acts vaguely, driven by unconscious impulses. Its action is so far planless and disorganized. When trial and error have led to some few little successes, it then begins to organize its life in a more definite way—how? By watching its environment. By *discriminating*. By engaging in a sort of action which involves, in a sense, a temporary resignation of all more immediate efforts towards self-expression. This stage of growing intelligence surrenders itself to what, in us men, becomes the deliberate undertaking to describe the facts of experience as they come, and so to win indirectly a plan for what may prove to be the expression of the Self.

This effort, to be sure, is still a kind of action. It is creative as well as passive. It involves in its least movement an acknowledgment of what is *not* given, as well as an observation of what *is* given; for, as we have seen, there is no rational conception of experience except by means of a linking of present and past experience; and this act of linking is always a transcending of what is merely found. But then, this watchful, discriminating activity is seeking to attend to what is conceived as already there in the vast background of the world; and it abandons, for the time, the immediate effort to win the expression of any other purpose but the purpose to wait, and to distinguish. So (to use an example from what appears to us as the workings of a far lower form of intelligence than our own) I see, from my library window at home, sometimes, a young cat, despairing for the time of succeeding in her cherished desire to catch the gray squirrels that play about from branch to branch in the trees, and that occasionally tempt her to vain crouching and springing when they descend to the ground in pursuit of nuts. She has long hoped to find the world the expression of her Internal Meaning by getting her claws upon them. But these swift phenomena still baffle her finitude. They escape her sly approaches with a maddening agility. They scold her from above, and throw down bits of bark to insult her. At length she abandons all apparent efforts at direct attack. It becomes her will to lie for hours nearly motionless, simply watching them. She chooses, as it were, to pursue science rather than any more drastic course of action. She will learn their ways, and discriminate one of their habits from another. In her dull patience, she seems to give herself over to the study of the World of Description. It is an enlightened patience of a sort somewhat similar to this that has created for us our sciences.

Now my purpose just here is not to define the methods and the tests that are used in any special science, but to point out the most fundamental conceptions to which this way of taking the world leads us, so long as we try to abstract it from any more deliberately creative fashion of viewing things. It is plain that in this way we can hope for no final view of the whole truth of things. We shall be dealing with a realm of abstractions, yet they will prove to be fruitful abstractions, everywhere founded upon final truth, although in themselves not final. For, that the world permits us, up to a certain point, to describe it, does help to throw light on the true nature of things. For the rest, I shall of course attempt here no account of the psychological genesis of our describing intelligence, or of its categories. I am concerned only with the logical genesis of these ideas, that is, with the way in which their simpler forms determine their more complex ones.

We return then to the view that the real world consists of facts which are, so to speak, waiting for us to attend to their presence. What constitution must such a world possess?

In reply to this question, I must next point out certain accompaniments of the process of discrimination which are of fundamental importance for our interpretation of the structure of any realm that we are to conceive as an object of possible attention. If I discriminate attentively between two facts in space, such as two marks on a blackboard, or two sides of the same coin or die, I observe, in general, that there is something *between* these two discriminated objects, and also that there are regions of space *between which* these two distinguished objects are to be found. So that, in such a case, *one* discrimination demands, as it were, *another*. One analysis of a whole into elements calls for further analysis. And every union of discriminated elements into a new whole (as, for instance, the two sides of the die form, when taken together with the material between them, a single whole), — every such union, I say, leads us to distinguish only so much the more clearly between this new whole and the "rest of the world," which limits the observed portion so as to set it between other portions. Thus, at all events in such cases as our own consciousness of the extended world, our process of attentive discrimination tends to become a Recurrent Process,[1] *i.e.* a process in which every step leads to conditions which demand, or at least appear to demand, a repetition of the very type of act that led to the step in question itself. For if I have discriminated, then, at least in this sort of instance, I have found a basis for a repetition of discriminations.

Now it is also plain, at least in case of such an object as the world of extended things, that this very recurrent character of our process of discrimination becomes to us a motive for interpreting what we take to be the "real structure" of space itself. Because we are led, upon any clear distinction of positions in space, to an observation of an interval between two positions, while this interval itself becomes the basis for new discriminations between the positions that lie once more within that interval, we find ourselves started upon a process which we can define as recurrent, that is, as capable of repeating itself indefinitely; and since we see no reason why this process should meet with any limit in the nature of extended facts, we come to the familiar postulate of the infinite divisibility of space. And because every such observed collection of spatial objects, once discriminated, and then viewed as a whole, turns out to be between still other regions of space, which its very presence leads us to discriminate from itself, this process of discrimination

[1] See the Supplementary Essay to the First Series, p. 495, *sqq.*, for the general definition of such a process.

also becomes recurrent, and we are led to the other familiar postulate of the boundlessness of space.

What such an instance shows is: (1) that, in certain cases at least, our tendency to discriminate *two* objects leads us by itself to discriminate a *third* object, *m*, as between them, and to distinguish other objects, let us say *f* and *l*, *between which* both *a* and *b* are; (2) that this observation may of itself lead to new discriminations, and so become, or tend to become, recurrent; and (3) that the result hereof *may* be to give us an idea of an infinitely complex objective structure which we are then disposed to ascribe to a system of facts (such as the points in space). So here the law of our discriminating process gives us a conception of a law of structure in the world of facts. This law may then be to any extent confirmed by further experience.

That not only space, but also time, suggests similar recurrent processes of discrimination, is familiar.

Now these well-known instances lead us to a more general question. Is this character of the process of discrimination something general in its nature, so that, *wherever* we discriminate, the conditions of such recurrent processes of finding new differences are present, or is the tendency to look for points between points, and so forth, a tendency determined by special conditions, such as those of our experience of space and time? And what follows with regard to the conception that we tend to form of the structure of the world of facts?

At first, the answer would seem to be that we may, upon occasion, come to perfectly clear limits in our discriminations. In the world of our pure conceptions, we find that between successive whole numbers, such as 2 and 3, 3 and 4, it is impossible to conceive other whole numbers inserted, so long as one takes the whole numbers in their natural order. And the same holds true, in the world of empirical things, regarding any simple series of objects whose type is that of the whole number series, where every object of the series is followed by a *next* one, with *nothing between* that belongs to the series. A series of this type we shall hereafter call, in accordance with recent mathematical usage, a Well-Ordered Series. But, on the other hand, as our Supplementary Essay showed at length, any collection of objects in the world is part of some infinite collection; and so the objects of any well-ordered series are themselves portions of the expression of a recurrent process, or of a well-ordered series of such processes. And in every such process, as was shown in the Supplementary Essay, an infinite number of discriminations are already implied. Hence, although it is indeed possible to find cases where we can no longer look for objects between a given pair of objects which have already been discriminated, it still appears that discriminations which are logically completed, merely by our distinguishing between *two* objects, are not to be found. Discrimination seems to be not merely of *pairs*, but of *triads*, or of larger systems of facts.[1]

[1] For the sake of later use, it is proper to note here, regarding the definition of the Well-Ordered Series just given, that, while its type is that of the whole-number series, in so far forth as every term has a *next following* term, recent mathematical usage has extended the concept to include the so-called Transfinite Well-Ordered Series of Cantor, in which infinite series may follow infinite series without end, but so that every term has its own next following term.

It is then worth while to examine the matter a little more closely. For if we can find whether or no *every* discrimination logically leads to some such recurrent process as the empirical instance of our consciousness of space has just exemplified, we may come to a result of great importance for the formulation of the Categories in terms of which we conceive the structure of the world of facts, so far as we view them merely as objects of possible discrimination.

And may I venture already to anticipate something of what this result will prove to be? Matters of this kind are not to be studied, except by a consideration of very subtle and abstract logical relationships. The inquiry, even in the fragmentary form here adopted, can be tolerable, in this context, only by virtue of its bearings on more concrete issues. May I, therefore, say, at once, regarding the outcome, simply this? I hold that by studying more closely what the process of discrimination logically implies, *we shall be led to see something regarding what enables us to view all acknowledged facts as linked in a single Ordered System, in which countless definable Series of real facts are interwoven;* and hereby *we shall be led to a more definite idea of what is meant by the acknowledgment of Law in the natural, in the social, and in the moral order of the world.* Thus our notions of the Unity of the world will become, in one aspect at least, more concrete.

How come we to the recognition of Law as an aspect of the real world? By means of some primal "intuition," which (despite its name) inflicts itself upon us as an opaque assurance? Our Idealism knows of no such primal assurances. Every assertion must bear criticism.

No assertions can escape such a test by pleading that they are "primal." Or again, has the Creator, in making our souls, stamped upon them a system of principles which is in preëstablished harmony with the real order, so that our metaphysical theory, if true, will teach us that our ideas of order must correspond to an order present in the facts beyond us? With Kant we reject such a *Präformations-System der Menschlichen Vernunft.* Our special reason for rejecting it is contained in our thesis, so fully set forth in Lecture VII of the previous Series, to the effect that correspondence is never the most fundamental relation between Idea and Object, and that, accordingly, the world is not *merely* a world of facts to which our knowledge conforms. Our own view has in common with Kant (from whom we, of course, derive this portion of our fundamental doctrine) the thesis that the laws of the objective world are the expression of Categories which the nature of every subjective process, and the Unity of Apperception wherein all truth is embraced, together determine. Only, for us, the Categories are not stamped, as Kant's Categories were, upon a foreign matter, but are in some measure, *i.e.* as far as they are really valid at all, at once objective and subjective. This last thesis we have in common with many forms of recent Idealism. But our own doctrine is not wholly identical with any of these forms. The *differentia* of our doctrine will be found, however, in the method whereby we define the special Categories, and in the special form that we accordingly give to them. Our logical genesis of the concept of real Law will determine the definition that we shall give to the term. It will also determine the limits of the subjection of fact to law in the universe. It will free us from that bugbear of popular metaphysic, the superstition that whatever is, is somehow subject to an absolutely rigid Necessity. We shall see that necessity is only one aspect of the fact-world, and the more abstract one, which is a valid aspect only in so far as it serves to make possible Individuality and Freedom.

To my mind, as I may at once say, our best single word for expressing what is essential to a lawful order in the world of facts is the term Series. Facts are subject to law in so far as they are arranged in definable series, or in systems of interwoven serial orders. The relation of physical cause and effect, whose consideration we have so often postponed in our previous discussions, becomes a definite relation at all only when it is viewed as an instance (and by no means the most important instance) of the existence of series of facts in the universe. All comprehension of particular facts which goes beyond a bare abstract classification of them, and which still falls short of a satisfactory teleological view of their meaning, depends upon conceiving them as in the same series, or system of series, with other facts. This is the essential nature of the categories that have to do with Law. As we shall see, the general concept of Series is common to the World of Description and to the world of the actual life of the Will. Only the types of Series differ in these two worlds, the Well-Ordered Series being characteristic of the life of the Will just in so far as it is self-conscious, and consequently always knows *what next to do*, while the World of Description is characterized, in general, by another and less perfect type of serial order.

To illustrate empirically of what wide application the concept of Series is, and how it is present wherever the concept of Law is present, and *vice versa*, is useful in beginning a discussion of this category, although anything like present completeness in such illustrations is hopeless. You find serial order wherever you look in the world of definitely conceived or of exactly describable fact. Space and Time illustrate our principle in their every detail. They and the Number-Series are the most familiar of the forms in which serial order appears to us. As for more special classes of instances, I conceive my own life as a particular and connected series of events, and yours in the same way. All the more significant social relations involve, directly or indirectly, the establishment of serial order-systems such as those of debtors and creditors, of friends and neighbors, of fellow-citizens, of teachers and pupils, of official superiors and inferiors, of the various grades of relationships in families, and so on indefinitely. For a social relationship of the type of debtor, friend, neighbor, fellow-citizen, teacher, superior, ancestor, cousin, has the logical character illustrated by saying that if A stands in this relation to B, B may, and frequently does, stand in the same relationship to C, C to D, and so on, — the collection of social individuals A, B, C, constituting in this way an ordered series, sometimes of a very limited, but more often of a very widely extended scope. In natural history, the classification of living forms, the study of the structures and functions of organisms, the accounts of the evolution and decay of all types of life, involve the conception of ordered series. Geology, on its descriptive side, is similarly a science of serial order-systems of rocks, fossils, formations. Nor does this character cease to mark the conceptions of science when one passes to chemistry, to physics, to astronomy, or to mechanics. The serial system of the chemical elements, which forms so important a topic of consideration in recent chemistry, is a notable example of how various masses of facts which once seemed in certain respects ultimate and mutually sundered, tend, upon further examination, to assume their places as stages of a single, though highly complex, order-system. Any natural process which is capable of a mechanical description, — such as the processes studied in the more exact regions of physical science, — is made comprehensible by conceiving all of its occurrences as stages in a single series, or system of series, of what the mathematicians call "transformations." Such a series of transformations is exemplified by the successive states of a body cooling under definable physical conditions, or by the successive configurations of a system of bodies moving under the influence of definable forces. In astronomy, the apparent places of the stars are reduced to order by the use of a system of astronomical coördinates, just as we reduce to order our knowledge of geographical positions on the earth's surface by the conceptions of latitude and longitude. But such ways of viewing facts are conceptions of definitely complex order-systems of places. In recent astronomy, moreover, the classification of the stellar spectra has led to a still tentative arrangement of stars in order-systems whose bearing on problems of evolution seems to be important. At all events, one thus finds a new sort of definable relation between the physical processes occurring in the very bodies that would appear, from one point of view, to be amongst the most disconnected and mutually sundered objects of the visible universe.[1]

And now, as to the more universal meaning of this serial structure of our world of facts, we may note in passing still one further consideration. It is a commonplace that the exact sciences of Nature have owed their exactness, up to the present time, and in the main, to their *quantitative* treatment of facts. The logic of the conception of Quantity has its own very complex problems; but thus much is clear: Any system of quantities, such as distances, times, masses, temperatures, pressures, is a serial order-system of facts, or is a complex of such serial order-systems. For the relationships, Equal, Greater, and Less, which mark systems of quantities, involve arrangements in serial order-systems. Therefore, one has much to say for the thesis that the whole logical value of the quantitative conceptions in science is due, not to any peculiar advantage of the concept of quantity, as such, but to the exactness of the forms of serial order which are discoverable in case of any quantitative realm of facts. From this point of view it is not, then, the quantitative character of exact science which is its most essential feature, but the precision and relative exhaustiveness of its reduction of its own ranges of fact to serial

[1] That plans of action, reflective systems of Ideas, and the structure of the Self in general, illustrate the concept of Series in the form of the Well-Ordered, or self-representative Series, we have shown in the Supplementary Essay, and we shall have occasion to return to that fact soon.

order-systems. Not Quantity, but Order, is the fundamental category of exact thought about facts.[1]

Now what is the logical derivation of the category of serial Order? The answer to this question requires us to return to the study of what is logically implied in coming to discriminate between any two objects. To such a study I must devote a little space, despite the painfully abstract nature of the topic.[2]

IV

In certain cases, as we have seen, to compare attentively two objects, as to their differences and likenesses, is to observe a situation which implies that something is *between* the two, and that the two themselves are again between another pair of objects. The process of discrimination and of synthesis thus initiated proves, at least in some such cases, recurrent, or self-repeating, and leads us to form postulates about the objective structure of the system of facts to which the things in question belong. In order to estimate more carefully the meaning and the uni-

[1] I am principally indebted for the substance of this remark to Mr. Charles Peirce, and to the study of Dedekind and Cantor. See the article on the Logic of Relatives in the *Monist*, Vol. VII, p. 205, *sqq.*, by Mr. Peirce.

[2] The best way of forming, from a psychological point of view, a general sense of the practical importance of the process of conceiving facts in series, is to read the brilliant passages on the topic in Professor James's larger Psychology (Vol. I, p. 490; Vol. II, pp. 644–669). What Professor James there takes as a fundamental psychological feature of the process of comparison, I here try to analyze in certain of its logical aspects. The discussion in the Supplementary Essay in our First Series has already dealt in full with that primary form, the Number-Series. Here we deal mainly with a derived type of Order.

versality of such processes, we next need *a generalization of the relation expressed by the word between.*

Such a logical generalization has been suggested, although for a purpose decidedly different from that of my present inquiry, by Mr. A. B. Kempe, in a very remarkable paper on "The Relation between the Logical Theory of Classes and the Geometrical Theory of Points."[1] If I venture to follow out the suggestion of Mr. Kempe's work, it is in my own way, and his discussion must not be viewed as responsible either for the intent or for the outcome of my speculations. In Mr. Kempe's research, what is most important for us at the moment is that a relation of a logically identical character is shown to exist in two apparently very different cases. When three points are on the same line, one of them is said to be *between* the two others. But when two logical classes of objects, *a* and *b*, are so related to a third class, *m*, that this class *includes* all the objects which are common to both *a* and *b*, and at the same time *is included within* the class of the objects which are *either a* or *b*, then Mr. Kempe defines the class *m* as a class *between a* and *b*. The interest of the identification of the relation *between* in the geometrical and in the logical realms, lies in the proof, given at length by Mr. Kempe, that the exactly definable properties of any complete system of logical classes, or "Universe of Discourse," are, up to a certain limit, *identical with the properties of*

[1] Published in the *Proceedings of the London Mathematical Society*, Vol. XXI, for the year 1890. Another statement of his main results was printed by Mr. Kempe in *Nature*, Vol. XLIII, pp. 156–162. These papers have been far too much neglected by the students of exact logic to whom they were addressed. Their interest goes far beyond that of the special idea which I here borrow from them.

a geometrical system of points. Mr. Kempe shows, in fact, that the system of points possible in a space of any number of dimensions differs from the system of logical classes possible in any "Universe of Discourse," merely by the addition of a single new property, viz. that which is geometrically expressed by saying that two straight lines have only one point in common. This very striking identification of laws belonging to the kinds of orderly arrangement present in such different realms as a system of ideal logical classes and a system of points in space is associated, in Mr. Kempe's discussion, with an observation regarding the nature of the generalized relation *between*, which I here propose to use, although I have no time to state either fully or very exactly the reasoning that I found upon this observation.

If one visible point were between two others on a line, and if all three were (to fix our ideas) luminous points, and if you went just far enough away from the line to be unable longer to observe the place of the point *a* as diverse from that of the point *b*, so that the two blended to your eye in one luminous point, then obviously *m*, the intermediate point, would blend with both of them. Just so, however, if you abstract from the difference between the classes *a* and *b*, while still recognizing, in a measure, the possibility of objects that, as a fact, belong to one or to another of them, then, so long as you thus regard the two classes as equivalent, it makes no conscious difference to you whether an object is in the class *a*, or in the class *b*, or both at once. So that you do not observe, in that case, Mr. Kempe's intermediate class *m* as a class different from either *a* or *b*. The same result follows if you not merely neglect or abstract from the difference of the two classes, but positively know them to be identical classes. For in that case both *a* and *b* become identical with *m*.

Generalizing from these cases, one may go quite beyond Mr. Kempe's instances of the classes and the points and say, Let there be any system or collection of objects such that, if they are really different, these objects can be discriminated by an attention once properly directed. Let it be also possible for a given intelligence *not* to discriminate two objects belonging to that collection. Or again, let it be possible for this intelligence, although discriminating them, still to regard two of them at will as "equivalent," that is, as such that their difference does not count for a given purpose. Then let an object *m* of the system in question be so related to *a* and to *b* that *if* you, either by inattention, neglect, or deliberate choice, disregard their difference, so that in any way they blend or become equivalent, *m* thereupon of necessity blends with both, or becomes equivalent to both. In this case we shall say that, in the generalized sense, *m* is such a member of the system in question as to lie *between* *a* and *b*. The mathematical way of symbolizing this relation would be briefer. It would take the form of merely saying: "*m* is such that, if $a=b$, then $m=a=b$. And *if* this is the case, *m* is regarded as *between* *a* and *b*."

Now the advantage of this formal generalization is the power that it here gives us of facing an important logical aspect of all discrimination, comparison, and differentiation. We usually say that the relation between *a* and *b*, where we discriminate them, or regard them as unequal, is a relation of the *pair* of them, a *dual* relation. The generalization here founded upon Mr. Kempe's paper will show us that contrast and comparison involve, in general, a relation of at least *three* objects, viz. *a* and *b*, and something else that *helps us to keep them apart*, or that *illustrates the point wherein they differ*, or that helps to *determine the sort, degree, or direction of their difference.* This something *may* be an object of the exact character here ascribed to *m*. That is, it may be conceived as an object such that, *if* *a* and *b* were to blend, or were to be viewed as equivalent, it would blend with both, or be viewed as equivalent to both. In such a case, the relationship emphasized by the contrast belongs not to the pair, *a* and *b*, but to the triad, *a*, *b*, and *m*. In other words, it is what one may technically name a *triadic* relation. The possibility of observing this relation is due to the fact that, since our discriminating attention is a voluntary act, possessed of its own internal meaning, we are able to see, by reflection, how one discrimination follows from another.

Let us look yet a little more closely at the considerations which come into view whenever we make any definite discrimination. I attend to *a* and to *b*. I note that they are different. It follows, as we saw at the outset, that they differ *in some character*, and that they also, although of course in another respect, agree as to this same character. It may be color in which they differ. Then they agree also in having color. In magnitude,— then they agree in having magnitude. Tell me the character in which they differ, and I will at once undertake to show you the sense in which, in respect to this same character, they also agree. I inevitably note, then, if I look closer, the "common nature" of *a* and *b*. Of course I can never, in any realistic sense, so abstract this "common nature" as to make it appear by itself as an object existing independently of their difference. Yet it is there, and arouses my interest. Otherwise I should not be comparing *a* and *b*. They, as they come to me, appear as specifications of this "common nature."

Now when I view them as such specifications, the problem of the One and the Many arises afresh. How can this One Nature be the same in these *two?* This ancient question is here a question of fact. It is a question about what I actually observe when I discriminate. As it comes to me, it is already a question about a Triad, not as yet of objects, but of aspects of the whole situation before me. There is an unity here. There is also the diversity of these two objects; and this unity is not something merely glued to this diversity in an external way. The situation is this: That a certain One (viz. the "common nature" of these two objects) is observed, not as something over and above these two, but as *in* them, — as *their* nature, diversified into their differences. Yet this one is itself, nevertheless, contrasted with these two; for neither of the two, *a* or *b*, is by itself the other member of the pair; while the "common nature" is expressed in them both. *How* this can be, I so far am led to inquire. But that this is so, the discrimination implies. Here, then, I have one of those "bare external conjunctions" of the One and the Many of which Mr. Bradley, in his *Appearance and*

Reality, has so much to say, and which, for him, constitute the insoluble problem of our finitude.

Now the effort to answer the question thus raised is not merely an idle subtlety of the philosophers. As a fact, *all* the sciences are full of specific contributions towards the answers to just such questions. Yes, even unreflective common sense daily undertakes to do something towards answering problems of the sort. Common sense and science, however, go about the matter more concretely than the philosophers have usually done. In ordinary life we recognize the problem of the presence of One in a pair of discriminated objects only by proceeding at once to look for *still another instance of the same kind of likeness and difference.* Baffled by the so formal triad just named, viz. the triad of the One nature and the two expressions, we help ourselves by searching out a more concrete triad. We compare, if possible, both objects with a third object, as concrete as themselves, which serves us as a "common standard." This third object is preferably an already known one, whose choice sums up the results of a long course of previous experience. To help us at all, however, it must obviously possess something of the "common nature" that interests us in *b* and *c*. It will, of course, differ from both of them. But most of all it helps us when it is so much like *a* and *b*, and yet so definitely unlike them, that the triad, *a*, *b*, *c*, leads us to definite observations of the sort characterized in the foregoing exact definition of the relationship *between*. If one of the triad is such that upon reflection we observe a particular order of dependence amongst the acts whereby we distinguish the three objects, *i.e.* if one object appears, as in our present sense, *between* the two others, then we have the first beginning of a single *series of distinctions.* And the rule of our discriminating intelligence is that, while the problem of the One and the Many is hopelessly baffling if we deal merely with two terms, and while it is equally hopeless so long as we deal with an indefinite number of objects *not* arranged in series, we begin to see the light so soon as we get *one of our objects between the two others*, and so begin to form a series possessing a definite character and direction. And by "direction" we here mean, not spatial or temporal direction, but direction of logical dependence.

And now why does this getting of one object between two others help us? I point out that the generalized definition of the relation *between*, which we owe to Mr. Kempe, suggests at once the answer to this question. I can comprehend the relation of One and Many just in so far, and only in so far, as I observe the unity of my own purpose demanding, itself of itself, a variety of expression.[1] Now, when I discriminate, I at first find the fact

[1] As our Supplementary Essay showed at length, the precise understanding of the relations of One and Many which we get in case of the Number-Series, or of any "self-representative system," is due to the fact that there our own purpose in creating the system is just such a consciously self-differentiating Unity. Hence, as I there said, the order of the number-system is the original type of all order in heaven and upon earth. But we are here following out a process that leads us to a conception of order-systems very different from the number-system. For in the latter, each term has a next following term. In the system that we shall now be led to conceive, no term has a next term. Yet we reach these other systems by means of the first form of order, since, as we shall see, the *recurrent* character of our discriminations is the source of these derived order-systems.

of difference as something that is indeed an expression of my attentive purpose, but that is still more an instance of the limitations of my insight. I look for light, and so far I find a problem. The object *a* differs from *b*. How? I cannot so far tell; for I do not yet see the *structure* of the difference as the expression of any one plan. But when I conceive, and then am able to find in experience, some third object *c*, which behaves like the *m* of my former definition, then, while my insight is still infinitely limited, I see the differences of *a*, *b*, and *c*, or, (as we may now say, in case *c* is the intermediate object of the triad), I see the differences of *a*, *b*, and *m*, as such that the recognition of the difference of *b* from *a follows* for me inevitably upon the recognition of the difference, either of *a* and *m*, or of *b* and *m*, or of both. I make this fact clear to myself by trying the ideal experiment of annulling or disregarding the difference of *a* and *m*, and of *b* and *m*. I can try this experiment with exactness, because, in making it, I am observing my own voluntary acts. I observe hereupon that the difference between *a* and *b* vanishes. In convincing myself of this fact, in seeing how the distinction of *b* from *a* follows from first distinguishing one of them from *m*, I gradually begin to find that the nature expressed in *a* is such that I am led over from *a* to *b* by a single definable process of drawing distinctions. Or again, I thus conceive the nature of *a* not as static and as merely given to me, but as a stage in a process that now has an actively appreciated and logically significant direction, — a direction determined by my own purposes, and also by the facts. Hereupon I can proceed in the direction of *b* by passing, in the course of this process, through *m*. For the very discovery of *m*, and of the dependence now in question, constitutes for me the direction of this ideal process. I now begin to construct the Many by one sort of activity. And in doing so, I also find what structure my objects themselves, as so far known to me, appear to possess.

It is perfectly true that such a process as this is far from answering *all* my questions about the One and the Many. On the contrary, it constantly arouses new ones. But it also suggests a systematic plan for attempting to move towards an answer to every such question. Let me find, if possible, by means of further experience, not only the triad, *a*, *m*, *b*, but also yet other objects similarly disposed, — a whole series of further intermediaries (m_1 between *a* and *m*, m_2 between *m* and *b*, and so on). If I succeed in my search, I then gradually get, by means of a well-ordered series of acts of my own, a series resembling a collection of points in order on one line, thus:

$$a \ldots . m_1 \ldots . m \ldots . m_2 \ldots . b.$$

But there is room, in this series, for the conception of new intermediate terms indefinitely; and I can continue the search for such in my experience. The objects of the series are such that any three form a triad, with one of the triad *between* the two others (in our present sense of *between*), while all the triads are thus linked in one series, beginning with *a*, ending with *b*, and having intermediaries such as are determined by a recurrent process of conceiving, and, if possible, of finding in experience, ever new triads within the series. The whole series, so far as I can conceive and verify it at all, will define stages of a single process of ideal construction, which I can conceive in volitional terms, as a process that expresses *how one can pass from a to b*, or (to borrow a mathematical term, again) can *transform a into b*. And the unity of this series, as the expression of a single volitional process, will be due to the fact that I can everywhere see, as I pass along the series, how *one distinction, or act of holding apart two objects, depends for its very existence on another and previous distinction.* For in this way my ideal process, going from distinction to distinction, establishes between every pair of distinct objects, an intermediary, which is viewed by me as *making their distinction possible*, or as *holding them apart*. Yet the intermediary terms, while they hold apart, also link.

V

This is, then, our general statement of how it is that every discrimination tends to lead us to the definition of series of objects, observed or conceived. At the same time we begin to see how and why every such series helps us to comprehend the structure of the world that we are to acknowledge as real. Now my main thesis here is that, in the World of Description, *all understanding of facts in terms of general laws* depends upon the conception and verification of such serial order in facts as I have been characterizing. The whole logic of our conception of general law in this World of Description turns, in my view, upon the single question, What for us is implied in discriminating *a* from *b*? For the world acknowledged as beyond is presented to us at every moment as a single whole, *within* which the facts are present. These facts are for us, in one aspect of their nature, *objects of possible attention.* Attention begins to succeed when we discriminate. And so we have for one postulate about the acknowledged facts this: *They are such that any pair of them could be known together through a single possible act of discrimination and comparison.* This is the primal notion of linkage. *Any* pair of real objects are thus linked. But this postulate leads to others. Whatever pair of objects there may be in that world, since both members of the pair could be the object of a single act of discriminating attention, those two objects are already *like each other and different from each other.* Hence the single discrimination of the two presents a new problem, that of the union of One and Many. What is the unity, what the variety of this pair? The only way that we have of proceeding towards a solution of this problem, so long as we are still ignorant in the concrete of what One Will is expressed in these objects, is by passing from the pair to the triad, and defining an object that lies *between* the members of the first pair, in the sense of Mr. Kempe's generalized definition of this relation. We then seek for this fact in experience. If we find it we are helped towards an understanding of the One and the Many. For in so far as we define such a triad, we discover how we could conceive one member of our original pair as *transformed* into the other, by means of a process that involves first distinguishing the intermediary between the two from one of the extremes, and then the other member from the object thus distinguished. The direction of the process of transformation thus defined is determined by the logical sequence, according to which *one distinction is observed to follow from another.* But because we are thus led better to comprehend what the objects discriminated are, we now make still a further and provisional postulate: *Between any two objects of the world there is always another to be found.* Our power to illustrate *this* postulate in our empirical investigations is very wide, but is also always limited. And the postulate itself would indeed fail wholly to receive application beyond a certain definite point, if we could only come to understand all the objects of our world as a single ordered series of the type of the whole number-series. For then any pair of directly successive objects would have no object between them. But, then, to be sure, the objects of the world, if so understood, would no longer *need* to be discriminated merely in pairs. They would be logically given, all at a stroke (like the whole numbers), as an expression of a single self-representative Purpose,[1] and we should have to look no further than this purpose for the transparent definition of all our facts. But in discriminating pairs and then triads of facts, we come as yet upon no purpose, but our own descriptive purpose, of trying to find the One in the midst of this given Many. Our own process of discriminating proves indeed to be recurrent, but it looks always for yet another object between any two objects already distinguished. Hence, while the process of defining the intermediate terms is a Well-Ordered Process, that leads us from each stage to the next one, it tends to make us conceive a series of facts in which no term has any next neighbor,

[1] See once more the Supplementary Essay, p. 501, *sqq.*

because, as we conceive, there is always another *between*. So the postulate: *Between any two there is a third*, is the working postulate of our process of comprehending things through our successive discriminations. And this is the process upon which all scientific description of given facts depends.

Now the definition of *between* suggested by Mr. Kempe's papers has quite freed us from the need of limiting the application of this postulate to the extended world, or to the numerical and quantitative aspects of things. The points on a line, as conceived by the geometer, the series of rational fractions arranged in order as greater and less, and the series of the real numbers, all indeed illustrate our postulate.[1] They are conceptual systems of objects especially wrought out by the mathematician in such wise as to conform to the postulate. And every homogeneous system of measurable and continuous quantities (masses, distances, durations, forces, temperatures, etc.) is conceived by our exact science as also to illustrate this postulate. Yet the formation of series has application to qualities as well as to quantities, — in fact, to whatever we can undertake to discriminate. Hence there is no obvious limit to the variety of objects that we can undertake to deal with in this way. We can compare colors and shades as well as points and magnitudes. Europe and America, compared geographically, or socially, or politically, lead us to attempt the formation of series of

[1] All these systems are so ordered that no term is conceived to have a next neighbor. Yet the process whereby we reach the conception of each is always a Well-Ordered Process, in which each of our own acts leads to the next one.

objects. Feelings, deeds, persons, lives, stellar spectra, chemical elements, processes of evolution, types of doctrine, modes of conduct, æsthetic values, in brief, beings of all grades, invite serial treatment as soon as they are compared. Various series, already conceived, can be combined in the most varied ways, so as to give us systems of objects that no longer can be arranged in any *single* serial order. We thus get Systems whose series are interwoven and interrelated in most manifold fashions. Mr. Kempe's example of the classes in a single "Universe of Discourse," while it by no means exhausts the complexity of the relations that are definable through conceiving various systems of series connected together, is so complex that the space of the geometer, we have seen, corresponds to one only of the special forms definable *within* that system.[1]

The conception of systems of facts such that any two members of the system may be viewed as linked by series of intermediaries, is thus indeed capable of application in

[1] Mr. Kempe's system illustrates, amongst other things, very definitely the fact that the generalized conception of a series of intermediaries, linking two given objects, *a* and *b*, is an infinitely variable concept. If two objects can be linked by one series, they can, in general, be linked by an infinity of other series of intermediaries. Thus *all* the classes in any Universe of Discourse are, by Mr. Kempe's definition, contained between any class *a* and the negative of that class, not-*a*. Again between any class *a* and a class *i* included within *a*, you can establish an infinite number of different series of intermediate classes. It is thus also in space, if you consider the various curves by which two points can be connected. But the spatial relation of points on a line is inadequate to express all the possibilities of the generalized relation of *between*. In Mr. Kempe's system the same object *x* can be defined as between *a* and *b*, *b* and *c*, and *c* and *a*, and can yet be different from all three.

the most widely sundered regions of our experience. If we disregard the empirical limitations that we constantly meet with in our attempts to find the desired intermediary terms, and if we consider only the foregoing postulates as defining for us how we are to conceive our world of acknowledged facts, we hereupon get a view of this world which may be summed up as follows: We may omit, for the time, from our notice, the before-mentioned possibility of a knowledge of the world that would reduce it to a *single* serial order of the general type of the Well-Ordered Series of whole numbers, where every term has one coming *next after* it. If we abstract from *that* possibility, we are left to the conception that *Between any two facts there are to be found various series of intermediaries* of the type now defined. The world thus regarded will consist for us of all these interwoven series, and will constitute a single System. The work of our knowledge, if we were to grow in knowledge indefinitely, on just these lines, would consist in the Description of this system. But this description would have the same general character that geometry illustrates in case of the space-world, which is only a particular example of such a linked system of interwoven series. Any such system would be capable of description in terms of Laws. The laws would express features common to various of the series present in this world. And the method of discovering laws would be, in its most general outlines, this: —

The whole system of the world may be viewed as made up of various different systems. For whole systems of facts can be discriminated from one another, and then linked by series of intermediate systems, precisely as *a* and *b* have been in our discussion of series in general. If, comparing two of these subordinate systems (let us say A and B), we conceive also, in some comprehensive fashion, a series of intermediary systems that link A and B together, we conceive what the mathematicians would call the "series of transformations," whereby we can, at least in our conceptions, if not in our observations, pass from one of these systems to the other. Thus, let A be, no longer, as in one of our earlier illustrations, a point in space, but a large solid body. And let B be this same body viewed by us at another time in another place, or else let it be another body of precisely the same shape and size as A, occupying another place. Let us suppose A and B compared together in one act of attention. Then we can conceive of a system of movements (consisting of translations from place to place, of rotations about one or another axis, or of a single translation followed by a single rotation), — a system whereby A could be brought to take precisely the place that B now occupies. Sometimes this serial system of movements can be actually observed. Or again, let A be the system of the characters, habits, and dispositions of the people of England just before the colonization of America; let B be the system of characters and habits and dispositions of the people of the North American Colonies at the middle of the Eighteenth Century. Then we can follow (although, in this case, only very inexactly) the series of transformations that English civilization early underwent in its passage to American soil. Other instances without limit could be named.

Between any two systems, A and B, there thus lie

intermediate systems of conceived, or, on occasion, of observed transformations, whereby one passes, in idea or in experience, from A to B. Now because of the general character of the relation *between*, as defined in the foregoing, all the intermediate transformations in any one system will be capable of being viewed as stages in a single definable process of passing from A to B. This process tends to acquire the unity of a single volitional act. And this process (if we abstract from certain complications that we need not here consider) may always be viewed as having *one* general direction, that leads *from* A to B, *through* the intermediary stages. But A and B will, as systems, resemble one another as well as differ. That depends upon the very nature of discrimination. And by virtue of the nature of the *between* relationship (just in so far as the intermediate process has one type and direction), all the intermediate stages will resemble each other in the very features in which A and B resemble each other. For all the stages between A and B are, by definition, facts that would not be viewed as different from either A or B, unless A and B were viewed as different each from the other. Hence all the intermediate stages must have in common the features that A and B have in common. These features then remain *unvarying* throughout the series of transformations in question. Denote these *unvarying features* (or, in the more technical way of stating the case), the "invariant characters of this system of transformations," by the letter I. Then the whole process here in question, whether it is merely conceived, or is observed, will be definable as "a series of transformations, beginning in A, ending (so far) in B, and leaving invariant the characters I."

Now all that we mean by the laws governing a system of facts is that within this system certain series of observed or of validly conceived "transformations" can be defined, such that throughout the whole series of transformations some definable characters of the objects that are undergoing the transformation do not vary. Wherever I can say that, in passing from A to B, through a series of stages which I have a right to view as real facts in the world, I observe, or validly conceive, that all the stages have certain uniform or "invariant" characters, I then have discovered a law which, in this way of interpreting the world, I conceive as expressing the nature and structure of the facts that I acknowledge as real.

Thus, moving a body from one part of space to another leaves, of itself, the shape of the body unchanged. Whoever discovers that, discovers the property of space defined by the so-called "axiom" or law of "free mobility." All physical and chemical changes, so far as known, leave the mass of matter unaltered. This is another example of law. All the transformations which a gravitating system of bodies undergoes are such as to leave invariant the precise system of relationships which that law defines. And so one could continue indefinitely. *What* laws our discriminating intelligence and our discovery of the serial linkages shall lead us to define, this view of our world leaves us unable to predict. But that *some* laws will come to be acknowledged, this is as certain as that the serial method of interpreting the structure of our world has, within its own limits, validity.[1]

VI

But what are the limits of this way of viewing things? What is the precise nature and range of its validity?

We have followed the logical genesis of the categories of what we may now call The World of Description, from their simplest forms to the point where we must abandon the attempt to develope here more fully their detail.[2]

The most fundamental of these categories is that of Likeness and Difference. Upon the basis of a consideration of the nature of this primal conception, we come to view the Objective World as, in one aspect of its Being, a realm of Objects of Possible Attention. The Categories of Relation, which have to do with the connections existing amongst these Objects, we could not

[1] The first systematic attempt to *classify* the laws present in a system by regarding these laws as the "invariants" of "systems of transformations" was, so far as I know, stated in Klein's *Erlanger Programm* of 1872: *Vergleichende Betrachtungen über Neuere Geometrische Forschungen.* Klein regarded the types of laws demonstrable in the various different sorts of geometry (Projective Geometry, Analysis Situs, etc.) as so many species, each definable in terms of the invariants of a Group of Transformations. The conception has since been extended to other fields of science. Owing to the irreversible character of many of the serial processes present in our experience, the "Group" character, in the narrower sense of that term, will be absent from many of the systems of transformations with which science has to deal. But a law will still be the expression of the "invariants" of a system of transformations.

[2] We shall return, in our Fourth Lecture, to the consideration of these categories as they appear when applied to our actual study of nature.

exhaustively study. Only the fundamental relation *Between*, in the generalized sense, attracted our closer attention, and has represented for us, in this discussion, all the Categories of Relation, although, of course, the very nature of serial order implies also the existence of countless other relations. On the basis of this conception we reached the Category of Ordered Series, although not in its only form. For the Category of Number, and of the Self-Representative System, or Well-Ordered Series, was fully discussed in our Supplementary Essay, and is here presupposed. Nor have we attempted to discuss the Category of Continuity, which would find a place in a full treatment of the Ordered Series. On the basis, however, of the Concept of Series, we indicated the nature of the more complex Category of the Ordered System, in which many series are interwoven. And thus we were led to an indication of the scope of the Category of Law as it appears in the World of Description.

So much for the mere list of concepts. Plainly these are indeed fundamental notions regarding the realm of the facts that we ought to acknowledge. But are they exhaustive? Has our world of fact no other aspect than this?

I answer at once, the world of the objects of my present possible Attention, where attention means simply the discrimination of what is already assumed to be there, is by no means the final or determinate world that the Will seeks. For, first, it is on its face a world of abstract aspects, and not of finality. It is a world of Validity, and not explicitly a world of Individuals such as our Fourth Conception demands. It is, moreover, defined in terms of a fundamental postulate that always has an alternative over against it, the alternative expressed by saying that were the world concretely viewed as a Self-Representative System, then, for one who grasped the facts in the order of that system, the recurrent process of the interpolation of intermediate terms in series already recognized would no longer express the final truth. And finally, this conception of the World of Description, although it is constantly suggested by certain aspects of experience, meets constantly its empirical limitations. We frequently make discriminations that we have to accept as final, without being able to comprehend them any further through discovering, in our experience, new intermediate terms. So it is when we find a limit to our power to observe finer distinctions of shades lying between two shades of gray. So it is, still more markedly, when we fail to find definite signs that between two individuals whom we believe to be real (as, for example, between two men), there are all the possible intermediate grades of individual men. Our empirical world appears to us often discrete. The problem of the "missing link" is not confined to the well-known instances that the theory of evolution brings to our notice. And it is, above all, individuality, wherever experience suggests it to us, that seems associated with a certain discreteness.

Now it is perfectly sure that, so long as we view the world merely as the field of possible discriminations, of consequent series, and of intended abstract descriptions, we deal with all these empirical failures by noting that to discriminate two objects and yet to be unable to find an intermediary, is, so far, to be baffled as to the relation of the One and the Many. Hence, so long as we are trying merely to describe what we find, and possess no other clew, we postulate, where we do not observe, the intermediaries. Our thinking, under the influence of such postulates, moves in the direction of conceiving every discrete series as a mere fragment of a continuum. And to "understand" the world, in terms of ideal continuity, is often our provisional goal. But the deepest principle of our procedure, even in this case, is the assurance that the One and the Many *can* be reconciled, and that the real world is the expression of our Purpose. In conceiving the World of Description, we view the facts, however, as if the only purpose that they could fulfil was the purpose of being discriminable. But perhaps even this purpose can be reached better in some other way. Perhaps the real world forms in its wholeness a Well-Ordered Series of a discrete type. For such, as we saw in the Supplementary Essay, is the characteristic form in which Selfhood is expressed.

Let us look, however, a little more closely at the sense in which this World of Description is also a world of abstraction. Here our attention is at once attracted by a consideration that I have so far kept in the background. Our principle has so far been this, "The real world is even now virtually present to my thought at every moment, as that whole which I acknowledge. My task in trying to come to clearer consciousness about the world is to discriminate *what* it is that I acknowledge." It is indifferent, from this point of view, where I begin. *Any a* and *b* will do to start my investigation.

Observe facts, and then look for their linkages. That is the one maxim of my procedure, — the maxim of descriptive science stated in its most abstract form. The choice of a specialty is indeed a personal matter ; and because of human narrowness any one man has to confine himself to his own specialty. But all specialties have, from this point of view, their place in the endless task of describing the world. *Was haben Sie neues gefunden?* — this is the question which they ask of the laboratory specialist in Germany. *Anything* will do, if only it belongs to the range of one's specialty. The great world is there in the background all the time, awaiting the discriminating attention, now of this and now of that specialist. What you find must indeed be *new*, and, nevertheless, capable of being linked to the old. For, after all, even mere discrimination is an expression of the will, which seeks novelty. But the plan of one's discriminating procedure is indeed a self-surrendering plan. There is a heroism of sacrifice about it. I will give myself up to the facts so far as in me lies. I will find myself, only by losing myself in attentive observation of what is already there. My construction shall always be merely an acknowledgment of what I find.

But now, for such a method of work, not only any fact will do to begin with ; but *any* point of view from which I set out will lead me to the *same* ideal result if only I continue this process of description. This world of facts, arranged in these abstractly conceived series, is *anybody's* world. All of us start from different points of view. We all, if we find this sort of truth, shall come in the end to define our results in terms of corresponding series.

And this variety of possible points of view is not merely a chance accompaniment of description, but a necessary consequence of the way in which this series-forming-process of looking for what lies between any two objects proceeds. For from this point of view *there is nothing about the objects, as thus discriminated, which makes it necessary to take them up in your investigation in one order rather than in another.* Projective geometry deals with the facts of space in one way. Metrical geometry deals with them in another way. A higher development of mathematical thought shows how, by the addition of certain conceptions, one can pass from the series of conceived objects and relations of objects that projective geometry finds in space, to the series of the metrical geometer, and *vice versa.* And now there seem to be *two equally justified* ways of portraying the metrical properties of space. Or, in another field, in preparing the way for the description of the process of evolution, the historians and the geologists, the botanists, the zoölogists, the astronomers, — all contribute their various series of facts to be linked together in the larger generalization; and it is a mere historical accident in what order, or by what specialty, the particular series are brought to light. Hence, in general, since the discriminations upon which the formation of series depends might be made in any order, beginning with any *a* and *b*, the World of Description is, even apart from our human social conceptions, a world where the *same* results are valid for *various* methods of approaching and so of expressing these results. It is a world, therefore, where truth is never discovered in its complete and final individual form. For the various possible ways of defining series of facts are all equally justified. But to say this is to admit that they are all equally abstract and inadequate.

When you count eggs, it "makes no difference" in what order you count them. But when you are to enjoy a Symphony, a great deal depends on the precise order in which the notes are played. When the astronomer makes a catalogue of stars, the stars appear indifferent to the order in which their positions are set down. But when you undertake to perform any rational task, such as getting through your day's duties, or serving your country, or growing in a sense of your relations to God, everything turns upon the order in which you do your work. Whatever expresses a single purpose has, as the expression of that purpose, an irreversible succession. One deed comes first, another next, and so on forever.

And now this holds true as to precisely the personal, the truly volitional aspect, of even those very processes of a descriptive sort (counting eggs, cataloguing stars, discriminating facts in their series), — such as I have here used to exemplify the apparent indifference of the serial systems of the world of description to the order in which you, or other observers, take note of their presence. The eggs and the stars appear unconcerned about the order in which you chance to take up your task of describing their serial variety. But *in your life*, that is, or ought to be, as orderly as the symphony or as serving God and your country, it makes a great difference *to you*, when you count the eggs, whether or no you count "six" after having counted "five," or skip in counting one or more of your well-ordered number-names. And in the life of the astronomer, considered as a man coöperating in a social task with other astronomers, the order in which the catalogue is made may be as sacred as any other moral task. Now the Reality is not the world apart from the activity of knowing beings, — it is the world of the fact *and* the knowledge in one organic whole.

It follows that we simply do not tell the whole story of our live relations to the world when we report the results of our formation, through successive discriminations, of series of facts. The world is unquestionably there to be known. Its facts are objects of possible attention. They can be discriminated. They do form series. But that is not the whole truth about them. The world is *also* there to express a perfectly determinate and absolute purpose. Its facts are incidents in a life, — yes, in a life of many lives, — *a rationally connected social system of beings that embody purposes in deeds.* The facts can therefore not only be discriminated, but, in so far as we ever come to be conscious of their true sense, they are linked in a teleological unity. And this unity determines not merely what is *the same for many points of view*, but what is uniquely present, once for all, from the divine point of view, as the one true Order of things. And the true Series is that of the Self, and of its expression in life. The true variety is that of various individual Selves, who together constitute, in their unity, the Individual of Individuals, the absolute. Beyond our own circle of concretely known facts, there are not merely series of data to be discriminated, but volitional processes to be estimated, appreciated, and conceived in their true serial order, as the stages of the world's life.

Now this conclusion is suggested, apart from our own special Theory of Being, by any fair reflection upon what happens when discriminations are made, when series of facts are found and described, when various observers, proceeding from different starting-points, reach, like the projective and the metrical geometer, or like two students of an experimental science, the *same* abstract results. For, as a fact, one has only to reflect in order to see, as we just saw in the case of counting the eggs, or of cataloguing the stars, that the process of discrimination, or of forming series, is itself an incident in a life whose Internal Meaning lies not merely in the acknowledgment of facts, but also in the creation of novelties. Our interest in discriminating is expressed in the joyous "I see" of the discoverer. But this is the joy of living, of creating, as well as finding, a world. For in merely acknowledging facts one may indeed be said to *find* (in the sense that I here have in mind) something that, as one conceives, *another* might have found as well. But one is conscious of creating, only in so far as one believes that the expression of one's purpose is an unique and individual fact, that has nowhere else in the world of Being its likeness.[1] In consequence, the whole truth is that one discriminates, indeed, at every step, and in doing so acknowledges what one does not regard as one's present creation. But this very act of discrimination is, in the life of one who sees, a present, an individual, and in so far a creative expression of purpose. And the world, *in permitting this ex-*

[1] See the discussion of the relations between freedom, activity, and individuality in the First Series of these lectures, p. 466, *sqq.*

pression, reveals its true essence better than the mere description of the serially arranged data reveals the final truth of things. Whoever observes merely the series of linked and discriminated facts, has therefore but to reflect in order further to observe that *one's discrimination and linking of facts is itself also a fact*, yet not a fact in the series discriminated, — but rather one stage in a life of self-expression. Thinking, also, is living. Science is justified as a type of action. And this is why we never can be content with discovering that the world is describable, but must note that all description is valuable as a process occurring in a life. That is why, moreover, we must always hold that the very facts themselves which we can at present interpret only in terms of Description, are the incidents of an orderly life of divine Self-Expression.

VII

All then that we said at the outset about the presence of the world in the background, as the acknowledged reality *in* which we are to discover all the facts that ever we are to come to acknowledge in the concrete, was, as far as it went, valid. And the conclusion that we drew as to the way in which we, from our point of view, must undertake to solve the problem of the One and the Many by the serial discrimination and linkage of facts, expresses a significant, although partial, aspect of our search for truth. But the other aspect of the truth returns of itself whenever we reflect. The world is indeed there in the background. But it is there as embodiment of Life, and not merely as the object of discrimination. It is a world with which we stand in Social Relations. Its life coöperates with ours.

And now, as to the true serial order of this world of Life, we have, from the outset of our exposition of our Fourth Concept, recognized that, whatever the world contains, it contains in the form of a Self-Conscious Being. In our Supplementary Essay we showed at length that a Self, as a real being, has a certain form of expression, which inevitably involves a serial structure, but that *this* serial structure, in its main outline, is most truly represented by the form of the series of whole numbers, rather than by the form of a series between any two of whose terms, further terms without end are interpolated. A series of the latter type is indeed describable. Nor is it in the least objectionable by reason of the infinite complexity of its conceived structure. For, as the Supplementary Essay showed us, the real world is certainly infinitely complex in structure, and there is no contradiction in conceiving an infinitely complex object as real. But, from our point of view, the world of a Self, whatever continuity of internal structure it may in some aspects possess, is *in its principal form of expression embodied in a discrete series of acts, of individual expressions, of stages of self-representation and of self-revelation.* We cannot here repeat the argument by which this result was reached in the Essay in question. But experience at any moment shows how I am conscious of my own deeds, of my progress, of my acts of attention, and of my approaches to selfhood in any way, in the form of a *discrete series, in which one stage or act of life is followed by the next.* The principle of *my* life, as I come to myself, and, knowing what I want, proceed to do it, is a principle *winning novelty through Recurrence. Again* and *again*, I proceed, *from* one act *to* the next, and so always to new acts. But neither an interpolation of deeds *between* my own deeds, nor yet a consciousness of unbroken continuity in my own acts, would help me to understand myself. *My* order, then, so far as I grasp it at all, is, like the order of the number-series, discrete. That is shown in my very process of discriminating something *between* any two accepted facts, so far as it is *my own process*. For that process, as we saw, is a recurrent one. I find that *a* is not next to *b*, but has *m* between. Then I conceive m^1, inserted, then m^2, and so on. But as I do this, my act of conceiving the new intermediaries comes next after a former act; and another act of conceiving intermediaries between *a* and *b* comes, in *my* life, next after this one.

Now if, with this fact in mind, I look back on the world which I attempted thus to describe, I find that the limitation which experience often seems to set to my postulates about the discrimination of facts, may well be founded in the deepest nature of things. The true world, the World of Values or of Appreciation, as rightly viewed by an absolute insight, would be a world of Selves, forming in the unity of their systems One Self. This world would appear to such an insight as a Social Order. For the categories of the World of Appreciation, as we shall later more fully see, when we come to the study of our human Social consciousness, are the categories of the Self in Social form and expression. But as I discriminate the world, taking account now of *a* and now of *b*, my discrimination, determined as it is by the interest of my individual development, does not seize upon the facts in the order in which they are actually determined by the Will whose expression is the world. As I take the facts, they come to me as incidents in my individual life. Since I fail to grasp the One in the Many in these cases, I postulate the intermediaries, and have a right to do so in so far as that can further my own purpose of comprehension, which itself is a part of the world-purpose, and which is accordingly sure, within its limits, of representing one aspect of the truth. The true world, however, is not the world of description, but the world of socially interrelated Selves. And the world as we describe it, is the world viewed in the order of our own processes of description, which as incident in our human life, have their value, but are expressions of the true world order, only in so far as they reveal to us the life of things. Our conclusion is that the true series of facts in the world must be a Well-Ordered Series, in which every fact has its next-following fact. The series discoverable by us in the World of Description are characterized by the prevalence, for our view, of the relation *Between*. Hence they do not appear to us as Well-Ordered Series. But just in so far they are inadequate expressions of the truth.

We are now prepared to consider the more special form which these general categories will take when we come to study our human experience of Nature and of our fellows. But before we make that transition, there is still something to be said regarding one further fundamental conception, — that of Time.

LECTURE III

LECTURE III

THE TEMPORAL AND THE ETERNAL

THE world of the facts that we ought to acknowledge is, in one of its aspects, present (so we have maintained) as the Object of Possible Attention, in every act of finite insight. Finitude means inattention to the wealth and organization of the world's detail.

An obvious objection to this thesis is furnished by the nature of Time. How can Past and Future, which "do not exist," be in any sense "present," in the undistinguished unity of the facts which any finite thinker at any instant acknowledges?

In the Ninth Lecture of the First Series, we briefly considered the topic of temporal Being.[1] We have to return to it here with more detail. There is an ancient distinction of the philosophers between the Temporal and the Eternal. It must be plain at this point, that we ascribe to the true world a certain eternal type of Being. Yet how shall we reconcile this with our equally obvious treatment of the world as existing in time? Plainly we have here a question that is of great importance for any understanding of the categories of experience. It belongs, then, in the context of these earlier discussions of our present series of lectures. Moreover, it is one that will constantly meet us later. The relation of Time to

[1] p. 407, *sqq.*, pp. 420–421.

Nature will be of central concern to us. When we come to deal with the individual Self, we shall again have to face the question: In what sense has the Self of the individual a purely Temporal, and in what sense an Eternal type of reality? And before we can answer this question we must be more precise than we have yet been in defining the terms Time and Eternity. The issue here involved has a significance not only theoretical, but also intensely practical. It will need therefore a close and deliberate scrutiny. Time, as we shall soon see, is a concept of fundamentally practical meaning. The definition of the Eternal, on the other hand, has very close relations to the question as to the ultimate significance of all that is practical. Any rational decision as between a pessimistic and an optimistic view of the world, any account of the relations between God and Man, any view of the sense in which the evils and imperfections of the Universe can be comprehended or justified, any account of our ethical consciousness in terms reconcilable with our Idealism, — in brief, any philosophical reconciliation with religion and life, must turn in part upon a distinction between the Temporal and the Eternal, and upon an insight into their unity in the midst of their contrast. The problem at issue is one of the most delicate and, at the same time, one of the simplest of the great issues of philosophy. I shall here have to deal with it at first in a purely theoretical fashion, and shall then proceed to its practical applications. For both aspects of the question we are now fully prepared.

I

Time is known to us, both perceptually, as the psychologists would say, and conceptually. That is, we have a relatively direct experience of time at any moment, and we acknowledge the truth of a relatively indirect conception that we possess of the temporal order of the world. But our conception of time far outstrips in its development and in its organization anything that we are able directly to find in the time that is known to our perceptions. Much of the difficulty that appears in our metaphysical views about time is, however, due to lack of naïveté and directness in viewing the temporal aspects of reality. We first emphasize highly artificial aspects of our conception of time. Then we wonder how these various aspects can be brought into relation with the rest of the real world. Our efforts to solve our problem lead very easily to contradictions. We fail to observe how, in case of our more direct experience of time and of its meaning, various elements are woven into a certain wholeness, — the very elements which, when our artificial conception of time has sundered them, we are prone to view as irreconcilable with one another and with reality.

Our more direct perceptions of time form a complex sort of consciousness, wherein it is not difficult to distinguish several aspects. For the first, some Change is always occurring in our experience. This change may belong to the facts of any sense, or to our emotions, or to our ideas; but for us to be conscious is to be aware of change. Now this changing character of our experience is never the whole story of any of our clearer and more definite kinds of consciousness. The next aspect of the matter lies in the fact that our consciousness of change, wherever it is definite and wherever it accompanies definite successive acts of attention, goes along with the consciousness that for us something comes first, and something next, or that there is what we call a Succession of events. Of such successions, melodies, rhythms, and series of words or of other simple acts form familiar and typical examples. An elementary consciousness of change without such definite successions we can indeed have; but where we observe clearly what a particular change is, it is a change wherein one fact succeeds another.

A succession, as thus more directly experienced by us, involves a certain well-known relation amongst the events that make up the succession. Together these events form a temporal sequence or order. Each one of them is over and past when the next one comes. And this order of the experienced time-series has a determinate direction. The succession passes *from* each event *to* its successor, and not in the reverse direction; so that herein the observed time relations notoriously differ from what we view as space relations. For if in space *b* is next to *a*, we can read the relation equally well as a coexistence of *a* with *b*, and as a coexistence of *b* with *a*. But in case *b* succeeds *a*, as one word succeeds another in a spoken sentence, then the relation is experienced as a passing from *a* to *b*, or as a passing over of *a* into *b*, in such wise that *a* is past, as an event, before *b* comes. This direction of the stream of time forms one of its most notable empirical characters. It is obviously related to that direction of the acts of the will whose logical aspect interested us in connection with the consideration of our discriminating consciousness.

But side by side with this aspect of the temporal order, as we experience this order, stands still another aspect, whose relation to the former has been persistently pointed out by many psychological writers, and as persistently ignored by many of the metaphysical interpreters of the temporal aspect of the universe. When we more directly experience succession, — as, for instance, when we listen to a musical phrase or to a rhythmic series of drum-beats, — we not only observe that any antecedent member of the series is over and past before the next number comes, but also, and without the least contradiction between these two aspects of our total experience, we observe that this whole succession, with both its former and later members, so far as with relative directness we apprehend the series of drum-beats or of other simple events, is present *at once* to our consciousness, in precisely the sense in which the unity of our knowing mental life always finds present at once many facts. It is, as I must insist, true that for my consciousness *b* is experienced as following *a*, and also that both *a* and *b* are *together* experienced as in this relation of sequence. To say this is no more contradictory than to say that while I experience two parts of a surface as, by virtue of their spatial position, mutually exclusive each of the other, I also may experience the fact that both these mutually exclusive parts go together to form one whole surface. The sense in which they form one surface is, of course, not the sense in which, as parts, they exclude each other, and form different surfaces.

Well, just so, the sense in which *b*, as successor of *a*, is such, in the series of events in question, that *a* is over and gone when *b* comes, is not the sense in which *a* and *b* are together elements in the whole experienced succession. But that, in *both* of these senses, the relation of *b* to its predecessor *a* is an experienced fact, is a truth that any one can observe for himself.

If I utter a line of verse, such as

> "The curfew tolls the knell of parting day,"

the sound of the word *day* succeeds the sound of the word *parting*, and I unquestionably experience the fact that, for me, every earlier word of the line is over and past before the succeeding word or the last word, *day*, comes to be uttered or to be heard. Yet this is unquestionably not my whole consciousness about the succession. For I am certainly *also* aware that the *whole* line of poetry, as a succession of uttered sounds (or, at all events, a considerable portion of the line), is present to me at once, and as this one succession, when I speak the line. For only by virtue of experiencing this wholeness do I observe the rhythm, the music, and the meaning of the line. The sense in which the word *parting* is over before the word *day* comes, is like the sense in which one object in space is *where* any other object is *not*, so that the spatial *presence* of one object excludes the presence of another at that same part of space. Precisely so the presence of the word *day* excludes the presence of the word *parting* from its own place in the temporal succession. And, in our experience of succession, each element is *present* in a particular point of the series, in so far as, with reference to that point, other events of the series are either *past*, that is, over and done with, or are *future*, that is, are later in the series, or are *not yet when* this one point of the series is in *this* sense present. Every word of the uttered line of poetry, viewed in its reference to the other words, or to previous and later experiences, is *present* in its own place in the series, is *over and done with* before later events can come, or when they are present, and is *not yet* when the former events of the succession are present. And that all this is true, certainly is a matter of our experience of succession.

But the sense in which, nevertheless, the whole series of the uttered words of the line, or of some considerable portion of the line, is presented to our consciousness *at once*, is precisely the sense in which we apprehend this line as one line, and this succession as one succession. The whole series of words has for us its rhythmic unity, and forms an instance of conscious experience, whose unity we overlook at one glance. And unless we could thus overlook a succession and view at once its serially related and mutually exclusive events, we should never know anything whatever about the existence of succession, and should have no problem about time upon our hands.

This extremely simple and familiar character of our consciousness of succession, — this essentially double aspect of every experience of a present series of events, — this inevitably twofold sense in which the term *present* can be used in regard to our perception of temporal happenings, — this is a matter of the most fundamental importance for our whole conception of Time, and, as I may at once add, for our conception of Eternity. Yet this is also a matter very frequently obscured, in discussion, by various devices often used to express the nature of the facts here in question. Sometimes, for the sake of a laudable attempt to define the term *present* in a wholly unambiguous way, those who are giving an account of our experience of time are led to assert that, since every part or element of any series of temporal events can be *present* only when all the other elements of the series are temporally non-existent, *i.e.* are either past or future, it must therefore be quite impossible for us to be conscious, *at once*, of a present succession involving a series of such elements. For how, they say, can I be conscious of the presence of all the successive words of the verse of poetry, when only one word is actually and temporally present at any one time? To comprehend how I can become in any sense aware of the series of successive words that constitutes the line of verse, such students of our problem are accustomed to say that when any one word as *passing*, or *day*, is present to my mind, the other words, even of the same line, can be present to consciousness *only* as coexistent memories or images of the former words, or as images of the expected coming words. From this point of view, I never really observe any sequence of conscious events as a sequence at all. I merely apprehend each element by itself; and I directly conclude from the images which in my experience are coexistent with this element, that there have been antecedent, and will be subsequent events in the series.

This interpretation of our consciousness of time is, however, directly counter to our time-experience, as any one may observe it for himself. For we do experience succession, and *at once* we do take note of facts that are in different times. For, I ask you, What word of mine is it that, as this single present word, you just *now* hear me speaking? If I pause a little, you perhaps dwell upon the last word that I utter before pausing, and call that the one present word. Otherwise, however, as I speak to you, you are conscious of series of successive words, of whole phrases, of word groups, of clauses. Within each one of these groups of words, you are indeed more or less clearly aware that every element has its own temporal place; and that, *in so far as* each element is taken by itself as present, the other elements either precede or succeed it, and in *this* sense are not in one time with it. But this very fact itself you know merely in so far as you actually experience series, each of which contains several successive words. These series come to you not merely by virtue of remembered facts, but also as experienced facts.

And in truth, were this not so, you could indeed have no experience of succession at all. You would then experience, at any one moment, merely the single word, or something less than any single word, together with the supposed coexistent and contemporaneous images of actually past or of coming words. But how, in that case, would your experience of time-sequences come to seem to you different from any experience whatever of coexistence? Nor is even this the only difficulty about the doctrine which supposes you to be unable to view a series of successive events as all at once presented to your consciousness. A still deeper difficulty results from such an effort to evade the double sense in which the facts of succession are known in your experience. If you can have present to you only *one* event at a time in a series of successive events, how long, or rather how short, must an event be to contain within itself no succession at all, or no difference between former and latter contents? In vain do you suppose that, at any time, you have directly present to your consciousness only one of the successive words that you hear me speak. Not thus do you escape our difficulty. For a spoken word is itself a series of temporally successive sounds. Can you hear at once the whole spoken word, or can you grasp at once this whole series? If so, my own foregoing account is in principle admitted. For then, in this presence of the facts of succession to your consciousness, there are our two former aspects, both of them, involved. *Each* element of the succession (namely, in this case, the elementary sounds that to your consciousness make up the word) is temporally present just when it occurs, but *not* before or afterwards, in so far as it follows previous elements and succeeds later elements; and also *all* the elements are, in the other sense of the term, *present at once* to consciousness, as constituting this whole succession which you call the word. If, however, you deny that you actually hear, apart from memory or from imagery, any single whole word at once, I shall only the more continue to ask you, What is the least or the simplest element of succession that is such as to constitute a merely present experience, with *no* former or latter contents within it? What apart from any memory or any imagery, and wholly apart from ideas of the past or the future of your experience, is present to you, in an indivisible time instant, just *Now?* The question is obviously unanswerable, just because an absolutely indivisible instant of mathematical time, with no former and latter contained within it, neither constitutes nor contains any temporal event, nor presents to you any fact of temporal experience whatever, just as an indivisible point in space could contain no matter, nor itself ever become, in isolation, an object of spatial experience. On the other hand, an event such that in it you were unable to perceive any succession, would help you in no whit to get the idea of time until you experienced it along with other events. What is now before you is a succession, within which are parts; and of these parts each, when and in so far as once your attention fixes it, and takes it in its time relations, is found as a present that in time both precedes and succeeds other facts, while these other facts are also just as truly before you as the observed element called the temporally present one is itself before you. And thus you cannot escape from our twofold interpretation of the experience of temporal succession. You are conscious of a series of successive states presented to you as a whole. You are also aware that each element of the succession excludes the others from its own place in time.

There is, to be sure, another frequent way of describing our consciousness of succession, — and a way that on the whole I find unsatisfactory. According to this view, events come to us in succession in our experience, — let us say the words of a spoken verse, — and *then* something often called the synthetic activity of the mind supervenes, and later binds together into unity, these successive facts, so that when this binding has taken place we *then* recognize the whole fagot of experience as a single succession. This account of the temporal facts, in terms of an activity called a synthesis, helps me, as I must confess, no whit. What I find in consciousness is that a succession, such as a rhythm of drum-beats, a musical phrase, a verse of poetry, comes to me as one present whole, present in the sense that I know it all at once. And I also find that this succession is such that it has *within* it a temporal distinction, or order, of earlier and later elements. While these elements are at once known, they are *also* known as such that at the briefer instant *within* the succession when any one of them is to be temporally viewed as a present fact, none of the others are contemporaneous with that fact, but all are either *no longer* or *not yet* when, and in so far as, that element is taken as the present one. And I cannot make this datum of experience any more definite by calling it a synthesis, or the mere result of a synthesis.

I have now characterized the more directly given features in our consciousness of succession. You see, as a result, that we men experience what Professor James, and others, have called our "specious present," as a serial whole, *within* which there are observed temporal differences of former and latter. And this our "specious present" has, when measured by a reference to time-keepers, a length which varies with circumstances, but which appears to be never any very small fraction of a second, and never more than a very few seconds in length. I have earlier referred to this length of our present moments as our characteristic "time-span" of consciousness, and have pointed out how arbitrary a feature and limitation of our consciousness it is. We shall return soon to the question regarding the possible metaphysical significance of this time-span of our own special kind of consciousness.

But it remains here to call closer attention to certain other equally important features of our more direct experience of time-succession. So far, we have spoken, in the main, as if succession were to us a mere matter of given facts, as colors and sounds are given. But all our experience also has relation to the interests whose play and whose success or defeat constitute the life of our will. Every serial succession of which we are conscious therefore has for us some sort of meaning. In it we find our success or our failure. In it our internal meanings are expressed, or hindered, thwarted or furthered. We are interested in life, even if it be, in idle moments, only the dreary interest of wondering what will happen next, or, in distressed moments, the interest in flying from our present fortune, or, in despairing moments, of wishing for the end; still more then if, in strenuous moments, our interest is in pursuing our ideal. And our interest in life means our conscious concern in passing on from any temporal present towards its richer fulfilment, or away from its relative insignificance. Now that Direction of temporal succession of which I before made mention, has the most intimate relations to this our interest in our experience. What is earlier in a given succession is related to what is later as being that *from* which we pass *towards* a desired fulfilment, or in search of a more complete expression of our purpose. We are never content in the temporal present in so far as we view it as temporal, that is, as an event in a series. For such a present has its meaning as a transition from its predecessors towards its successors.

Our temporal form of experience is thus peculiarly the form of the Will as such. Space often seems to spread out before us what we take to be the mere contents of our world; but time gives the form for the expression of all our meanings. Facts, in so far as, with an abstractly false Realism, we sunder them from their meanings, therefore tend to be viewed as merely in relations of coexistence; and the space-world is the favorite region of Realism. But ideas, when conscious, assume the consciously temporal form of inner existence, and appear to us as constructive processes. The visible world, when viewed as at rest, therefore interests us little in comparison with the same world when we take note of its movements, changes, successions. As the kitten ignores the dead leaves until the wind stirs them, but then chases them — so facts in general tend to appear to us all dead and indifferent when we disregard their processes. But in the movements of things lies for us, just as truly as in her small way for the kitten, all the glory and the tragedy, all the life and the meaning of our observed universe. This concern, this interest in the changing, binds us then to the lower animals, as it doubtless also binds us to beings of far higher than human grade. We watch the moving and tend to neglect the apparently changeless objects about us. And that is why narrative is so much more easily effective than description in the poetic arts;

and why, if you want to win the attention of the child or of the general public, you must tell the story rather than portray coexistent truths, and must fill time with series of events, rather than merely crowd the space of experience or of imagination with manifold but undramatic details. For space furnishes indeed the stage and the scenery of the universe, but the world's play occurs in time.

Now all these familiar considerations remind us of certain of the most essential characters of our experience of time. Time, whatever else it is, is given to us as that within whose successions, in so far as for us they have a direct interest and meaning, every event, springing from, yet forsaking, its predecessors, aims on, towards its own fulfilment and extinction in the coming of its successors. Our experience of time is thus for us essentially an experience of longing, of pursuit, of restlessness. And this is the aspect which Schopenhauer and the Buddhists have found so intolerable about the very nature of our finite experience. Upon this dissatisfied aspect of finite consciousness we ourselves dwelt when, in the former series of lectures, we were first learning to view the world, for the moment, from the mystic's point of view. As for the higher justification of this aspect of our experience, that indeed belongs elsewhere. But as to the facts, every part of a succession is present in so far as when it is, that which is *no longer* and that which is *not yet* both of them stand in essentially significant, or, if you will, in essentially practical relations to this present. It is true, of course, that when we view relatively indifferent time-series, such as the ticking of a watch or the dropping of rain upon the roof, we can disregard this more significant aspect of succession; and speak of the endless flight of time as an incomprehensible brute fact of experience, and as in so far seemingly meaningless. But no series of experiences upon which attention is fixed is wholly indifferent to us; and the temporal aspect of such series always involves some element of expectancy and some sense of something that no longer is; and both these conscious attitudes color our interest in the presented succession, and give the whole the meaning of life. Time is thus indeed the form of practical activity; and its whole character, and especially that direction of its succession of which we have spoken, are determined accordingly.

II

I have dwelt long upon the time consciousness of our relatively direct experience, because here lies the basis for every deeper comprehension of the metaphysics both of time and of eternity. Our ordinary conception of time as an universal form of existence in the external world, is altogether founded upon a generalization, whose origin is in us men largely and obviously social, but whose materials are derived from our inner experience of the succession of significant events. The conceived relations of Past, Present, and Future in the real world of common-sense metaphysics, appear indeed, at first sight, vastly to transcend anything that we ourselves have ever observed in our inner experience. The infinite and irrevocable past that no longer is, the expected infinite future that has as yet no existence, how remote these ideal constructions, supposed to be valid for all gods and men and things, seem at first sight from the brief and significant series of successive events that occur within the brief span of our actual human consciousness. Yet, as we saw in the ninth lecture of our former Series, common sense, as soon as questioned about special cases, actually conceives the Being of both the past and the future as so intimately related to the Being of the present that every definite conception of the real processes of the world, whether these processes are viewed as physical or as historical or explicitly as ethical, depends upon taking the past, the present, and the future as constituting a single whole, whose parts have no true Being except in their linkage. As a fact, moreover, the term *present*, when applied to characterize a moment or an event in the time-stream of the real world, never means, in any significant application, the indivisible present of an ideal mathematical time. The present time, in case of the world at large, has an unity altogether similar to that of the present moment of our inner consciousness. We may speak of the present minute, hour, day, year, century. If we use the term *present* regarding any one of these divisions of time, but regard this time not as the experienced form of the inner succession of our own mental events, but as the time of the real world in which we ourselves form a part, then we indeed conceive that this present is world-embracing, and that suns move, light radiates between stars, the deeds of all men occur, and the minds of all men are conscious, in this same present time of which we thus make mention. Moreover, we usually view the world-time in question in terms of the conceptions of the World of Description, and so we conceive it as infinitely divisible, as measurable by various mathematical and physical devices, and as a continuous stream of occurrence. Yet in whatever sense we speak of the real present time of the world, this present, whether it is the present second, or the present century, or the present geological period, it is, for our conception, as truly a divisible and connected whole region of time, within which a succession of events takes place, as it is a world-embracing and connected time, within whose span the whole universe of present events is comprised. A mathematically indivisible present time, possessing no length, is simply no time at all. Whoever says, "In the universe at large only the present state of things is real, only the present movement of the stars, the present streamings of radiant light, the present deeds and thoughts of men are real; the whole past is dead; the whole future is not yet," — any such reporter of the temporal existence of the universe may be invited to state how long his real present of the time-world is. If he replies, "The present moment is the absolutely indivisible and ideal boundary between present and future," — then one may rejoin at once that in a mathematically indivisible instant, having no length, no event happens, nothing endures, no thought or deed takes place, — in brief, nothing whatever temporally exists, — and that, too, whatever conception you may have of Being. But if the real present is a divisible portion of time, then it contains within itself succession, precisely as the "specious present" of psychological time contains such internal succession. But in that case, within the real present of the time-world, there are already contained the distinctions that, in case of the time of experience, we have heretofore observed. If, in what you choose to call the present moment of the world's history, deeds are accomplished, suns actually move from place to place, light waves traverse the ether, and men's lives pass from stage to stage, then *within* what you thus call the present there are distinguishable and more elementary events, arranged in series, such that when any conceived element, or mere elementary portion of any series is taken in relation to its predecessors and successors, it is *not yet* when its antecedents are taken as temporally present, and is *past and gone* when its successors are viewed as present. The world's time is thus in all respects a generalized and extended image and correspondent of the observed time of our inner experience. In the time of our more direct experience, we find a twofold way in which we can significantly call a portion of time a present moment. The present, in our inner experience, means a whole series of events grasped by somebody as having some unity for his consciousness, and as having its own single internal meaning. This was what we meant by the present experience of this musical phrase, this spoken line of verse, this series of rhythmic beats. But, in the other sense of the word, an element within any such whole is present in so far as this element has antecedents and successors, so that they are *no longer* or *not yet* when it is temporally viewed as present, while in turn, in so far as any one of them is viewed as the present element, this element itself is either *not yet* or *no longer*. But precisely so, in the conceptual time of our real world, the Present means any section of the time-stream in so far as, with reference to anybody's consciousness, it is viewed as having relation to this unity of consciousness, and as in a single whole of meaning with this unity. Usually by "our time," or "the real time in which we now live," we mean no very long period of the conceived time-stream of the real world. But we never mean the indivisible *now* of an ideal mathematical time, because, in such an indivisible time-instant, nothing could happen, or endure, or genuinely exist. But within the present, if conceived as a section of the time-stream, there are internal differences of present, past, and future.

For, in a similar fashion, as the actual or supposed length of the "specious present" of our perceptual time is something arbitrary, determined by our peculiar human type of consciousness, so the length of the portion of conceptual time which we call the *present*, in the first sense of that term, namely, in the sense in which we speak of the "present age," is an arbitrary length, determined in this case, however, by our more freely chosen interest in some unity which gives relative wholeness and meaning to this present. If usually the "present age" is no very long time, still, at our pleasure, or in the service of some such unity of meaning as the history of civilization, or the study of geology, may suggest, we may conceive the present as extending over many centuries, or over a hundred thousand years. On the other hand, within the unity of this first present, any distinguishable event or element of an event is *present*, in the second, and more strictly temporal sense in so far as it has predecessors and successors, whereof the first are *no longer*, and the latter *not yet*, when this more elementary event is viewed as happening.

Nor does the parallelism between the perceptual and the conceptual time cease here. The perceptual time was the form in which meaning, and the practically significant aspects of consciousness, get their expression. The same is true of the conceptual time, when viewed in its relations to the real world. Not only is the time of human history, or of any explicitly teleological series of events, obviously the form in which the facts win their particular type of conceived meaning; but even the time of physical science gets its essential characters, as a conception, through considerations that can only be interpreted in terms of the Will, or of our interest in the meaning of the world's happenings.

For the conceived time-series, even when viewed in relation to the World of Description, still differs in constitution from the constitution of a line in space, or from the characters belonging to a mathematically describable physical movement of a body, in ways which can only be expressed in terms of significance. Notoriously, conceptual time has often been described as correspondent in structure to the structure of a line, or as correspondent again, in character, to the character of an uniformly flowing stream, or of some other uniform movement. But a line can be traversed in either direction, while conceptual time is supposed to permit but one way of passing from one instant to another in its course. An uniform flow, or other motion, has, like time, a fixed direction, but might be conceived as returning into itself without detriment to its uniformity. Thus an ideally regular watch "keeps time," as we say, by virtue of the uniformity of its motion; but its hands return ever again to the same places on the face; while the years of conceptual time return not again. And finally, if one supposed an ideally uniform physical flow or streaming in one rectilinear direction only, and in an infinite Euclidean space, the character of this movement might so far be supposed to correspond to that of an ideally conceived mathematical time; except for one thing. The uniformity and unchangeableness of the conceived physical flow would be a merely given character, dependent, perhaps, upon the fact that the physical movement in question was conceived as meeting with no obstacle or external hindrance; but the direction of the flow of time is a character essential to the very conception of time. And this direction of the flow of time can only be expressed in its true necessity by saying that in case of the world's time, as in the case of the time of our inner experience, we conceive the past as leading towards, as aiming in the direction of the future, in such wise that the future depends for its meaning upon the past, and the past in its turn has its meaning as a process expectant of the future. In brief, only in terms of Will, and only by virtue of the significant relations of the stages of a teleological process, has time, whether in our inner experience, or in the conceived world order as a whole, any meaning. Time is the form of the Will; and the real world is a temporal world in so far as, in various regions of that world, seeking differs from attainment, pursuit is external to its own goal, the imperfect tends towards its own perfection, or in brief, the internal meanings of finite life gradually win, in successive stages, their union with their own External Meaning. The general justification for this whole view of the time of the real world is furnished by our idealistic interpretation of Being. The special grounds for regarding the particular Being of time itself as in this special way teleological, are furnished by the foregoing analysis of our own experience of time, and by the fact that the conceptual time in terms of which we interpret the order of the world at large, is fashioned, so to speak, after the model of the time of our own experience.

III

Having thus defined the way in which the conceptual time of the real world of common sense corresponds in its structure to the structure of the time known to our inner perception, we are prepared to sketch our theory both of the sense in which the world of our idealistic doctrine appears to be capable of interpretation as a Temporal order, and of the sense in which, for this same theory, this world is to be viewed as an Eternal order. For, as a fact, in defining time we have already, and inevitably, defined eternity; and a temporal world must needs be, when viewed in its wholeness, an eternal world. We have only to review the structure of Reality in the light of the foregoing analysis in order to bring to our consciousness this result.

And so, first, the real world of our Idealism has to be viewed by us men as a temporal order. For it is a world where purposes are fulfilled, or where finite internal meanings reach their final expression, and attain unity with external meanings. Now in so far as any idea, as a finite Internal Meaning, still seeks its own Other, and consciously pursues that Other, in the way in which, as we have all along seen, every finite idea does pursue its Other, this Other is in part viewed as something beyond, *towards* which the striving is directed. But our human experience of temporal succession is, as we have seen, just such an experience of a pursuit directed towards a goal. And such pursuit demands, as an essential part or aspect of the striving in question, a consciousness that agrees in its most essential respect with our own experience of time. Hence, our only way of expressing the general structure of our idealistic realm of Being is to say that wherever an idea exists as a finite idea, still in pursuit of its goal, there appears to be some essentially temporal aspect belonging to the consciousness in question. To my mind, therefore, time, as the form of the will, is (in so far as we can undertake to define at all the detailed structure of finite reality) to be viewed as the most pervasive form of all finite experience, whether human or extra-human. In pursuing its goals, the Self lives in time. And, to our view, every real being in the universe, in so far as it has not won union with the ideal, is pursuing that ideal; and, accordingly, so far as we can see, is living in time. Whoever, then, is finite, says, "not yet," and in part seeks his Other as involving what, to the seeker, is still future. For the finite world in general, then, as for us human beings, the distinction of past and future appears to be coextensive with life and meaning.

I have advisedly used, however, the phrase that the time-consciousness is a "part" or "aspect" of the striving. For from our point of view, the Other, the completion that our finite being seeks, is not *merely* something beyond the present, and is not merely a future experience, but is also inclusive of the very process of the striving itself. For the goal of every finite life is simply the totality whereof this life, in its finitude, is a fragment. When I seek my own goal, I am looking for the whole of myself. In so far as my aim is the absolute completion of my Selfhood, my goal is identical with the whole life of God. But, in so far as, by my whole individual Self, I mean my whole Self in contrast with the Selves of my fellows, — then the completion of my individual expression, in so far as I am this individual and no other, — *i.e.* my goal, as this Self, is still not any one point or experience in my life, nor any one stage of my life, but the totality of my individual life viewed as in contrast with the lives of other individuals. Consequently, while it is quite true that every incomplete being, every finite striving, regards itself as aiming towards a future, because its own goal is not yet attained ; we have, nevertheless, to remember that the attainment of the goal involves more than any future moment, taken by itself, could ever furnish. For the Self in its entirety is the whole of a self-representative or recurrent process, and not the mere last moment or stage of that process. As we shall see, there is in fact no last moment. A life seeking its goal is, therefore, indeed, essentially temporal,—but is so just as music is temporal,—except indeed that music is not only temporal, but temporally finite. For every work of musical art involves significant temporal series, wherein there is progression, and passage from chord to chord, from phrase to phrase, and from movement to movement. But just as any one musical composition has its value not only by virtue of its attainment of its final chord, but also at every stage of the process that leads towards this conclusion; and just as the whole musical composition is, as a whole, an end in itself; so every finite Internal Meaning wins final expression, not merely through the last stage of its life (if it has a last stage), but through its whole embodiment. And, nevertheless, as the music attains wholeness only through succession; so every idea that is to win its complete expression, does so through temporal sequences.

Since, at all events, no other than such a temporal expression of meaning in life is in any wise definable for our consciousness, our Idealism can only express its view of the relation of finite and absolute life by viewing the whole world, and in particular the whole existence of any individual Self, as such a temporal process, wherein there is expressed, by means of a Well-Ordered Series of stages, a meaning that finally belongs to the whole life, but that at every temporal stage of the process in question appears to involve, in part, a beyond,—a something not yet won,—and so a distinction both of the past and the future of this Self from the content of any one stage of the process when that stage is viewed as the present one.

In this sense, therefore, our doctrine is obliged to conceive the entire world-life as including a temporal series of events. When considered with reference to any one of these events, the rest of the events that belong to the series of which any one finite Self takes account, are past and future, that is, they are *no longer* and *not yet;* just as, when viewed with reference to any one chord or phrase in the musical composition, all the other successive elements of the composition are either past or future.

The infinite divisibility of the time of our ordinary scientific conceptions is indeed due to that tendency of our own discriminating attention to an endless interpolation of intermediary stages, — a tendency which we studied in connection with our general account of the World of Description. We have, however, seen reasons, which, applied to time, would lead us to declare that an absolute insight would view the temporal order as a discrete series of facts ordered as any succession of facts expressing one purpose would be ordered, viz. like the whole numbers. On the other hand, we have no reason to suppose that our human consciousness distinctly observes intervals of time that in brevity anywhere nearly approach to the final truth about the temporal order. Within what is for us the least observable happening, a larger insight may indeed discriminate multitudes of events. In dealing with the concept of Nature, we shall see what significant use may be made of the hypothesis that there exists or may exist, finite consciousness for which the series of events that we regard as no longer distinguishable from merely elementary and indivisible happenings, are distinguished so minutely as to furnish content as rich as those which, from our point of view, occupy æons of the world's history. Our right to such hypotheses is incontestable, provided only that they help us to conceive the true unity of experience. Nevertheless, in the last analysis, the Absolute Will must be viewed as expressed in a well-ordered and discrete series of facts, which from our point of view may indeed appear, as we shall still further see, capable of discrimination *ad infinitum*.

But now secondly, and without the least conflict with the foregoing theses, I declare that this same temporal world is, when regarded in its wholeness, an Eternal order. And I mean by this assertion nothing whatever but that the whole real content of this temporal order, whether it is viewed from any one temporal instant as past or as present or as future, is *at once* known, *i.e.* is consciously experienced as a whole, by the Absolute. And I use this expression *at once* in the very sense in which we before used it when we pointed out that to your own consciousness, the whole musical phrase may be and often is known *at once*, *despite* the fact that each element of the musical succession, when taken as the temporally present one, excludes from its own temporal instant the other members of the sequence, so that they are either *no longer* or *not yet*, at the instant *when* this element is temporally the present one. As we saw before, it is true that, in one sense, each one of the elements or partial events of a sequence excludes the former and the latter elements from being at the time *when* this particular element exists. But that, in another and equally obvious and empirical sense, *all* the members of an actually experienced succession are *at once* to any consciousness which observes the whole succession as a whole, is equally true. The term *present*, as we saw, is naturally used both to name the temporally present when it is opposed to whatever precedes or succeeds this present, and also to name the observed facts of a succession in so far as they are experienced as constituting one whole succession. In so far the term is indeed ambiguous. But even this ambiguity itself is due to the before-mentioned fact that, if you try to find an absolutely simple present temporal fact of consciousness, and still to view it as an event in time, you are still always led, in the World of Description, to observe or to conceive that this temporal fact is a complex event, having a true succession *within* itself. So that the *now* of temporal expression is never a *mere* now, unless indeed it be viewed either as the ideal mathematical instant within which *nothing* takes place, or else as one of the finally simple stages of the discrete series of facts which the absolute insight views as the expression of its Will.

As to the one hypothesis, an absolute instant in the mathematical sense is like a point, an ideal limit, and never appears as any isolated fact of temporal experience. Every *now* within which something happens is therefore *also* a succession; so that every temporal fact, every event, so far as we men can observe it, has to be viewed as present to experience in *both* the senses of the term present; since this fact *when* present may be contrasted with predecessors that are *no longer* and with successors that are *not yet*, while this same fact, when taken as an event occupying time, is viewed as a presented succession with former and latter members contained within it.

As to the other hypothesis, it seems clear that we human beings observe no such ultimate and indivisible facts of experience just because, so far as we observe and discriminate facts, we are more or less under the bondage of the categories of the World of Description.

But, in view of the correspondence between the universal time of the world-order, as we conceive it, and the time of our internal experience, as we observe it, the temporal sequences must be viewed as having in the real world, and for the Absolute, the same twofold character that our temporal experiences have for ourselves. *Present*, in what we may call the inclusive sense of the term, is any portion of real time with all its included events, in so far as there is any reason to view it as a whole, and as known in this wholeness by a single experience. *Present*, in what we may by contrast call the exclusive sense, is any one temporal event, in so far as it is contrasted with antecedent and subsequent events, and in so far as it excludes them from coexistence with itself in the same portion of any succession. These two senses of the term *present* do not contradict each other in case of the world-order any more than they do in case of our own inner experience. Both senses express inevitably distinct and yet inseparable connected aspects of the significant life of the conscious will, whether in us, or in the universe at large. Our view declares that all the life of the world, and therefore all temporal sequences, are present at once to the Absolute. Our view also maintains that, without the least conflict with this sense in which the whole temporal order is known at once to the Absolute, there is another sense in which any portion of the temporal sequence of the world may be taken as present, when viewed with reference to the experience of any finite Self whose present it is, and when contrasted with what for this same point of view is the past and the future of the world. Now the events of the temporal order, when viewed in this latter way, are divided, with reference to the point of view of any finite Self, into what *now* is, and what *no longer* is, and what *is to be*, but is *not yet*. These same events, however, in so far as they are viewed at once by the Absolute, are for such view, all equally present. And this their presence is the presence of all time, as a *totum simul*, to the Absolute. And the presence in this sense, of all time at once to the Absolute, constitutes the Eternal order of the world, — eternal, since it is inclusive of all distinctions of temporal past and temporal future, — eternal, since, for this very reason, the totality of temporal events thus present at once to the Absolute has no events that precede, or that follow it, but contains all sequences within it, — eternal, finally, because this view of the world does not, like our partial glimpses of this or of that relative whole of sequence, pass away and give place to some other view, but includes an observation of every passing away, of every sequence, of every event and of whatever in time succeeds and follows that event, and includes all the views that are taken by the various finite Selves.

In order to conceive what, in general, such an eternal view of the temporal order involves, or to conceive in what sense the temporal order of the real world is also an eternal order, we have, therefore, but to remember the sense in which the melody, or other sequence, is known at once to our own consciousness, despite the fact that its elements when viewed merely in their temporal succession are, in so far, *not* at once. As we saw before, the brief span of our consciousness, the small range of succession, that we can grasp at once, constitutes a perfectly arbitrary limitation of our own special type of consciousness. But in principle a time-sequence, however brief, is already viewed in a way that is not *merely* temporal, when, despite its sequence, it is grasped at once, and is thus grasped not through mere memory, but by virtue of actual experience. A consciousness related to the whole of the world's events, and to the whole of time, precisely as our human consciousness is related to a single melody or rhythm, and to the brief but still extended interval of time which this melody or rhythm occupies, — such a consciousness, I say, is an Eternal Consciousness. In principle we already possess and are acquainted with the nature of such a consciousness, whenever we do experience any succession as one whole. The only thing needed to complete our idea of what an actually eternal consciousness is, is the conceived removal of that arbitrary limitation which permits us men to observe indeed at once a succession, but forbids us to observe a succession at once in case it occupies more than a very few seconds.

IV

This definition of the relations of the Temporal and the Eternal accomplishes all the purposes that are usually in mind when we speak of the divine knowledge as eternal. That eternity is a *totum simul*, the scholastics were well aware; and St. Thomas developes our present concept with a clearness that is only limited by the consequences of his dualistic view of the relation of God and the world. For after he has indeed well defined and beautifully illustrated the inclusive eternity of the divine knowledge, he afterwards conceives the temporal existence of the created world as sundered from the eternal life which belongs to God. And hereby the advantages of an accurate definition of the eternal are sacrificed for the sake of a special dogmatic interest.

Less subtle forms of speculation have led to uses of the word *eternal*, whose meaning is often felt to be far deeper than such usages can render explicit. But as these subtle usages are often stated, they are indeed open to the most obvious objections. An eternal knowledge is often spoken of as if it were one for which there is *no* distinction whatever between past, and present, and future. But such a definition is as absurd as if one should speak of our knowledge of a whole musical phrase or rhythm, when we grasped such a whole at once, as if the *at once* implied that there were for us no temporal distinction between the first and the last beat or note of the succession in question. To observe the succession *at once* is to have present with perfect clearness *all* the time-elements of the rhythm or of the phrase just as they are, — the succession, the tempo, the intervals, the pauses, — and yet, without losing any of their variety, to view them at once as one present musical idea. Now for our theory, that is precisely the way in which the eternal consciousness views the temporal order, — not ignoring one jot or tittle of its sharp distinctions of past or of future, of succession or of duration, — but still viewing the whole time-process as the expression of a single Internal Meaning. What we now call past and future are not merely the *same* for God; and, nevertheless, they are viewed *at once*, precisely as the beginning and the end of the rhythm are not the same for our experience, but are yet at once seen as belonging to one and the same whole succession.

Or again, an eternal knowledge is often supposed to be one that abstracts from time, or that takes no account of time; so that, for an eternal point of view it is as if time were not at all. But to say this is as if one were to speak of observing at once the meaning or character of the whole phrase or rhythm by simply failing to take any note at all of the succession as such. The meaning is the meaning of the succession; and is grasped only by observing this succession as something that involves former and latter elements, while these elements in time exclude one another, and therefore follow, each one *after* its predecessor has temporally ceased, and *before* its successor temporally appears. Just so, we assert that the eternal insight observes the whole of time, and all that happens therein, and is eternal only by virtue of the fact that it does know the whole of time.

Or again, some doctrines often speak of an eternal insight as something wholly and inexplicably *different* from any temporal type of consciousness, so that *how* God views His truth as eternal truth, no man can say. But our theory regards the essential relation of an eternal to a temporal type of consciousness as one of the simplest of the relations that are of primal importance for the definition of the Absolute. Listen to any musical phrase or rhythm, and grasp it as a whole, and you thereupon have present in you the image, so to speak, of the divine knowledge of the temporal order. To view all the course of time just as you then and there view the whole of that sequence,—this is to be possessed of an eternal type of insight.

"But," so many hereupon object,—"it appears impossible to see how this sort of eternal insight is possible, since just now, in time, the infinite past,—including, say, the geological periods and the Persian invasion of Greece, is *no longer*, while the future is *not yet*. How then for God shall this difference of past and future be transcended, and all be seen at once?" I reply, In precisely the same sense all the notes of the melody except this note are not *when* this note sounds, but are either *no longer* or *not yet*. Yet you may know a series of these notes at once. Now precisely so God knows the whole time-sequence of the world at once. The difference is merely one of span. You now exemplify the eternal type of knowledge, even as you listen to any briefest sequence of my words. For you, too, know time even by sharing the image of the Eternal.

Or again, a common wonder appears regarding how the divine knowledge can be in such wise eternal as to suffer no change to occur in it. How God should be unchangeable, yet express His will in a changing world, is an ancient problem. Our doctrine answers the question at a stroke. The knowledge of all change is itself indeed unchangeable, just because any change that occurs or that can occur to any being is already included amongst the objects known to the eternal point of view. The knowledge of this melody as one whole does not itself consist in an adding of other notes to the melody. The knowledge of all sequences does not itself follow as another sequence. Hence it is indeed not subject to the fate of sequence.

And finally, a mystery is very generally made of the fact that since time appears to us as inevitably infinite, and as therefore not, like the melody or the rhythm, capable of completion, an eternal knowledge, if it involves a knowledge of the whole of time, must be something that has to appear to us self-contradictory and impossible. Any complete answer to this objection involves, of course, a theory of the infinite. Such a theory I have set forth in the Supplementary Essay, published with the First Series of these lectures. The issue involved, that of the positive concept of an infinite whole, is indeed no simple one, and is not capable of any brief presentation. I can here only report that the considerations set forth in that Supplementary Essay have led me to the thesis that a Well-Ordered Infinite Series, under the sole condition that it embodies a single plan, may be rightly viewed as forming a totality, and as an individual whole, precisely as a musical theme or a rhythm is viewed by our experience as such a whole. That the universe itself is such an infinite series, I have endeavored, in that paper, to show in great detail. If you view the temporal order of the world as also forming such an endless whole, expressing a single plan and Will (as I think you have a right to do), then the argument of the Supplementary Essay in question will apply to our present problem. The whole of time will contain a single expression of the divine Will, and therefore, despite its endlessness, the time-world will be present as such a single whole to the Absolute whose Will this is, and whose life all this sequence embodies.

V

In order to refer, as I close, to the practical interest which has guided me through all the abstract considerations even of this present lecture, I may be permitted to anticipate some of our later results about the Self, and, for the sake of illustration, to point out that from our point of view, as we shall later explain it more fully, your life, your Self, your will, your individuality, your deeds, can be and are present at once to the eternal insight of God; while, nevertheless, it is equally true that not only for you, but for God, your life is a genuine temporal sequence of deeds and strivings, whereof, when you view this life at the present temporal instant, the past is just now *no longer*, while the future is *not yet*. This twofold view of your nature, as a temporal process and as an eternal system of fact, is precisely as valid and as obvious as the twofold view of the melody or of the rhythm. Your temporal present looks back, as Will, upon your now irrevocable past. That past is irrevocable because it is the basis of your seeking for the future, and is the so far finished expression of your unique individual Will. Your future is the *not yet* temporally expressed region wherein you, as finite being, seek your own further expression.

That future is still, in one aspect, as we shall see, causally undetermined, precisely in so far as therein something unique, that is yours and yours only, is to appear in the form of various individually designed expressions of your life-purpose, — various individual deeds. Therefore, as we shall be able to maintain, despite all your unquestionable causal and moral determinations, there will be an aspect of your future life that will be free, and yours, and such as no causation can predetermine, and such as even God possesses only in so far as your unique individuality furnishes it as a fact in His world.

And nevertheless, your future and your past, your aspect of individuality, and of freedom, and the various aspects wherein you are dependent upon the rest of the world, your whole life of deeds, and your attainment of your individual goal through your deeds, — all these manifold facts that are yours and that constitute you, are present at once to the Absolute, — as facts in the world, as temporal contents eternally viewed, — as a process eternally finished, — but eternally finished precisely by virtue of the temporal sequence of your deeds. And when you wonder how these aspects can be at once the aspects of your one life, — remember what is implied in the consciousness *at once* of the melody or the rhythm as a sequence, — and you will be in possession of the essential principle whereby the whole mystery is explained.

It is this view, once grasped in its various aspects, that will enable us to define in what sense man is one with God, and in what sense he is to be viewed as at present out of harmony with his own relation to God, and in that sense alienated from his true place in the eternal world. And so, in discussing this most elementary category, we are preparing the way for a most significant result as to the whole life of any man.

The temporal man, viewed just now in time, appears, at first, to be sundered even from his own past and future, and still more from God. He is a seeker even for to-morrow's bread, — still more for his salvation. He knows not just at this instant even his own individuality; still less should he immediately observe his relation to the Absolute in his present deed and in his fleeting experience. Only when he laboriously reflects upon his inmost meaning, or by faith anticipates the result of such reflection, does he become aware of how intimately his life is bound up with an Absolute life. This our finite isolation is, however, especially and characteristically a *temporal* isolation. That inattention of which we spoke in the last lecture, is especially an inattention to all but this act, as it now appears to me. I am not one with my own eternal individuality, especially and peculiarly because this passing temporal instant is not the whole of time, and because the rest of time is *no longer* or else *not yet when* this instant passes. Herein lies my peculiarly insurmountable human limitation. This is my present form of consciousness. To be sure, I am not wholly thus bound in the chains of my finitude. Within my present form and span of consciousness there is already exemplified an eternal type of insight, whereby the *totum simul* is in many cases and in brief span won. But beyond this my span of presentation, time escapes me as a past and future that is at once real and still either no longer or else not yet. From the eternal point of view, however, just this my life is *at once* present, in its Individuality and its wholeness. And because of this fact, just in so far as I am the eternal or true Individual, I stand in the presence of God, with all my life open before Him, and its meaning revealed to Him and to me. Yet this my whole meaning, while one with His meaning, remains, in the eternal world, still this unique and individual meaning, which the life of no other individual Self possesses. So that in my eternal expression I lose not my individuality, but rather win my only genuine individual expression, even while I find my oneness with God.

Now, in time, I seek, as if it were far beyond me, that goal of my Selfhood, that complete expression of my will, which in God, and for God, my whole life at once possesses. I seek this goal as a far-off divine event, — as my future fortune and success. I do well to seek. Seek and ye shall find. Yet the finding, — it does not occur merely as an event in time. It occurs as an eternal experience of this my whole striving. Every struggle, every tear, every misery, every failure, and repentance, and every rising again, every strenuous pursuit, every glimpse of God's truth, — all these are not mere incidents of the search for that which is beyond. They are all events in the life; they too are part of the fulfilment. In eternity all this is seen, and hereby, — even in and through these temporal failures, I win, in God's presence and by virtue of His fulfilment, the goal of life, which is the whole of life. What no temporal instant ever brings, — what all temporal efforts fail to win, that my true Self in its eternity, and in its oneness with the divine, possesses.

So much it has seemed that I might here venture to anticipate of later results, in order that the true significance of our elementary categories might be, however imperfectly, defined for us from the outset. For all the questions as to our deeper relations to the universe are bound up with this problem of Time and Eternity.

LECTURE IV

LECTURE IV

PHYSICAL AND SOCIAL REALITY

We have now learned something concerning the general Forms in which we conceive the facts that we acknowledge as real. No psychological account of the genesis of these forms in the history of the individual mind has been attempted. We have considered only the logical significance of certain fundamental motives that guide us, from moment to moment, and from stage to stage of our intellectual development, in the interpretation of our world and of our relations to this world.

These motives are twofold: (1) The motives that lead us to the concepts of one type of Serial Order, of Law, and of the World of Description; (2) The motives that lead us to conceive Reality as a Well-Ordered Series, and as a realm of Appreciation, that is of values, of Selfhood, of life other than the life that is directly revealed to us, by our present conscious purposes, and so as a realm of various Selves. These twofold motives correspond to our own twofold limitations as finite beings. For we know, just now, *neither* the whole of what this will of ours, in its present dissatisfaction, really intends and means, nor do we know *how* this will is expressed in the facts of universal experience. The World of Description, as a conceived objective order, is the result of our attempting, through a process of serial discrimination, to make good the *second* of these aspects of our ignorance. The World of Appreciation we learn to recognize by coming to a better definition of what it is that our will even now seeks. For then we learn that our present will demands for its full expression, not merely *contents* or *facts that are yet to be discriminated*, but *other wills than this present conscious will of ours*, other purposes than we as yet observe within the limits of this instant's consciousness. Our reaction in presence of the world can become definite and rational, and in accordance with the Ought, only when we acknowledge, not merely data other than those now consciously present, but lives, selves, other than our own finite selfhood. Hence the World of Description, taken by itself, is never the whole truth. It needs to be interpreted in terms of the World of Appreciation.

What the criticism of fundamental categories has enabled us to see in general, is concretely exemplified by our knowledge of the Physical World and of Human Society. We proceed accordingly to apply our general theory to these special cases. We shall find motives that lead us to interpret the physical world as a World of Description, where, as we then conceive, series of phenomena are linked according to rigidly invariable laws. These laws enable us indeed to see how the One and the Many are in certain ways related, but do not appear as expressions of Purpose. On the contrary, the Social World, the realm of our human fellow-beings, is for us all primarily a World of Appreciation, that is, a world where other wills than our own present conscious will seem to be expressing themselves, in accordance with their own choices. Hence our customary interpretation of the world as known to men is profoundly dualistic. On the one hand we find in experience motives that seem to lead to Materialism. For Materialism is due simply to a one-sided emphasis laid upon certain aspects of the World of Description. On the other hand we are driven, by equally obvious empirical considerations, to interpret the social world as a realm of conscious voluntary processes, which occur because somebody finds it worth while that they should occur. Our ordinary common-sense view of things sets these two doctrines about the knowable world side by side, and in general despairs of seeing any comprehensible link between the two orders, viz. between the mental and the material, the social and the physical, the necessary and the free, the describable and the spiritual. Our own general criticism of the categories has prepared us, however, to understand, in terms of our Idealism, both the contrast and the unity of these two realms. In the present and in the subsequent lecture, I propose therefore to undertake a discussion of the concept of Nature, and to show its relation to our concept of Mind. We shall have to explain, in the first place, what are the main motives for our acknowledgment of the existence of the physical world; and secondly, we shall have to set forth in some detail the relations between our idealistic Theory of Being on the one hand and the empirical facts that men acknowledge on the other hand, in dealing with one another and with Nature.

I

No precise definition of the scope covered by the term Nature can be given in advance of a Theory of Nature.

It is easy to say that, by Nature, we mean the portion of the universe that our senses make known to us and that our special empirical sciences study. But the region of Being marked out by such a definition is no very precise one. What our senses make known to us means little enough until the data of sense have been organized through our conduct, and interpreted in the light of theory. Nature has therefore always been conceived by men very largely in supersensuous terms, from the days of magic lore down to the latest geological or physical or biological theories. And what our empirical sciences actually study is, according to all our beliefs about Nature, the mere fringe of a world that exists, but that we have not yet learned how to study with success. Nature is also often contrasted with Mind; but for the psychologist mental processes are a portion of the natural processes; while, for our own idealistic view, all Nature is an expression of Mind. In our own phraseology as used in these lectures, Nature has so far been contrasted several times with Man. But we of course all recognize a sense in which Man is to be conceived as a part of Nature; while on the other hand, nothing is clearer than that, for us, all our beliefs about Nature are determined by conditions which belong, in one aspect, to the mind of Man. A confessedly vague way of stating the definition of the term is to say that by Nature we mean a realm external to our own private experience, and yet *this side*, so to speak, of the ultimate Reality, — a realm, as it were, between the divine, viewed as the Absolute, and the knowing finite human Subject. But all of these expressions, while they are indeed in their various ways valid, indicate a problem rather than define its precise limits.

More to the point, at this stage of our inquiry, than a formally precise definition of Nature, is a consideration of the motives which lead us to acknowledge as real the facts that we all call physical,—viz. to acknowledge the existence of matter, the laws of natural processes, and the dependence of our own mental life upon these processes. To this aspect of the problem of Nature we accordingly at once proceed.

After all that we have now seen regarding the nature of human knowledge, it would be vain to assert that we perceive directly, through our senses, the existence of that which we call matter. The senses never show us, by themselves, the true Being of anything whatever. All truth is the object of acknowledgment, and not merely of immediate experience. Moreover, what has Being is, in itself, something Individual. And the senses never show us individuality, but only the presence of sense-qualities,—colors, sounds, odors, touch, impressions, and the like. On the other hand it is perfectly indubitable that the senses show, now to one and now to another of us men, all the data that, after comparing our various human experiences, *we interpret as the signs of the existence of matter.* The question is, however, this: In what way do we come by this interpretation?

We cannot say, at this point, that some innate conviction, some first and fundamental axiom, or some opaque "law" of the intellect mysteriously requires us to believe that matter is real. This we cannot now assert, just because our Idealism knows nothing whatever about a collection of principles called fundamental or innate assurances. Nor yet can we here, appealing to our more thoughtful and scientifically organized experience, assert that even the success of science, by itself, sufficiently warrants us in attributing to matter a valid Being, which, just because it is independent of our caprices, must remain valid in a realm wholly beyond that of the minds of men. For we know, from our former criticisms of Critical Rationalism, that a merely valid Being, taken by itself, is not yet a real Being. And the philosophical inquiry into the reality that lies at the basis of our experience of Nature, is only begun when we point out that, for our experience, the laws of Nature are valid. For the question at once arises, in what form of life, in what expression of the Absolute, in what Being of our own fourth or idealistic type, are our valid laws of Nature founded?

It follows that for us, at this stage, when once we raise the question regarding the Reality of Nature, the most ordinary conventional answers will in no sense serve. We must undertake the whole problem afresh.

As we do so, we next meet an account of the foundations of our belief in the external and natural world which is so frequently defended, and so familiar, that we cannot here pass it over in silence. It involves looking deeper into the nature of our idea of Being, than those look who simply say that we directly perceive by our senses the external existence of natural objects. And while it indeed appeals to a certain axiom, namely, to the supposed axiom of causality, it is usually more critical in its statement than are most of the views that make the whole issue depend upon irreducible innate convictions. And, furthermore, it has been urged by many noted thinkers who otherwise are of the most various philosophical tendency.

According to this view, we come by our belief in the physical world simply upon the ground of the Resistance which the solid material objects offer to our touch, to our movement, and especially to our muscular sense, and upon the basis of the various other ways in which Nature sets limits to our activity. And we reason from such experiences of resistance and of limitation to the external existence of things, upon the ground that there must indeed be a cause for every effect, and therefore, in this case, a cause which resists and sets limits to our will. As this cause is not found within ourselves, we assume it as external.

No theory of our belief in an external world seems to have had better fortune than this one in popular philosophy, or even in more serious metaphysical inquiry. And yet I regard it as precisely such a mingling of true and of false analysis as is especially adapted hopelessly to confuse our whole view of nature.

This view, as I hold, is indeed sound in laying stress upon a deep connection between our observation of the significant inner life of our own will, and our assurance that the universe in which we live has true Being. But, as I have maintained in developing our Fourth Conception of Being, while our finitude always shows us that we have not won the whole of Being, it is the fulfilment, — the always relative and imperfect fulfilment, — but still the fulfilment of our internal meanings, and not the opaque resistance which the world offers to these meanings, which both defines our warrant for finding that the universe has Being, and gives us, in the form of the Internal Meaning of our Ideas, our only and our valid means for defining wherein that Being consists. Our limitations do, indeed, send us beyond themselves for the truth. But the proof that a real world is here about us, is never the *mere* opaqueness of fact, the blind presence of something which besets and hinders us; but rather it is the relative transparency of our inner life, the observed manifestation of meaning in our experience, which constantly tells us that we are in an universe where, in view of our present incompleteness, rational truth beyond us is to be found. What is, is the completion of our incompleteness, and not any fate that merely overcomes us. This we have fully illustrated in the foregoing discussion of the Categories.

Furthermore, the view that we here criticise makes the whole case depend upon an appeal to the principle of causation. The resistance that my will meets, needs explanation. It is explained by the hypothesis of a material cause which resists us. But hereupon I respond to the defender of this theory, What is, then, your principle of causation? Is it not this, namely: that whatever happens needs, from your point of view, to be explained, and finds, as a fact, its explanation in its relation to other facts? And if this be your belief, as it doubtless is, is not your principle of causation for you a principle somehow first known to govern the real world which your experience of resistance is said to make manifest to your senses, before you can use the principle to prove the existence of matter? But if this be true, is not your principle of causation, your assurance that the real world is one where facts stand in rational relations, and where what happens is explicable, already presupposed not only as valid, but *as valid for a real world beyond you*, from the very outset of your whole inquiry? Is there not here, then, a belief deeper than your mere experience that your will is at any time resisted? For unless you had this principle of causation in your possession, and unless you first believed the principle to be applicable to a realm beyond your private experience, your will would be resisted in vain, so far as your power to learn about a real world would then go. For you would then learn nothing thereby but the blind fact that you felt limitations, as an infant feels them when he hungers. But if you already possess your principle, and believe it applicable to Reality in general, then indeed you can apply it to explain, after a fashion, any fact that you please. Already, however, in assuming that you are somehow able to know that the principle of causation applies to a realm beyond your own present will, you have found out, apart from all experience of resistance, that there is the real external world within which the principle of causation is valid. And, in that case, you have *not* discovered the reality of the physical world through the fact that it resists your will, but have presumed, in advance of all feeling of resistance, that there is a real world, beyond yourself, whose facts, whatever they are, are linked by a law of causation to your own experience. For surely you do not mean that the principle of causation itself, by resisting your will, forces you to believe in its reality as the cause of such resistance.

If you look closer you soon see, however, as to our belief in causation, that somehow or other it helps us more clearly to grasp the internal sense, the observed inner significance, of some of our conscious states, to observe what we call their causal connections. In observing these connections, so far as they fall *within* our own range of experience, we there find somehow our own rational Will better expressed, or embodied, than it would be without this idea, and thereby we better win our own inner clearness. In assuming, now, that some such connection as this has validity *beyond* us, in a realm external to ourselves, we have begun by defining this outer realm, not as a realm that primarily resists or thwarts our Will, but as a realm that first of all embodies one of our own deepest and most rational purposes. If the external world, said to be material, is, as this view holds, above all causal, and is such as to explain the particular facts which are found in our experience, then, that world is above all a real embodiment of the very purpose which, in us, appears as our purpose of explanation.

Properly examined, then, the view here in question becomes only a form of Idealism, — a sort of primary assurance that the nature of things is rational, and fulfils our purposes. And so the problem about our belief in the existence of Nature must be solved in explicit relation to our Fourth Conception of Being. If we are to understand what we mean by Material Nature, and why we believe it to be real, we must ask, What internal meaning of ours seeks and demands an embodiment such that, to our minds, only outer Nature can furnish this embodiment? But so far, indeed, we have not seen what grounds distinguish our belief in matter from our belief in any other sort of Reality. What we are seeking, however, is an account of how our belief in the material world, as distinct from any other realm of acknowledged facts, is to be explained and defended.

Moreover, as has occasionally been pointed out, in the course of various recent discussions of this view, the natural truths which are of the most theoretical importance to us, are often truths that result from an indirect interpretation of facts with which the sense of resistance in any direct muscular sense has very little to do. Do the geometrical laws force themselves upon us by resisting our will (except, to be sure, our will exhaustively to know them)? The heavens have long been a type of the apparently everlasting character of Nature. When did the stars show themselves to be real by resisting our will, except indeed by arousing questions that we cannot at present answer?

II

In proceeding to suggest what I regard as a more adequate account of the warrant for our belief in the physical world, I must call attention to a plain fact which, as I conceive, has far too often been wholly neglected in the discussion of this subject. Our belief in the reality of Nature, when Nature is taken to mean the realm of physical phenomena known to common sense and to science, *is inseparably bound up with our belief in the existence of our fellow-men*. The one belief cannot be understood apart from the other. Whatever the deeper reality behind Nature may turn out to be, — *our* Nature, the realm of matter and of laws with which our science and our popular opinions have to do, is a realm which we conceive *as known or as knowable to various men*, in precisely the same general sense in which we regard it as known or as knowable to our private selves. Take away the social factor in our present view of Nature, and you would alter the most essential of the characters possessed, for us, by that physical realm in which we all believe.

How significant this aspect of our belief in Nature is, you may see if you will look a little more closely at the facts. There is much, indeed, in the realm of Reality in general, apart from Nature, which a man need not view as accessible to all men, in so far as they are men. As a matter of religious faith, one might well believe, for instance, that upon a given occasion God had revealed his will to a single prophet, or other inspired person, and that this revelation not only remained, but had to remain, by God's will, a secret quite inaccessible to all other men. In the reality of the revelation in question one might nevertheless believe, simply because, by hypothesis, God would be conceived, by a believer in such a revelation, as a real person, and the prophet as also a real person. And whatever occurs to one person, as a fact of his inner life, and whatever passes between two persons, may remain a secret inaccessible to all other persons, in so far as these persons are finite individuals. Or again, I now believe in your mind as a reality, external to mine; yet I also view your mental life as, in its own direct presence to you, something inaccessible to all human beings besides yourself. But while Reality as such does not imply that what is real is directly accessible, in its details, to the private and finite experience of any or of all men, it is different with the sort of reality which we ascribe to what we usually regard as the material world.

Suppose that I told you that I was well acquainted with the existence and the properties of a material object which I had now and here before me. Suppose that I assured you that I could see, touch, weigh, and otherwise test the reality of this material object, but that I was quite sure that neither you nor any other man could conceivably see it or touch it, or otherwise get the least experience of its presence. Suppose, as a fact, that nobody else ever did verify my report; but that I continued to insist upon the reality, observable for me, of my material object. What would you say of that object of mine? The answer is plain. You would say that my object might indeed be real, but was real solely as a physical phenomenon, to wit, as a collection of states in my mind, in other words, as a certain fixed hallucination of mine. And now I, myself, if indeed I remained sane while I asserted all this, should not hesitate to agree with you, just as surely as I retained my present definition of my material world. For by my material world, I certainly mean a collection of actual and possible experiences of mine such that you too can agree with me about the presence and the describable characters of these experiences, precisely in so far as you have equal opportunities with me to verify their presence and to test with me their peculiar type of Being. The fact that we men find Nature here, implies for us, then, that we are so constituted as to find the same sort of natural phenomena. The realm of the physical phenomena, whatever inner Being may be behind it, is, for us, primarily *this common realm of human experience.* Upon this consideration the very definition of what we call Nature depends.

It is, of course, true that any one of us, when alone, supposes himself to be still in the presence of Nature. It is also true that this supposition would lose its present meaning just as soon as we supposed not only that we were alone with Nature, but that, even if our fellows had the same opportunities as ourselves, they would still be wholly unable to verify our observations. A nature that is not only by accident observable just now to me alone, but that also is such that nobody else amongst all men besides myself can observe it, becomes, at once, to my mind, either one of two things, viz. either something that is explicitly my own dream, or fancy, or hallucination, or other mental state, or else something that I should view, if I continued to believe in it, as a reality belonging to a realm of spirits, whom I might then suppose to exist apart from men. In either case, such fact, observable by me alone, is no longer to be conceived as belonging to the well-known material world of common sense and of science.

III

Our belief in Man, then, is logically prior to our interpretation of Nature. And any theory of Nature must undertake to explain, not merely how these data of sense appear to any one of us in this order, and subject to these valid laws, but how all men come to possess this connectedness and interrelated unity of their common experience, despite the apparent separateness of their individual states of mind.

But what then is the source of our belief in the reality of our fellow-men? To this question the customary answer is quite the reverse of the answer which I mentioned a few moments since, when I began to speak about the physical world. If it is common to say that we believe in external Nature as something that thwarts or hinders or resists our will, it is usual, on the other hand, to assert that we believe in our fellow-men because we detect in their conduct expressive fashions of behavior, which are analogous to those whereby we express and accomplish our own will. I do various things, and know what they mean. The present theory supposes that I observe in my fellow-men deeds similar to those whose meaning is already known to me. By analogy, one continues, I attribute to these deeds an inner meaning of their own, analogous to my own inner meaning. Here, as you see, it is no longer the thwarting of my will, which is said to prove the reality of external things, but the positive expression of something analogous to my will in the deeds of my fellows, — it is this, I say, which is believed to be an evidence that, beyond my life, there is another life fulfilling ends analogous to my own.

This view of the reason why we believe our fellow-men to be real is, therefore, more in harmony with our own Fourth Conception of Being than is the ordinary account of our belief in material Nature. For what I learn to view as real is here defined rather as what is in harmony with my Internal Meaning than as what thwarts my meanings. Yet even this customary way of explaining our belief that our fellow-men exist is still, to my mind, inadequate. It is not the analogy with ourselves which is our principal guide to our belief in our fellows. The view that analogy mainly guides us is defective as an account of the psychology of our social consciousness, and is inadequate as a statement of the reasons why our social consciousness is well founded in the truth of things. Here too, then, we shall have to alter the conventional theory.

As a matter of psychology, *i.e.* of the natural history of our beliefs, a vague belief in the existence of our fellows seems to antedate, to a considerable extent, the definite formation of any consciousness of ourselves. This thesis, which will later prove important for our whole theory of the individual human Self, will be again illustrated in connection with that theory. We are social beings first of all by virtue of our inherited instincts, and we love, fear, and closely watch our fellows, in advance of any definite ideas about what our fellows really are. Our more explicit consciousness that our fellows exist is due to a gradual interpretation of these our deepest social instincts. Our belief in the existence of our fellows, therefore, does not come to our consciousness, through a mere argument from analogy, whereby we use the previously developed observation of our own nature and powers as a basis for the estimate of the inner life of other men. Our assurance about our fellows arises by means of those very interests whereby we gradually come to our own self-consciousness. It is nearer to the truth to say that we first learn about ourselves from and through our fellows, than that we learn about our fellows by using the analogy of ourselves. Not even now do we mainly trust to analogy to guide us in interpreting what we most want at any instant to know about the inner life of our fellows. In an excited crowd, or in any assembly of the type of a mob, even the mature man is often much more aware of the feelings of other people than he is of his own. He often, in such cases, loses sight of himself in a certain passion of sympathy. And again, when at present we converse with people, we become conscious of their inner life rather in terms of their contrast with ourselves, than by means of their analogy with us. A man who expresses himself in a way that is new to me, seems to me often all the more a real person, with an inner life of his own, just because I fail to trace any close analogy between his meanings or his expressions and my own. His difference from me makes him seem more real to me. Thus the truly original poet, the Shakespeare or the Goethe, seems to us, as we study him, to possess his own wondrous inner life, just because, while we read him, we meet novelty. Wonder arouses the social sense more vigorously than does recognition. The child's period of liveliest growth in social insight is his questioning age, when every new mind is a mysterious realm to be explored by inquiries.

And now as to the logic of our social consciousness, the simplest way to express the whole sense of the evidence that impresses upon us, at every moment, the reality of our fellows, is to say, Our fellows are known to be real, and to have their own inner life, because they are for each of us the endless treasury of *more ideas*. They answer our questions; they tell us news; they make comments; they pass judgments; they express novel combinations of feelings; they relate to us stories; they argue with us, and take counsel with us. Or, to put the matter in a form still nearer to that demanded by our Fourth Conception of Being: *Our fellows furnish us the constantly needed supplement to our own fragmentary meanings.* That is, they help us to find out what our own true meaning is. Hence, since Reality is through and through what completes our incompleteness, our fellows are indeed real. Wondering, in a doubtful case, what to do, we wait to see what other people do. Here we use no analogy with our own deeds as the basis of our interpretation of their inner life. While we wait for the social verdict, we stand halting, — our ideas fragmentary, our meanings in search of their own wholeness, our finitude desiring its own Other. Our fellows act, and we perhaps follow suit. *Now* our doubts are all set at rest. We have won the desired decision. But where did we look for that decision? The answer is, We looked to our fellows. Now, in general, the Real, as our Fourth Conception has asserted, is precisely our own whole meaning, which we seek as beyond ourselves, even because we know it in advance as ours, but have not yet won it in fulness as a present conscious fact. This our fuller meaning, however, our hidden Reality, the object sought when we turn to our fellows for help, we find as something imparted to us by their deeds. We therefore afterwards view this meaning as having been real beyond us, namely, in the minds of our fellows, before it became present in us, namely, as our own conscious meaning. And this is why we ought to acknowledge our fellows to be real. This is the way in which the general category of the

Ought gets, in the World of Appreciation, the special motives that warrant us in acknowledging particular facts that embody will.

Just so it is, too, when we ask a question, and get an answer, or inquire the way in the street, or look in the paper for the news, or read a book, or listen to another man's arguments, or in any way learn our fellows' ideas. All these ideas, just in so far as they interest us, are sought as some meaning not yet consciously our own, but needed as a supplement to what so far is consciously our own. As a needed supplement to our own meaning, these meanings which we seek have their place in Reality before we consciously find them. That they have such a place is a consequence of that whole conception of Reality which our own former series of lectures so fully analyzed. The only question is, What place have they? Our whole social experience, in case of our ideas of our fellows, tends to give such ideas their more precise localization in our finite world, as the ideas which our fellows express, by voice, by gesture, by writing, and by countless other significant deeds. Our fellow-man, when he is genuinely alive to us at all, is therefore precisely such a storehouse of meanings, — such a thesaurus of needed ideas. The Internal Meaning of which his Being is the outward embodiment, is, in general, *our own conscious aim to have our questions answered, and to win novelty by insight into our world.* That he exists at all we can therefore logically know only upon the basis of an essentially idealistic interpretation of the universe. In a world where all true meaning is eternally embodied, the only question that arises about a particular finite meaning which I just now seek, but do not consciously possess, is the question, Where and how is it embodied? To this question my social experience answers whenever my fellow speaks to me, or acts expressively.

That my fellow is also far more than a mere storehouse of opinions and plans, that he is, as a human Individual, the proper object of countless unique interests, such as win our love, or move our hostility or our rivalry, — all this is indeed true. But all this too is secondary to our empirical ground for believing that, whatever as Individual or as Self he further may prove to be, he is in any case something real, and something other than any conscious life of our own. This ground is found in the fact that he is a local centre for the imparting to us of meanings, — a dynamo of ideas. That all his ideas have their fulfilment in the Reality, our general Idealism assures us. What our fellow empirically shows us is the way in which certain more or less imperfect expressions of meaning find their place in Being. This, then, is the particular shape which the World of Appreciation, discussed in its general form in a previous lecture, takes when interpreted in the light of our special human experiences.

But now, with the life of this my fellow, when he is viewed in his relations to me, there is bound up the fact that, as our social intercourse constantly shows, we can treat certain facts which each of us for himself experiences, as if they were facts common to both of us. And herewith we are prepared to return to the conception of material Nature.

IV

The organism of my fellow-man is directly known to me as a phenomenal object, moving about in what my experience presents to me as space, and in time. But side by side with my experience of my fellow, I experience the presence of countless other objects, which also interest me, but which I do not primarily interpret as expressions either of his life, or of the life of any other comrade. Now the notable feature of all these objects, in so far as they are normally to be found in the realm of sight and of touch, is, that my whole social intercourse with other men confirms me in my belief that these objects somehow exist for my fellows as well as for myself. My fellow points out to me these objects, and I find them in company with him; he expresses in these objects interests similar to those which I too share. Our discriminating intelligence also wins in all of us the same success in dealing with them. That is, my fellow *describes* these objects as I do; our science makes them topics of investigations in which we all share; and our civilization depends upon using these objects together, and upon finding the same laws present in those series of them which interest us. In the same realm in which I see my fellow expressing his meanings, I observe many of these objects passed from hand to hand, or otherwise made the instruments of our common human tasks, enjoyments, inquiries, and contests. These objects then, and above all, *the objects of my combined senses of sight and touch*, become for me through and through saturated with a meaning that I also can never completely find embodied in my private experience, and that only my fellow's experience of these objects can aid me to interpret in harmony with my own socially colored ideas. These objects then, as from infancy I learn to hold, are in their true meaning *common to my fellow and to myself.*

As my experience of the problems of life grows, I learn to view my fellow's inner life more and more as a realm remote from my direct observation. Under the influence of the tendency to discriminate facts more and more sharply I become increasingly individualistic in my interpretation of my own social presuppositions. I learn to conceive of my fellow and myself as falsely sundered, or even as Independent Beings, whose isolation from one another becomes emphasized by well-known social motives, — for example, by the conflicts of social rivalry, by the class distinctions and estrangements of a complex social order, — in brief, by all that makes man forget that he and his fellow together are empirically known as fragmentary hints of the real unity in variety of the life of the Absolute. Childhood, whenever the capricious fears of its bashfulness are not in question, easily accepts all minds in whose expressions of meaning it chances to be interested, as akin to itself. Adult life, under civilized conditions, exaggerates the mystery of our apparent sundering from one another, and forgets that only the community of our meanings, and the fact that we are local centres wherein the ideal unity of the world gets various and contrasted expressions, enables us to communicate with each other at all.

But, however far we seem to grow remote from one another, and to be independent centres of life and of meaning, there remains a realm that, in the sense discussed in our Second Lecture, appears as *between* us; that is, it is such that our sharp distinction from one another depends upon our distinguishing it from every Self. The realm of the objects that each of us experiences for himself, but believes to be also objects for the other men, remains thus as a link which seems to bind our actual lives, in a relatively external way, together. Our individual minds come to seem sundered; but all of us together seem to be in relation to matter. But in order that this our common relation to the physical phenomena should remain conceivable, in spite of our apparent isolation from one another, common sense has to learn to regard matter as something outside of all our minds, and as therefore capable of coming into an equally close, and also equally remote, relation to all of us. Here then, is a special instance of the application of the category of the *between*. It leads to the triad: My fellow and Myself, with Nature between us.[1]

I see the sun shining. My fellow, as I learn, sees the sun shining also. This I first learn as a part of my interpretation, not of external nature, but of my fellow's inner life. Now the shining of the sun is hereby shown to be not a fact for me alone, but for other minds. Other men, however, see the sun, as I learn, when I do not see it. Hence its existence goes wholly beyond that of my private

[1] Only from the special point of view here in question is this relationship especially characteristic of Nature. In the further growth of dualism Nature very generally loses this character, and is regarded not as *between* two minds, but as foreign to all minds, in a way that we shall later follow. But in ordinary social dealings of various men with the *same* material objects, the conception of the material object commonly involves the triad here noted.

consciousness, and persists in my absence. While I sleep in darkness, men in other lands, as social communications teach me, observe the sun. Various men die ; yet the sun is still seen by the survivors. I learn, by common report, that it shone for men long before I was born. I come to believe that it will shine for future generations after we are all dead. Such knowledge, all of it socially derived, goes to show that the sun shines apart from the experience of any particular man, while the shining of the sun is still something which every man can verify. It is in a sense common to all of us. It is in a sense relatively independent of each of us. It is a part of a vast realm of phenomena all of which have this same general character, — that of needing no particular human experience to verify their presence, while all men alike can under suitable conditions agree in such a verification.

A confirmation of this theory of the reason why we regard certain of our experiences as indications of the existence of material objects, is furnished by the well-known fact that not all our sensory perceptions, but especially those of sight and touch, are regarded by us as showing to us the presence of the external physical world. We may well ask, then, *why* it is that, as I observed a moment since, the sight-touch world of extended objects seems to be most of all the world where material reality is at home. Why do we so readily reject as not revealing the true nature of material things, the tastes and odors, although these latter, in the mind of many an animal, and even in our own childhood, would seem to have been the most interesting characters of nature? At the age of six months, the child is frequently fond of investigating the taste of things. Yet taste, despite its importance as a possibility of experience, goes far into the background of our interpretation of nature, and does so very early. If one asks as to the real reason of all this, I should point out that precisely all those socially significant experiences of our common dealings with natural objects occur most definitely when we deal with the world of the visible and tangible things. Hearing is indeed the most important sense of social communication in all the more abstract regions of our intercourse. But, on the other hand, in case you and I are together dealing with natural objects, the field which is common to the senses of sight and touch has the very important character that in this field one observes one's fellows' dealings with objects. I can see you touching an object. I can even, in the ordinary social sense, be said, by virtue of familiar interpretations, to see you looking at an object. And, just so, if we grasp a pole or a rope together, or lift a weight together, I feel your grasp of the object, just as truly as I feel the object. But in no corresponding sense can I be said to hear that you hear an object, nor can I taste your tasting of an object, nor can I smell your smelling of an object; while I can both see and touch processes which I interpret as your seeing and touching of the object. Hence it is that the objects with which you and I at once deal, as well as the objects which on occasion can exist independently for either of us, come to be viewed as the objects of the field of sight and touch. The later developments of our describing consciousness confirm this tendency. What is seen and touched can be described more exactly than can the objects of other senses. And Nature, as we shall still further see very soon, comes to be viewed as, above all, a World of Description.

V

Our assurance that outer nature exists apart from any man's private experience, is thus inseparably bound up with our social consciousness. But now, what shall we say of our ordinary modern interpretation of the principal characters that are to belong to this material world, when once the existence of Nature has been admitted? This interpretation is in general, to the effect that the material world is, indeed, the classic instance of the application of the categories of Description. Whatever its inmost essence may be, it is regarded by us as something wholly unlike our own minds. Nature we no longer ordinarily view as sentient, or as conscious, or as a direct result or expression of purpose. It appears to us as something very like a mechanism. Its laws are describable, but are not such as seem to embody will, or any moral or æsthetic meaning. We, therefore, often call it lifeless; and the generalizations of the doctrine of Evolution, which show us that, despite this apparent lifelessness of Nature, our own lives have come into Being, as an outgrowth from Nature, seem to us only the more to show the impenetrable mystery of our place in the Universe. "Dead matter" seems to us the extreme opposite of mind. "Nature's mechanism" appears to be hopelessly opposed in its essence to the interests of our will and of our emotion. And now whence this idea of a vast separation between material nature and the significant inner life of our fellows?

I answer, here too, it is first the way in which material nature enters into our common social life together which fixes our attention upon this contrast between persons and things, and which, when certain dualistic motives grow more prominent, makes the contrast seem ultimate. The difference between minds and material objects is for the civilized man so vast, not by virtue of any experience which gives him a right to assert, positively, that Nature is utterly opposed in its essence to Mind, but by virtue of the fact that our practical and human relations to the material world have a social significance which becomes more and more contrasted with our practical relations with living men, the more our ethical consciousness becomes organized, and the more our power to mould natural phenomena to our human purposes becomes prominent in our minds. Man becomes, as we grow wiser in practical affairs, more and more our live fellow-being. By contrast, Nature grows more and more our socially significant tool. We appreciate Man more and more sensitively as we grow more civilized; but we describe certain of the more important phenomena of Nature more and more carefully as we grow more skilful. Our interest in both aspects of this process is profoundly human and social. The nature that our industrial art controls is just Man's Nature; and our science is an extension into the realms of theory of precisely the control over Nature that we seek when we use tools. And the very interests that make our science and our art grow are interests in Man, in his life, in his wisdom, and in his power. But because the Nature that we describe and control permits our science and our art to succeed by virtue of whatever is rigid, uniform, predictable, explicable, and in a measure, mechanical, about our experience of Nature, we come to lay exclusive stress upon just these aspects of the material world, and to conceive them as the deepest and most essential aspects of that world. And because our science and our art in their turn humanize our life, and enrich our civilization, they lead to a constant increase of our sense that all men are live and sentient beings, whose will and whose interests are related to our own, despite all our social estrangements. In consequence, our civilization leads to a contrast of the mental and the material worlds in a fashion which is distinctly due to a perspective effect. The narrow clearness of our civilized consciousness tends to make us materialists when we view the world apart from man, and sensitive appreciators of life whenever we consider our fellows. And that is why, in our own age, theoretical Materialism has flourished side by side with the growth of a wide Humanity of sentiment. Both are expressions of social motives. Neither is sufficiently broad in its view to express to us the whole of our true relations to Being.

As to the social aspect of the process of growth in civilization which we have thus summarized, there can be, of course, no doubt. It is for us a growth of our concrete World of Appreciation. The civilized man lives in spiritual relations to his fellow-men, — relations, many of which are wholly unintelligible to the savage. It is not merely that the civilized man has sympathy with more men, but that his conduct involves an organized system of responses to a human environment that he acknowledges as mental, conceives in terms of its values and purposes, and views as a more or less clearly connected whole, — a social order, such as is one's own country, or humanity. Such an environment is conceived, so far as one gives the notion of it any clearness at all, in idealistic terms. For the social order itself is no independent realistic entity, since it is the very breath of life for me, the social being. Nor does it consist of mutually independent selves. It is an organism. Nor is it a mystical entity, since it has articulation and differentiation of structure within it. It is no merely Valid Being, since in the social consciousness of us men it is consciously alive. It can be adequately conceived only in terms such as our Fourth Conception has defined, although it is indeed not the Absolute, but itself only a fragment of a larger whole.

On the other hand, the natural world, as the civilized man comes to conceive it, bears the same general relation to the social world which, in our second lecture, we found the World of Description bearing to the World of Appreciation. Men have always been trying to find out how to coöperate with one another. Their only way of finding out has been to seek to unify the One and the Many in their experience, by discriminating, in their common realm of physical phenomena, what objects, what series of objects, and what unvarying laws of these series of objects they could agree upon as the common basis of definite acts of coöperation. For only by means of their common relations to the natural phenomena are the men able to give, one to another, definite signals as to what their intentions are, or to define extensive plans of action in socially intelligible terms. Taken by themselves, however, and apart from their relations to the men, the natural phenomena fail to furnish a basis for any definite interpretation of their order as the expression of a Will such as men can concretely understand. And this proves to be more and more the case as men grow critical, and define their own social purposes and plans in more definite and rational ways. For the animistic savage all nature was vaguely alive. The civilized man has too definite a life of his own to tolerate this vagueness. In consequence our civilized view of Nature has tended, in many ways, towards Dualism. Nature is no longer conceived as *between* the various socially related pairs of conscious beings, in the sense discussed above. It is viewed, more and more, as foreign to them all. There remains, in case of the natural phenomena, then, the one rational resource of undertaking to describe them, by the use of precisely the categories which, in their most general form, we discussed in our second lecture. Discrimination, an effort towards a comprehension of the One and the Many in Nature through a discovery of the *between*, a watchful search for Series of phenomena, a socially critical comparison of the experience of many men in order to find out what series of natural phenomena are verifiable in our common human experience, a constant disposition to the hypothetical construction of conceptual series, whereby what we cannot yet observe is defined as ideally observable *if* men only possessed sufficiently keen sense-discrimination: such are the familiar devices by which the special sciences constantly undertake to extend our descriptive knowledge of Nature.

All these processes are indeed kept under rigid control by means of a conception whose origin is social, but whose application to natural phenomena gives us a definite critical standard for distinguishing between the natural facts that we acknowledge, and the fables or errors that we reject. This conception is the one already discussed at the outset of the present series of lectures, — the conception of Human Experience as an organized totality. As we saw, no one of us ever verifies the fact that there exists any such totality. Yet, upon an obviously social basis, we tend to make a constantly sharper distinction between what ought to be recognized as confirmed by this common experience of humanity, and what cannot be thus confirmed. Now what this ideal totality called Human Experience is conceived to have discriminated, to have recognized as the orderly series of phenomena, to have reduced to definable laws by the discovery of the "invariants" of a given order-system of phenomena, — this we are accustomed to view as the one accessible revelation of what Nature is. The "necessity" which is often said to "force" upon us the recognition of particular facts and series, and laws as belonging to this realm of human experience, unquestionably exists; but it is to but a small extent, in the case of any one of us, even if he be the most earnest empirical investigator, a necessity of present sense-experience. It is a necessity expressible in terms of the Ought; and the most deeply rational warrant for this necessity is social rather than sensuous. Not to accept the "verdict of human experience" would be to cut ourselves off from definite social relations. To accept this verdict, not blindly, but with constantly renewed criticism, and with a frequent addition of personal verification, so far as that is possible,—this is to keep ourselves in touch with the civilized social consciousness.

VI

But now we come to the point where it is necessary to deal with the precise sense in which the physical world, when conceived as the object of such common description and verification, is also conceived as subject to rigid and unchangeable Laws of Causation. This conception, as I hold, is one of only a relative validity. Human experience, as we shall see in the next lecture, cannot be said actually to have verified it, even when we take the term *human experience* to mean the totality of the verifications that all the various men have ever made. What we verify, are more or less permanent rules relating to the routine of nature phenomena. In other words, our common experience discovers states, more or less persistent, of what our American philosopher Chauncey Wright used to call "cosmic weather," habits, more or less enduring, of the behavior of phenomena. Yet we are indeed accustomed to conceive that our common human experience *ought to show us*, were it broad enough and discriminating enough, rigidly uniform natural laws, whose general character may be summed up in the well-known thesis that, "The same antecedents (when the truly causal antecedents are taken into account) are *invariably* followed by the same consequents." Now, why do we conceive nature as subject to such *invariable* laws, when our common experience, however wide you conceive its range to be, can only show us particular instances of persistent behavior on the part of Nature?

If one answers by generalizing the foregoing thesis into the axiom that "Whatever is must have a cause which determines, of necessity, *what* it is," — then, at this stage of our inquiry, we have no difficulty in saying that *this* principle, unless made more specific, is so hopelessly ambiguous, as to be merely trivial. From our own point of view, the realm of Being is indeed such an unity that the Many, whatever they are, must in *some* sense be the resultant and expression of the One. But the true rational link between the One and the Many, between the universal and the particular, or between the World and the Individual, may be very different from a link of rigid necessity. We shall hereafter expound more fully that doctrine of the freedom of the Individual which we briefly stated in the closing lecture of the former series, and shall show that our unity in God actually demands our individual freedom in a limited, but perfectly definite sense. Or again, from our own point of view, the Internal Meaning of every idea demands as its complete expression the whole universe, containing infinitely numerous other Internal Meanings. But here the link *between* this instant's passing meaning and the universe is a causal one, only in the most trivially abstract sense of the term cause. And in fact, when one merely asserts in general that *whatever is must have a cause*, one may mean only that nothing finite can be understood by itself alone, or that *some* kind of explanation, relation or tie, binds every particular in the world to every other. But since the explanations and ties which may interest a given inquirer may be of any sort, teleological or mathematical, æsthetic or mechanical, — according to the sort of conception that happens to be in question, and since, in the most general logical sense, even what at first appeared as the absence of ties or of relations between two objects would be itself only a new kind of tie and relation, the general principle, "Whatever is, is somehow linked to others," so far amounts to the assertion that whatever is, is in the world *with* others. Over such an axiom one need not dispute; but it needs specification before it can give light as to the linkage of facts.

A Cause, in the narrower sense of *physical cause*, means, however, a certain group of antecedents linked in a certain way, with a consequent. The term, as thus defined, applies to series of events. The question about the validity of the principle is the question why we conceive *every natural event as preceded by a group of events such that whenever that group as a whole recurs, that same consequent must follow.*

The answer to this question depends, as I conceive, upon *two* considerations. The first I discussed briefly in our second lecture. Conceive any ordered series of describable systems of events, such as, in the passage referred to,[1] we exemplified. Such a series, if once clearly discriminated by an observer, and then carefully considered in its whole sequence, would possess *some* features that would remain unvarying throughout the

[1] See above, p. 89, *sqq.*

set of "transformations" of which just *that* ordered series consists. This, so far, is due to the very conditions of the discrimination of serial order. The more careful the discriminations, the more minute the examination of the series in question, the more certain it is that a rational observer of any such connected series of events could, if he chose a sufficiently large range of phenomena for his observation, find *some* "invariant" of the "system of transformations" in question. So far the result is that: *Any series of events which you can exactly describe, exemplifies a law of succession which remains invariant at least throughout this series.* This is a consequence merely of the conditions of description. For I do not define any series of events as connected unless I find all the members of this series *between* a chosen beginning and a chosen end of the series, and can discriminate the precise order of succession of the events thus *between.* But so to find the facts is to find certain relations persistent throughout the series. For upon such persistence the recognition of the serial order depends. The persistent relations, as we earlier saw, are those involved in the very definition of *between.* For the whole process of discovering these relations is a finding of the One in the Many. Moreover, if I conceive the series (as, in the World of Description one does conceive it) as in its nature either altogether continuous, or at least composed of stages between stages that I discover by continuing to interpolate indefinitely, — then all the more my conception of the continuous, or at all events "compact" whole of the series, gives me grounds which enable me to define the series as possessing throughout "invariant" characters. So far, then, wherever there is an exactly described series of natural events there is *a law of that series.*

But the assertion of the existence of causal connections does indeed go much further than this. If one says, "*Whenever* certain given antecedents recur, certain consequents follow," one declares that, *at various times, or in various parts of the universe,* which may themselves be as *dis*connected with one another as is possible, there are, or may be found, series of natural phenomena which follow the *same* describable laws, or *possess the same "invariants."* But thus one indeed goes beyond the mere observation that every describable series inevitably illustrates its own law, *within* its own limits. One goes far beyond the individual series to assert that if you conceived it transported to other regions of space or of time, it would still retain the same "invariants." As has often been noted, this assertion amounts simply to saying that *the true laws of nature are independent of particular places and times.* The independence here in question is of course not the independence that Realism ascribed to its Independent Beings, but is merely the relative independence of an "invariant." For we are here dealing with what one might call an "invariant" character of the second degree. The assertion is that in any series of natural events you can find not merely something "invariant" within that individual series, but also *some* character such that if you passed to other places and times, this character would remain unchanged in the series that were there to be found. Our principle, as thus interpreted, while applicable to the various parts of the world in space, refers especially to the *temporal invariance* of natural law, and we may confine our attention to that aspect. There are then, so one asserts, laws of nature, or "invariants" of any given series of changes of natural phenomena, which do not change with time. These, then, are not only the "invariants" of the series of phenomena originally considered. They are also the "invariants" of *any* such conceived series of substitutions or of transformations as enables you in mind to transfer the original series into some other *part of time*, and to study its behavior there. This is the meaning of the principle now in question. This principle is consistent, as everybody knows, with very vast changes in the aspect of nature, and is rather ill defined as the principle of the mere "uniformity" of nature. For, as one conceives the case, if the sun collided with another large cosmic body, the aspect of nature, so far as our senses now take account of it, would hereabouts be unrecognizably altered in an instant of time; yet the conceived "invariants" of thermodynamics would, as we suppose, find application to the transformed system after the collision as well as before.

After these further definitions of our principle, the inquiry reduces to this: Why should we conceive that, *The lapse of time, or a transfer to another part of time, makes no difference to what we call the "true" laws of nature?* We are aided in answering this question by the perfectly obvious consideration that, in a World of Appreciation, in the life of a Self, in a realm where what is done at any time is founded upon what has been done before, in brief, in any Well-Ordered Series of events, the thesis just stated, far from being an axiom, is simply not universally true at all. Countless aspects of a Well-Ordered Series of voluntary acts, due to some Self, *may*, and in all sufficiently complex and important instances of the sort *must*, indeed remain "invariant" *either* throughout the whole life of this Self, or else from some one point onwards; but these "invariants" are never *all* the "true" laws of the series; for the essence of a Well-Ordered Series (such as the number-series, or any more concrete instance of a self-representative process), is that, just by means of recurrence (that is, of the reapplication of unvarying principles in new cases), *new* events, *new* objects, are constantly produced; and these new objects are in some respects such as to exemplify new laws. A Self is always passing to new tasks even by virtue of the recurrent nature of its activities. For while it carries out the "same plan," it continually applies this "same plan" in new ways, because its new creations are founded upon its former deeds, and take up what went before in order to give it new significance.

It occurs to us, however, to remember that, just because our social life belongs to the World of Appreciation, its endless novelties in life and activity *can only be organized in definite ways, in case many people agree to coöperate by adopting the same plans.* If they adopt these same plans, and persist in them, a basis of customs, of social habits, is found. But these habits, applied in recurrent fashion in the lives of rational beings, will lead to constantly novel results, just because, in the conscious life of social beings, each new act will be founded upon the results of former acts, and each new social agent will join his act to what has been done by others. The mason's habits in laying down each brick, and in applying the mortar, are, for instance, relatively unvarying. But just thereby, since he lays each brick upon the former one, each of his deeds has an individual value, and he passes constantly to new stages of constructions. And even so, just in order that any Well-Ordered Series of socially planned deeds should involve, at every stage, significant novelties, and still retain definite relations to what has gone before, there must indeed be unvarying *aspects* belonging to all the social customs that lead to such rationally planned results. These unvarying aspects are the more permanent laws, customs, habits, of the social order.

But, if you look closer, you see that such definite social habits, or plans of action as can be *communicated by one man to another* or *passed down*, like the industrial arts of early peoples, *from generation to generation*, depend upon discovering, and fixing by our attention, *such uniformities of natural law as enable men to conceive, and to describe to one another, definite plans of action.*

Hence, in the history of mankind, the discovery of seemingly unvarying laws of Nature, has been *the condition for the organization of definite customs.* And just because Nature has thus come to be conceived as the socially significant tool, *that aspect of Nature which suggests such unvarying laws has come to be looked upon as the most characteristic of the aspects of the objective physical world.*

Irregularities in our experience of Nature either have no interest for the social order, and remain neglected, or else, like the irregularities of the weather, or of our own bodily health, they are practically so important as to fix in our minds the thought that only by finding, through further experience, laws which *shall* remain invariant through successive periods of time, can we hope to organize our conduct in definite ways in response to these phenomena. We make the effort to find such regularities, our ideal. We conceive it as the goal that our common human experience may be able to reach. But, observe, whenever we reach that goal, *then* one man can describe a given uniformity to his fellow, or can make exact predictions (as the astronomers predict the eclipses); and many men together can verify the prediction. In such cases then, the social test of what constitutes an externally real physical fact can be applied with a peculiarly impressive exactness; and the natural uniformity can be verified as belonging to our common objects. On the other hand, where natural phenomena remain baffling and irregular, our descriptions of series of events remain either less definite, or else less widely verifiable by the social test. We are accordingly able, in such cases, to assume that it is our individual ignorance, or our subjective bias, or the lack of socially verifiable definition of facts, which so far hinders us from finding out what the natural order really is. Hence we form the general conception that in so far as laws that remain temporally "invariant," have not yet been found, our subjective ignorance *may be* responsible for the result, while *in so far as definite laws that do not vary with time have been discovered, exactly described, and repeatedly verified, we are dealing with the objective constitution of Nature.* Our reason for this view is then simply the principle, that the more we know of unvarying natural laws, the more widely can our social tests be applied, and the better can the physical phenomena bear the scrutiny which depends upon thinking that they must be the same for all of us. ×

Hence the so-called axiom of the unvarying character of the laws of nature is no self-evident truth, is not even at once an empirically established and an universal generalization, and possesses its present authority because of the emphasis that our social interests give to the discovery of uniform laws where we can discover them.[1] That we do discover and verify them over a very wide range of our experience of Nature, is an unquestionable fact, and one of which every Philosophy of Nature must take account. But it is much to know that this discovery is not due to any innate idea, or to any first principle of the reason, but is an empirical, although by no means an universal generalization, which we have been led by social motives *to emphasize and to extend as far as possible*, and so to conceive as if it were universally characteristic of Objective Nature.

In the history of human thought about Nature it is easy to follow the influence of the social motives here in question. The savage certainly had no innate idea of absolutely uniform natural laws. Industrial art, commerce, and social custom, were the three early sources of interest in the uniformities of natural phenomena.

[1] Cf. the admirable paper of Mr. Charles Peirce on "The Doctrine of Necessity," in the *Monist*, Vol. II, p. 321. Mr. Peirce's doctrine as to natural law is not the one here discussed; but I owe much to his keen criticism of the "dogma of Necessity."

The arts needed uniform and persistently plastic materials to work upon, — clay, stone, metals. Otherwise the arts themselves could not be definitely taught and traditionally handed down; and no sufficiently definite social activities could be founded upon the use of the products of these arts. Men sought, at first unconsciously, then deliberately, for *materials whose behavior, while plastic for the purposes of their arts, still remained unchanging through time.* Men found such materials, although never with perfect success. For the pottery and the stones broke or wore out, and the tools and the weapons lost their edges, or were in time shattered. But the discovery of such relatively unvarying, socially common, objects and natural laws, first made the uniformity of nature something *consciously recognized as an objective fact*, — a fact for all. Commerce, for its part, led to disputes which the processes of weighing and measuring could either prevent or decide. Human ingenuity was thus led to observe the unvarying laws of *measurable* objects, and so, out of the search for such social community of conduct as commerce made men anxious to win, there grew a new idea about Nature. And thus the bases for all Quantitative Science were laid. Moreover, various social customs of a complex social type, relating to recurrent religious ceremonies, or to seed-time and harvest, led men to search for common natural phenomena whereby to organize such activities, and to fix their times; and from such motives men were led to a recognition of natural law in the heavens. The special sciences later sprang as much from the industrial and commercial arts, as from early philosophical speculations. The concept of the unvarying character of the laws of Nature, freed at length from its practical motives, became universal, and has inflicted itself as a dogma upon more recent thought. Yet its origin was social.

VII

The value of this dogma, as of all the concepts of the World of Description, is relative. It reveals no absolute truth. From our own point of view, there can indeed be no doubt that our experience of the objects of Nature *does* prove to us that there exists, in the universe, a vast realm of fact *other than* what human minds consciously find present within their own circles of individual or private apprehension. And so, for us, Nature is indeed a part of Reality, and the social tests do indeed prove that this is true. But when we ask *what* reality Nature possesses, we must beware of letting our social interests, and the general motives that lead us to conceive the World of Description, blind us to the true principles upon which an interpretation of experience should be founded. The sharp contrast between Matter and Mind, the sharp dualism between the World of Description and the World of Appreciation, — we have seen from what motives in our own lives all such contrasts result. We shall no longer take this dualism too seriously. We have seen its relative justification, and its limitations.

In any case, in viewing Nature as a realm of law, we must distinguish between what our common experience permits us to verify, in the way of our own conceptual constructions of Nature, and what our experience of Nature warrants us in asserting as the truth regarding a realm external to man's consciousness. It is with our more modern sciences as it was with early industrial arts. If an industrial art succeeds, that is because Nature actually furnishes us with empirical materials that are plastic for the purposes of this art. We have, however, no right to assert, upon that account, that all natural phenomena, viewed in themselves, and apart from man, already must be so constituted *a priori* as to be adaptable to the purposes of our human art. The primitive artists who produced the pottery of our American Pueblo Indians, were skilful in finding out just the right sort of clay for their purposes. But had they formed a theory that Nature is in itself essentially a storehouse of good potter's clay, they would have generalized quite as ill as did primitive Animism when it conceived all Nature as alive in the same sense in which our capricious wills are alive, and are in us subject to our moods and to our senses.

Now, as I have said, our science is a sort of theoretical extension of our industrial art. What the arts do with their tools, the student of science does with his conceptions. That is, he wins over the phenomena of our experience to the service of our human purposes. He does this by processes of selection, of construction, and of an endless process of trial and error. A conception used by any empirical science is an ideal tool, or a sort of mechanical contrivance. Using it, we work over the data of our common experience until these data become subject to our purposes of prediction and of description. With the successful conception in the mind, we can pass from fact to fact, from prediction to execution, from expectation to observation, with ease, exactness, and socially verifiable success. Precisely so, however, with the good material tool, or with any other mechanical contrivance, we can adjust our material objects to our common ends. Just as the railway may carry me from an experience of London to your presence in Aberdeen, so a good scientific conception enables the worker in any science to pass from the experience of one set of facts, through definite processes of prediction, of experiment, and of observation, to the presence of certain other facts, which he calculates in advance of finding them, precisely as the traveller purchases in advance his railway ticket for a certain destination.

And now, not only are the conceptual constructions of science thus similar to the contrivances of an industrial art; but the processes involved in the one case are actually continuous with those which are used in the other. Amongst the contrivances of any industrial art, none are successful except when guided by minds whose ideas are adjusted to their tools. Amongst the constructions of empirical science, the internal processes of scientific theory are inseparable from the diagrams, laboratories, and other contrivances, in which scientific plans of action get expressed. All industrial art, upon its intelligent side, implies scientific conceptions of certain objects in material nature. All science, in so far as it is concerned with natural objects, expresses its conceptions in the form of certain processes of classification, of description, of experiment, and of prediction, which are as material in their embodiment as the works of an industrial art. While science deals with natural facts in a far more universal way than does any industrial art, its purposes are no less human than are those of its fellow. Both coöperate to the end of *man's mastery over Nature.* Both succeed by selection from the mass of materials offered, by rearrangement of what is found, and by skill in adjustment.

And, therefore, both give us much the same sort of right to speculate as to Nature's inner constitution. Both involve the same sort of relatively narrow clearness as to just our human place in the mists of finite experience. Both indicate a truth that is in some sense valid beyond ourselves. Both have essentially the same kind of limitation when we undertake to view them as revelations of what that truth in itself is and implies.

But we have long since given up assuming that the success of our industrial art is, by itself, any sufficient revelation of the innermost nature of things. It does not now occur to us to say that Nature exists, apart from man, as a mere storehouse of materials for the contrivances of our industrial art, — for example, as a collection of banks of good clay for the potters, or (to use the example that Hegel cited) as a storehouse of good corks for our bottles. A certain simple-minded teleology used indeed often to view Nature in very much this trivial way. The coal measures were especially prepared for man's use. The metals were preordained for his forges and furnaces, for his machines, and for his ornaments and his money. The animals grew to provide him with food and with furs and with feathers. Even the heavens moved regularly in order to equip him with time-pieces. We have abandoned such simple views. We observe that Nature indeed is such as to permit man not only to live, but to give his life constantly richer meaning through his arts. But we also know that man wins his arts by his own struggle and skill, and that it is as nearly right to speak of his ceaseless conflict with hostile Nature as it is to lay stress upon Nature's kindness in furnishing him the instruments for his success in the conflict. Not thus, however, is our deeper insight into man's unity with Nature to be won or expressed.

And yet, despite this our emancipation from the trivialities of a simple teleology, there are those who even now would laugh at regarding Nature as predestined to be man's storehouse of clay and coal and corks and furs and metals, and who, nevertheless, view Nature, because of the actual success of our empirical science, as in itself, and by its inmost constitution, a treasure-house of purely mechanical laws, — as a thesaurus of concepts, of calculable relations, of rigid necessities, or as a realm of mathematical formulas.

Now the one of these two views of nature — the ancient view of a trivial teleology, and the other, the so-called mechanical conception of nature — is as crudely anthropomorphic as the other. Man's insight into the known laws of Nature is precisely as much due to a struggle with the complexities and irregularities of his experience of Nature, as his industrial arts are due to a conflict with Nature's seeming chaos of climates and of materials. A rigid selection, a long search, and a deliberate rearrangement of the facts offered to us by raw experience, wins, in the one case as in the other, not with any *a priori* certainty, but at times, and to a limited extent, and by virtue of our skill and patience. Nature, as we empirically know it, just as truly seems to resist our efforts to explain the phenomena, as in certain regions it permits us to win. When we win, when we explain and predict, doubtless that is indeed because external Nature is in itself such as to permit us to do so. But the same Nature permits us to find the clay and the coals and the metals.

Neither by our empirical science nor by our art do we then directly discôver anything but this: Namely, *that our human Internal Meanings do indeed possess some reference to a vast finite realm beyond ourselves, within which we men find our place.* Out of this realm we ourselves have proceeded through the processes of evolution. Into this realm, at death, we seem to return. This realm is called Nature. It doubtless has its own meaning. This meaning is doubtless in itself deeply linked to ours. And this meaning is such as to permit us with varying, but on the whole, with vastly increasing success, *both to develope our human arts, and to work out the relatively successful, but also distinctly human and social, descriptions and predictions of our science.* Both our art and our sciences are due, however, quite as much to our conflict with the facts that our experience directly furnishes, as to any essential plasticity of these facts, either to the practical purposes of our art, or to the ideal purposes of our science. Nature permits us to mine metals and to construct our railways. Just so Nature permits us to form our mechanical conceptions, to make our computations, and, upon occasion, to predict thereby future facts. Nature could permit our success in neither case unless, indeed, Nature had *some* actual and inner relation to the existence of our own life and meaning. But what this relation is, is not directly to be read from a mere enumeration of these our successes. For we also fail as well as succeed; and Nature is sometimes as stubborn to our art and to our science as, at other times, Nature seems plastic to both.

Where we, indeed, succeed, the success is at least as much due to our skill in selection and in conception as to the essential plasticity of Nature. As a great work of industrial art remains a monument rather to the engineer's skill than to Nature's kindliness, so, as Auguste Comte well said, the heavens declare the glory of Newton and of Kepler, whenever successful prediction shows how skilful were the astronomical tools that these thinkers invented, and the theoretical structures that they built upon the basis of these conceptions. That Kepler was thinking God's thoughts after him, is, indeed, also true; but the divine thoughts in question were at least quite as much God's thoughts regarding man's skill, as any divine plan present in outer nature.

My conclusion, then, is this: It is especially through the success of certain of our scientific conceptions that we have been led to a mechanical view of Nature, and to the consequent doctrine that Mind and Matter are utterly contrasted entities. Therefore, this very contrast is one whose origin lies in our human way of viewing the facts of our experience. It is our interest in social organization that has given us both industrial art and empirical science. As industrial art regards its facts as mere contrivances that have no life of their own, but that merely express their human artificer's intents, so a philosophy of Nature, founded solely upon our special sciences, tends to treat the facts of Nature (regarded in the light of our cunningly contrived conceptions) as having no inner meaning, and as being mere embodiments of our formulas. Both doctrines are perfectly justified as expressions of the perspective view of Nature which we men naturally take. Neither view can stand against any deeper reason that we may have for interpreting our experiences of Nature as a hint of a vaster realm of life and of meaning of which we men form a part, and of which the final unity is in God's life.

LECTURE V

LECTURE V

THE INTERPRETATION OF NATURE

WE reach at length, after perhaps too lengthy a study of the problem of man's knowledge of Nature, our own attempt to bring our theory of Nature into explicit harmony with our Fourth Conception of Being.

In the foregoing lecture we have seen how man comes by his belief in the material world, and how he has come to set that world in sharp contrast with the realm of Mind. We have seen how this contrast is made to seem especially hopeless by reason of the mechanical view of Nature upon which our more developed consciousness of natural law has led many thinkers to insist. At the last lecture, we also saw that this very view of Nature is a product of distinctly human and social motives. These motives have great value as bases for the conceptual constructions of our science. They have no right to pretend to reveal to us essential truth about the ultimate nature of things. Perhaps, then (so we reasoned), at bottom, the contrast between Mind and Matter is not as ultimate as it seems. Perhaps a deeper view may annul the apparent contrast, and may show how closely linked to Nature this life of ours is, and how akin to our own inner consciousness is much that we take to be most remote and foreign in the life of Nature.

Now what at the last time we approached from the side of the social origin and the human motives that have determined our conceptions of Nature, we now need to approach from another side. Whatever the origin of our ideas about Nature, these ideas unquestionably have a basis in extra-human truth. This is what all our previous analysis has shown us. Moreover, these ideas, however they have grown up in us, are very certainly a combination of two factors. In part they are due to an observation of the facts of our common experience. These facts many men have verified, both separately and together, until we can be reasonably sure that such facts are not matters of any man's private experience, but that they have a basis in what is beyond the inner life of any or of all men. These facts form what we might call our relatively literal knowledge of Nature. Examples of such facts are: the existence of a world that now appears to us as material, and the occurrence in this world of the more or less regular routine of Nature's phenomena, such as the tides, the weather, and the moon's phases. In part, however, our ideas about Nature take the form of more recondite and ideal theoretical constructions, such as experience only indirectly verifies. All our more mechanical theories of Nature as a whole belong to this class of ideas. These ideas are of such sort that Nature, whatever it really is, permits us to use them successfully, within certain limits, as the tools of our science. So much, then, we may here premise. We now propose to lay aside inquiry as to how all these ideas came to grow up in our minds. We accept them, for the moment, as they come to us, and with them in hand, and with the mere memory that the two sorts of ideas in question are not of equal value as evidences of the ultimate truth of things, we turn back to Nature itself, and try once more the task of interpreting, more in detail, the problem set us by what we have already called the greatest apparent contrast in Nature, namely, the contrast between Consciousness and what seems to us to be unconscious Matter.

I

At one extreme of Nature, we find a world which we are accustomed to conceive as a world of inwardly changeless substances, of material particles, whose changing external relations are determined by rigid and relatively mechanical laws. These laws the sciences of physics and of chemistry define. At the other extreme we find a world with whose inner character we are well acquainted, little as we know many of its laws. In that world, the world of our consciousness, all the stream of fact flows, and nothing abides but the meanings. This world is indeed not lawless, but its facts seem to bear no resemblance to those of inorganic matter. I need not further dwell on the apparent contrast of these two worlds. It has now been enough discussed.

What I here wish first to bring to notice is the fact that the doctrine of Evolution, in its modern form, is our largest generalization of all our human view of Nature, and that this doctrine seems to show, that, if the extremes are in seeming here endlessly far apart, yet somehow, in Nature, the gulf is bridged. Between what seems to us, from our ordinary social point of view, the highest of accessible mental life, and what we take to be the manifestation of lifeless matter, there is, in the process of mental evolution apparently no breach of continuity anywhere. And upon numerous recent thinkers the question has therefore been forced constantly afresh, What, then, is the real link that thus unites these uttermost extremes? What we call the manifestation of dead matter can certainly pass over into states where Nature, as embodied in the organisms of our fellow-men, shows to us all the signs of mind. The transition can be and constantly is made in the reverse order. Nor is the transition such as any longer to suggest to us miraculous extranatural interferences. Its manifold exemplification, through ages of natural evolution, seems to make clear that in this transition we have simply a normal indication of the true nature of things. And I must repeat, it is precisely this apparent continuity which is the most impressive of all the inductions that the study of evolution has lately forced upon the attention of all who have taken Nature at all seriously. Now, if man's experience of Nature has any sound basis at all, the modern doctrine of Evolution seems to be an account of a process that has a real basis in the essence of things. I shall here assume as known the general outlines of this doctrine, and the general sort of evidence upon which it rests. I shall ask, What light does this doctrine tend to throw upon our problem?

When two objects A and B, say a mass of inorganic matter and an organism with a rational mind, seem to differ as widely as possible, and when, nevertheless, things of the type of A seem pretty obviously to pass by a nearly continuous series of changes into objects of the type of B, that is, when from inorganic matter beings with minds evolve, and when B seems with even greater ease to pass back into A, the first presumption very naturally is that you are dealing with somewhat deceptive appearances. And, if you are sure, as the students of evolution are now for their own purposes rightfully sure, that the approximate continuity itself is not the deceptive appearance, and that A does really pass by nearly continuous gradations into B and *vice versa*, then the next natural presumption about A and B is that it is their wide difference which actually constitutes the deceptive appearance, and that A and B are really at heart very much alike. Now this is what a great many thinkers have supposed about the appearances called Mind and Matter. The continuous transition from the one of these appearances to the other is precisely what constitutes the most fascinating part of the seeming history called evolution. One may say that this approximate continuity is nowadays, at least, as sure as anything that we know about Matter itself, the more distant and really the more mysterious of the appearances.

Yet, singularly enough, when thinkers have proceeded to define the way in which these two apparent extremes could be identified, or could be regarded as mere appearances of some truth which lay deeper than at least one of the extremes, many such thinkers have undertaken the task of regarding Mind as a mere appearance of Matter, rather than that of conceiving material nature as a mere appearance behind which lies Mind. That is, they have said: Matter is very probably, in the main, what we take it to be, viz. permanent, rigid in its laws, naturally unconscious, mechanical in its processes. But it is Mind that we fail to know. Of the extremes A and B, Matter and Mind, such thinkers, regarding matter as fairly well known, have chosen to conceive B, namely Mind, as a curiously confused phenomenon, a mere resultant or show of certain of the properties of A, which we call Matter. Yet the result of such efforts to interpret evolution — efforts which have been very frequent — is, as any student of evolution knows, rather unpromising.

Meanwhile it is easy to see why such efforts should often have been preferred. Matter is actually the more mysterious of the two extremes. But it does not always seem so; for Mind, as we know it in men, is an unstable process, which all sorts of physical conditions appear to derange. But Matter, as a physical science conceives it, is, for the reasons mentioned at the last time, viewed by us as subject to stable laws and to definite predictions. Minds pass away from our ken. Material phenomena persist. Minds, capable of intelligibly communicating with us, are rare exceptions in the natural order. But the natural world seems full of the physical appearances called masses of matter. It is natural then for men to try to explain the unusual by the usual, to regard the unstable as the mere appearance of the stable, and to view the stable itself as the really better known of the two. Yet the persistent hopelessness of the whole undertaking, the absolute impossibility of explaining how mental life, whose appearance at least we know so well in its fleeting beauties, should be a mere show of the properties of that which, when we take its mere appearance as true, seems to be the permanent substance now conceived as Matter, — the persistent hopelessness, I say, of this whole undertaking, has led many to reflect afresh, and to ask, Do we so well know the mere appearance called by us Matter as to be sure that its apparent properties, its stability, its mechanical rigidity of lawful behavior, are its ultimately real characters? Suppose, after all, that this stable appearance were a delusion. Suppose that even material nature were internally full of the live and fleeting processes that we know as those of conscious mental life. Suppose that these processes constituted the inmost essence and foundation of what seems to us to be Matter. Would that be wholly inconsistent with what we know of the natural world? In that case, however, what we call matter would be a mere external appearance of the very sort of fact that we ourselves better know as Mind. And then the true secret of the evolution of mind would get an entirely different reading.

In order to judge what may be the true worth of such speculations, it is well to go still a little deeper than we have yet done into special problems of the Philosophy of Nature. Yet, as I do so, I shall, for the time, keep my Idealistic Theory of Being in reserve. That theory furnishes a deep warrant for the speculations here in question. But let us next give these speculations a merely empirical basis. Then, when our Idealism returns upon the scene, it will find the facts ready to accept its authority.

II

And first, let us for the moment merely assume as true the ordinary presuppositions of science. Let us ask ourselves how much, in that case, we can really pretend to know of the inner nature of things when they are judged upon a purely empirical basis, as science judges them. We are by this time well aware that no empirical science pretends really to know what the inner nature of things is at all, and least of all, to know the ultimate nature of Matter. What empirical science can try to tell you is not what things are in themselves, but how they behave, and to what laws they are apparently subject. The question as to how deep into the truth of Nature our empirical science goes is then the question: How far do the laws of Nature that science makes out agree with any natural truth that is valid wholly beyond the range of the human point of view, and that can be said to hold more or less apart from our mere human appearances? And when, with this inquiry in mind, we pass in review our natural sciences, we have already had good reason to assert that the most exactly stated of the laws of the World of Description, explicitly represent not directly observed facts, or any immediately verifiable and literally true statement about things as we men can experience them, but rather only extremely ideal ways in which science finds it convenient to conceive facts for the purposes of a brief theoretical description of vast ranges of experience.

In order to adapt this, our former general result, to the present inquiry, let us, for instance, consider our very valuable scientific theories of atomic and of ethereal processes. Nobody has observed atoms, or ether waves. These are interpolated series of ideal objects conceived as *between* the systems of facts that we can observe. The laws of atomic and of ethereal processes are very ideal constructions, whereby we are able to summarize, after a fashion, vast numbers of facts, or to construct in an abstract way the relation of One and Many. Even the law of gravitation, one of the most exact of material laws, is an extremely ideal statement of a formula whose direct truth nobody precisely verifies at any time. What we observe, and what, by the aid of the formula of gravitation, we can predict and verify, are planets moving, stones falling, and the rest of gravitative phenomena. Nobody ever directly observes any force, such as the ideal force called gravitation. A very ideal statement about the conceived mutual attractions of particles of matter enables us to summarize all the observed facts of the realm of gravitation in one formula. The truth of the formula lies in its summary application to vast ranges of phenomena. Nobody can pretend that this formula is known to express directly the observed inner nature, or even the directly observed genuine behavior of anything. The science of the future may come to observe phenomena which will explain gravitation as a mere appearance of some much more genuine natural process. Many of our most exact laws of Nature are thus, as it were, explicitly ideal constructions, products, so to speak, of the present methods of bookkeeping used by science in keeping our accounts of facts. Such laws are true enough as convenient conceptions whereby we summarize observed facts. They are true as ledger entries and balances are true summaries of business transactions. But they are not laws which are known to express anything final even about the observed behavior of things. Nobody can doubt the value of such summary theories of physical things. Nobody can doubt that they are ideal constructions. The science of the future may enter its accounts by other methods of bookkeeping.

In strong contrast, however, with such more ideal laws of Nature stand certain other generalizations of science and even of common sense. These other generalizations are often perfectly literal statements of how the facts of Nature are known to behave. For instance, there is the law that an organism grows old, but never grows young. But the Nature that we all acknowledge is full of just such irreversible processes as is the process of growing old. Science knows many more of such processes than does common sense. When in winter the heat of your chimney radiates into space and comes not back, when the spilt milk is wept over in vain, when china once broken refuses to mend, common sense observes a set of processes which science, in great measure, generalizes in the principles (1) of the tendency of energy to pass from available to unavailable forms, and (2) of the tendency of matter to pass through similarly irreversible series of changing configurations. In all such irreversible processes of nature, you are dealing with profoundly instructive ways of behavior of the natural world. These ways of the world's behavior are certainly just as real as is Nature herself. Here surely you touch "hard fact," that is, fact that you ought to acknowledge in case you accept the verdict of our social experience at all. Here then we get not, perchance, at the inmost nature, but certainly at the real behavior of things. The most widely generalizing science recognizes such processes and dwells long over them. They constitute one of the most interesting problems of the general theory of energy. The most simple-minded common sense also feels them. These, as far as they go, are thus literally true laws of Nature's behavior.

But now observe that, for this very reason, the laws of these processes differ in a very marked way from those ideal laws such as science states in the theory of ethereal or of atomic processes. The latter laws, the exactly ideal laws, are convenient hypothetical summaries of vast ranges of experience,—but in a highly conceptual, in a mathematically artificial form. They are laws that explicitly stand for the way in which it is just now convenient to keep the books of science. They are typical examples of formulas of the World of Description. They are true, but they are verifiably true only from a certain point of view. They conceive the physical world *as if it were so*, or so observable when it is *not* so observable. The science of the future may, therefore, substitute other theories for them. But the laws of the other sort, the laws about the irreversible processes, tell you, in a much more literal fashion, how Nature actually behaves.

And now, closely connected with this contrast is another. The ideal laws, of the type of the laws about the ethereal processes, are laws which are valid, so far as they are valid at all, only for Matter as such. They serve by their very exactness to make Matter seem very remote from Mind. But the other laws, the laws of the irreversible processes, *are in their most general type, common to Matter and to Mind, to the physical and to the moral world.* They tend to be, in some measure, applicable everywhere, to conscious as to apparently unconscious processes, to the dissipation of energy as to the facts of the moral world. Your beloved dreams, that slip away while you wake, are shattered like china, are dissipated like radiant energy, — in brief, are cases *of the law of the irreversibility of certain natural processes.* The poets, too, sing of precisely the principle that the students of energy report to us, namely, of this very irreversibility of certain processes of nature. "When the lamp is shattered," sings Shelley ; and Tennyson tells of the "tender grace of a day that is dead." Both poets reporting not mere feelings, but laws of nature. They are telling of the tendency of natural energy to pass from available to unavailable forms, as heat passes according to the second law of thermodynamics ; and the poets are observing that certain inner conscious processes have a tendency, just because these processes are in connection with all Nature, to follow a precisely similar, but often extremely inconvenient course, often, namely, a course from the irrevocable to the mere memory thereof. So, then, it is precisely the more literally actual, the more directly observable of our two sorts of natural processes, that is, apparently, a sort of process common to material and to mental phenomena. But these more ideal laws of nature, like the laws of the conceived ethereal processes, are at once peculiar to what science conceives as Matter, and are also laws which need not, in literal fact, represent any ultimately actual or directly observable behavior of Matter at all. One sees thus that, if we are not deceived by the mere book-keeping of science, if we distinguish between the ideal constructions of scientific theory, and the directly verifiable behavior of natural facts, we begin to see less contrast between Matter and Mind.

III

Taking a very broad view of the laws of Nature, in the rough, we can as a fact say that conscious Nature shares with what we regard as apparently unconscious and material Nature four great and characteristic types of processes. (1) Both regions of Nature are subject, as we have just seen, to some condition that demands the irreversibility of great numbers of their processes. In both realms, namely, there are numberless sorts of facts that return not again, so that an irrevocable passing away of states once reached, pervades the stream of experience in both realms alike. This is a very deep principle of universal Nature. It is certainly as genuinely real as is Nature herself. The irreversibility of many of Nature's processes, so far as it exists, suggests, therefore, some very genuine, if hidden, inner fluency about material Nature itself; and the hypothesis at once occurs that very possibly material Nature is a show of a process that is inwardly fluent, just as the mental process in us is fluent, only at some very different rate.

Here, then, is our first very instructive relation between the most remote and the nearest regions of Nature. It is an analogy that has attracted considerable attention.

I do not think that it has received, however, enough attention. But it is not the only pervasive analogy.

For (2): Both regions of Nature, the apparently mental and the apparently material region, are subject to processes which involve in general a tendency of one part of Nature to *communicate*, as it were, with another part, influencing what occurs at one place through what has already occurred at another place. Ideas in the same consciousness tend to assimilate other ideas, to communicate their own nature to these other ideas, to win the latter over to agreement with the first. Minds tend, in social intercourse, to be influenced by other minds. Now these vast and pervasive processes of conscious communication possess both a close similarity to, and a continuity with, certain still more vast and pervasive series of natural processes which, described indeed as so-called wave-movements, are amongst the phenomena best known to science. In both cases the tendency is one towards *the mutual assimilation of the regions of Nature involved in the process.* In both cases, the process of communication has, in general, an at least partially irreversible character. This second sort of analogy between the material and the mental worlds is again not exceptional, but of universal type. I cannot dwell upon it at length here. It has attracted some attention. It has been noticed by M. Tarde, and has been especially insisted upon by Mr. Charles Peirce as a basis for a remarkable hypothesis regarding evolution.

But (3): Both the material and the mental worlds show a tendency, under favorable conditions, to the appearances of processes resembling those which, in the life of a mind, we call Habits. Here again both Mr. Charles Peirce and Mr. Cope, as well as other students of evolution, have pointed out the analogy of Matter and Mind thus involved. The tendency can of course be stated in terms of descriptive concepts. Fechner, a generation ago, developed the principle of the "tendency to stability" in material systems. Let a complex material system, subject to certain general restrictions, once begin a series of movements. Then, in the long run, as Fechner showed, this system, if let alone, will tend to assume a somewhat stable series of rhythmically repeated movements, the more irregular movements being eliminated by a sort of natural selection. Spencer attracted attention to a somewhat similar character of Nature in his famous chapters on the "Rhythm of Motion" and "Equilibration." But whether or no one undertakes to conceive such phenomena as results of absolutely unvarying laws, certain it is that physical Nature is full of *approximate rhythms.* Now an approximate rhythm is a *temporary* law of Nature. It is a law to the effect that a given observable process *tends* to repeat itself over and over, as, for example, the rhythm of day and night or of the seasons is repeated. Such laws, I say, may be amongst the literally true accounts of what actually happens in the world. But laws of this sort may be, and often are, mere empirical generalizations whose validity is indeed temporary. For at all events *most* of Nature's apparent rhythms are mingled with processes of irreversible change, and of such change as runs in one direction, and as accordingly tends, in the long run, *to disturb and destroy the rhythm.*

The interest of science in ideally complete theories leads, indeed, to an effort to conceive the literally true, but usually only imperfect rhythms of Nature as special cases of those more ideal laws which we mentioned before. But the more ideal laws remain, as we said, matters of the book-keeping methods of our present science. *Nature, as actually observed, shows us rhythms that tend, within limits, to be pretty constant. Take them in long periods, and these rhythms tend to pass away and to be lost in irrevocable decay.* The rhythm of a man's heart-beat is a typical case. It has its normal variations, its normal regularity, and its long-continued but still limited persistence. Just so the rhythm of the earth's rotation on its axis, or of the now relatively stable movement of the planets, is a genuine, but not an everlasting process of Nature. The tides retard the one rhythm. The meteors, not to mention other disturbances, will, in the long run, ruin the planetary rhythm. Such observable and approximate routine in Nature is closely analogous to what constitutes a great deal of the life of habit in the internal processes of a mind. Habits are just such tendencies to routine, to rhythm, in conscious life. They are only approximate rhythms. They are mixed up with all sorts of irreversible tendencies, which in the end tend to overwhelm them one and all. But while they last they are instances of natural law. Like the rhythms of external Nature, they arise, last awhile, and seem to pass away; but so far as they go they are certainly genuine fashions of the behavior of Nature.

Our interest here lies in the fact that while those

ideally constant laws of Matter, which scientific book-keeping demands, but which are not literally and directly verifiable, seem to establish an ultimate contrast between Mind and Matter, these literally verifiable but not literally constant laws of observable Nature, these approximate rhythms, are common to conscious and to unconscious Nature, and when taken together, form a graded series of truths about the routine of Nature. The graded series suggests that the inner nature of things is not so much ideally constant, as merely relatively stable, so that in the fluent life of our consciousness, we directly know a process of which the apparently absolute stability of the conceived material processes is really only another instance, whose inner fluency is concealed from us by the longer intervals of time demanded for important changes to take place.

The fourth class of processes apparently common to unconscious and to conscious Nature are the very processes of evolution themselves. And we now see that these evolutionary processes, which seem so continuous from inorganic to organic and finally to conscious Nature, do not stand alone, but are only one instance, amongst many, of the processes whose type is common to conscious and to apparently unconscious Nature.

Taking all four of these types of processes together, what general impression of Nature do they give to us? I confess that, wholly apart from any more metaphysical consideration of the deeper nature of Reality, they suggest to me, as they have more or less suggested to others, who have considered one or other of them, an impression which I may as well briefly summarize for what, as a mere result of a rough induction, and as a mere hypothesis for further testing, it may so far be worth.

IV

My impression and my hypothesis are as follows: (1) The vast contrast which we have been taught to make between material and conscious processes really depends merely upon the accidents of the human point of view, and in particular upon an exaggeration of the literal accuracy of those admirable theories of atomic and ethereal processes which, as I have said, belong to the mere book-keeping of the sciences. Many of the processes of Nature can be conceptually described by very exact formulas whose value as conceptions nobody can question, but whose literal accuracy nobody verifies. Take those formulas as literally true, and then, indeed, the material world seems to become one of absolutely rigid substances, of absolutely permanent mathematical formulas, and of a type such that a transition from material to conscious Nature looks perfectly unintelligible. The only resort would then be that, if one still accepted the continuity of evolution, one would conceive consciousness as a chance resultant, as a show, as an illusory affair, whose true essence is not known to us; or as a sort of delirium to which the world of the atoms is occasionally subject, — a delirium wherein the world forgets that it is nothing but an embodied system of differential equations, and takes itself to be — well, let us say: —

> "An infant crying in the night,
> An infant crying for the light,
> And with no language but a cry."

For just some such incorporated system of differential equations gone mad would be, according to such a theory, any conscious being, even if, for instance, he chanced to be that dignified and considerate speculative and mathematical physicist who, by hypothesis, is to be aware that all this account of Nature is true. But then this account is not true; nor does science, rightly viewed, in the least demand or desire that it shall be true. The mathematical formulas are conceptions. They constitute admirable and, for their purpose, invaluable ledger entries in our accounts with Nature. For they help us to compute, to predict, to describe, and to classify phenomena. But they do not as literally express the directly observable behavior of any independent facts of Nature as does many a much humbler empirical observation, such as a man makes when he observes himself growing old, or as an evolutionist makes when he observes the growth and division of a cell. We know that Nature, as it were, *tolerates* our mathematical formulas. We do not know that she would not equally well tolerate many other such formulas instead of these. But we do know, meanwhile, that the processes called by us growth and decay are facts as genuinely real as any natural facts whatever. For one does grow old; and the cells do grow and divide.

Abandoning, then, the ideal contrast of Mind and Matter, and coming to their continuity and analogy, my present hypothesis runs: (2) That we have no right whatever to speak of really unconscious Nature, but only of uncommunicative Nature, or of Nature whose mental processes go on at such different time-rates from ours that we cannot adjust ourselves to a live appreciation of their inward fluency, although our consciousness does make us aware of their presence. And (3): My hypothesis is that, in case of Nature in general, as in case of the particular portions of Nature known as our fellow-men, we are dealing with phenomenal signs of a vast conscious process, whose relation to Time varies vastly, but whose general characters are throughout the same. From this point of view, evolution would be a series of processes suggesting to us various degrees and types of conscious processes. These processes, in case of so-called inorganic matter, are very remote from us; while, in case of the processes which appear to us as the expressive movements of the bodies of our human fellows, they are so near to our own inner processes that we understand what they mean. I suppose, then, that when you deal with Nature, you deal with a vast realm of finite consciousness of which your own is at once a part and an example. All this finite consciousness shares with yours the character of being full of fluent processes whose tendency is twofold, — in one direction towards the formation of relatively stable habits of repetition, in the other direction towards the irrevocable leaving of certain events, situations, and types of experience behind. I suppose that this play between the irrevocable and the repeated, between habit and novelty, between rhythm and the destruction of rhythm, is everywhere in Nature, as it is in us, something significant, something of interest, something that means a struggle for ideals. I suppose that this something constitutes a process wherein goals, ideals, are sought in a seemingly endless pursuit, and where new realms of sentient experience are constantly coming into view and into relation to former experiences. I suppose that the field of Nature's experience is everywhere leading slowly or rapidly to the differentiation of new types of conscious unity. I suppose that this process goes on with very vast slowness in inorganic Nature, as for instance in the nebulæ, but with great speed in you and me. But, meanwhile, I do not suppose that slowness means a lower type of consciousness.

For next, to complete my hypothesis in this direction, I observe that the relation of our own consciousness to Time is something very arbitrary. Our consciousness, for its special characters, is dependent upon a certain fact which we might well call our particular Time-Span. If we are to be inwardly conscious of anything, there must occur some change in the contents of our feelings, but this change must not be too fast or too slow. What happens within what we describe as the millionth or the thousandth of a second necessarily escapes us. We can note, at best, only the mere enduring after-effects of such a happening. So it is when an electric spark or a dynamite explosion occurs. For us the event itself is then no separate matter of experience. We confuse the event with its after-effects. On the other hand, whatever lasts longer than a very few moments no longer can form part of one conscious moment for us. But suppose that our consciousness had to a thousand millionth of a second, or to a million years of time, the same relation that it now has to the arbitrary length in seconds of a typical present moment. Then, in the one case, we might say: "What a slow affair this dynamite explosion is." In the other case, events, such as the wearing of the Niagara gorge, would be to us what a single musical phrase now is, namely, something instantaneously present, and grasped within the arbitrary present moment. Such relations to time would be no more arbitrary, no less conscious, no more or less fluent, and no more or less full of possible meaning, than is now our conscious life. In our lecture on Time and Eternity we considered such relations in their more general forms. Here we simply apply the general considerations to special cases.

Well, applying this simple consideration to our hypothesis, we should at once suppose that the actually fluent inner experience, which our hypothesis attributes to inorganic Nature, would be a finite experience of an extremely august temporal span, so that a material region of the inorganic world would be to us the phenomenal sign of the presence of at least one fellow-creature who took, perhaps, a billion years to complete a moment of his consciousness, so that where we saw, in the signs given us of his presence, only monotonous permanence of fact, he, in his inner life, faced momentarily significant change. Nature would be thus the sign of the presence of other finite consciousness than our own, whose time-span was in general very different from ours, but whose rationality, whose dignity, whose significance, whose power to will, whose aptness to pursue ideals, might be equal to or far above our own without any relation to whether the appearance of this consciousness, in the facts of outer Nature, seemed to us like an inorganic process or not. Common to all these conscious processes would be their fluency, their inner significance, and their constant intercommunication, whereby more or less novel facts were transferred all the time from one to another region of this conscious world. How this world was individuated, in what sense its minds, so intimately linked by universal intercommunication, were still in a sense sundered into the lives of relatively separate Selves, our hypothesis would leave for a deeper consideration elsewhere. But we should thus already be prepared for a general, if extremely hypothetical, view of evolution.

Evolution, we should now say, is due to the constant intercommunication of a vast number of relatively separate regions of this world of conscious life.[1] This intercommunication takes place as a simply universal process of finite experience. As it takes place, new and significant realms of conscious experience arise within the already existing temporal world of finite consciousness. If you wish to see how this can be, turn to the world of your social intercourse, where the communications of one being, or of a group of fellow-beings, can so enter into another's preëxistent, but still undeveloped consciousness, as to awaken there new ideals, a new selfhood, a relatively novel individuality. If, as I myself suppose, personal individuality is an essentially ethical category, then a new person exists whenever, within a conscious process of a given time-span, intercommunication with the rest of Nature results in the appearance of processes significant enough to express themselves in new ideals, and in a new unification of experience in terms of these ideals.

[1] In a later lecture, after our study of the problem of the Self, we shall be able to interpret this "intercommunication" as a process occurring not wholly between various beings, but rather in one aspect, *within* the life of an inclusive Self.

Meanwhile the evolutionary changes of the whole conscious world would be based upon processes whose basis would be viewed as threefold. First, they would be fluent processes, full of significant change, more or less obviously governed by the pursuit of ideal goals. Secondly, they would be processes determined, as our own are, by a constant communication with processes going on in other regions. Thirdly, they would be processes that, amidst all the changes, tended, as far as the novelty and the irrevocable passing of life's facts permitted, to the acquisition of definite habits. As these definite habits, so far as acquired at all, would be established under the influence of intercommunication from the whole of the finite world, and as the habits, whenever they appeared, would tend to take the form of repeated rhythms, which, if once more observed from without, would communicate their own nature in the form of an appearance of rhythmic monotony, we should expect to get, in a summary search through Nature, precisely that superficial impression of an endless repetition of the same types which inorganic Nature, in the uniformity of its Matter, seems to show us. The conceived atoms, all of the same size, the vibrations of the molecules of incandescent hydrogen, all of the same pitch, — these would be appearances of what, in their inner essence, are only extreme cases of habits rendered uniform by intercommunication, like the customs of a nation, or like the sounds of a given language appearing in many men's speech. The apparently absolute monotony in such cases would, of course, be itself, in great part, illusory, just as it is illusion when foreigners say that we who speak English merely hiss monotonously, like snakes or like geese. Just so, our spectroscopes find the hydrogen vibrations monotonous. But our time-span is very short, and our spectroscopes do not interpret to us the foreign tongues of Nature.[1]

Meanwhile, in one respect, evolution would indeed be in part what we before called a perspective effect, due to the limitations of human experience. It would not be true that Nature sometimes, in an exceptional way, pursues ideal goals. On the contrary, every natural process, if rightly viewed from within, would be the pursuit of an ideal. There would be no dead Nature at all, — nothing really inorganic or unconscious, — only life, striving, onflow, ideality, significance, rationality. Only for us Nature appears to be growing from death to life as the processes grow more like our own, and so more intelligible. But we should have to unlearn that atrocious Philistinism of our whole race which supposes that Nature has no worthier goal than producing a man. Perhaps experiences of longer time-span are far higher in rational type than ours. The evolution of Man would be but the appearance of a type of individuality whose time-span is short, and whose grade of rationality is doubtful, but presumably at least a little lower than that of the angels, and whose degree of significance depends partly, of course, upon our fatally determined place in Nature, but partly upon the use that we make of the countless communications that we receive from

[1] The relations of the formation and the persistence of habits to the two conceptions of the Well-Ordered Series and the series formed by the interpolation of new intermediaries between former terms, we shall consider later, in the lecture on the Place of the Self in Being.

our brethren of all grades, and of all time-spans. For my hypothesis would leave ample room for supposing that, whatever part of the total field of finite consciousness you choose, what happens there depends not merely upon the communications sent in, or upon the fatal onflow of experience, but upon the significant choices there made. For every region of this universally conscious world may be, in some sense, a centre whence issues new conscious life, for communication to all the worlds.

Meanwhile, our hypothesis supposes that, in case of the animals, we may well be dealing not with beings who are rational in our own time-span, nor yet with beings who are irrational. The rational being with whom you deal when you observe an animal's dimmer hints of rationality, may be phenomenally represented rather by the race as a whole than by any one individual. In that case, this individual animal is no rational person, but he may well be, so to speak, a temporally brief section of a person, whose time-span of consciousness is far longer than ours. Just as one word of a sentence represents a part of a meaning but not the whole, so an animal may represent phenomenally real conscious life, that in a longer time-span has a definite, an ideal, yes, — in its own way, — an ethical rationality, however noxious or unethical or irrational the animal, who is not himself a person, but a fragment of a person, may seem to us to be. Hence our theory at once justifies, but does not exaggerate, the meaning of our human companionship with animals. In general, our hypothesis holds that we can never know how much of Nature constitutes the life of a finite conscious individual, unless we are in intelligent communication with that individual's inner life. Hence, I do not suppose that any individual thing, say this house, or yonder table, is a conscious being, but only that it is part of a conscious process.

Finally, as to the origin and as to the end of human individuals, our theory suggests that we are differentiations from a finite conscious experience of presumably a much longer time-span than our present one. This finite consciousness of longer time-span, indicated to us in the phenomena of memory and of race-instinct, is individuated, is rational, is a live being, and is continuous in some sense with our own individuality. The birth and death of an individual man, from the point of view of the longer span, mean changes of time-span, or the occurrence of something interesting in a shorter or longer time-span. We might, if we chose, speak of death in those terms, — not as a relapse into unconscious Nature, but as merely a change in time-span of the life here involved. In what sense such a change could still preserve in fact our individuality, is a problem that this lecture still leaves open for later consideration.[1]

V

The hypothesis now roughly put before you belongs to a type nowadays not infrequent. As it stands, it pretends to be nothing but an hypothesis that takes account of a considerable range of real and verifiable

[1] Compare the further considerations in the lecture on the Place of the Self in Being.

natural facts, but that does not pretend to exclusive possession of the field. It is related, partly by derivation, partly by resemblance, to several other cosmical hypotheses, amongst which that of Mr. Charles Peirce[1] is, in my own mind, rather prominent. Yet this hypothesis is not identical with any of these others. Why I prefer it, I have not had time in any complete way to tell you. I have preferred so far to let the hypothesis stand as such. What we most of us need, in this field, is a breaking up of our traditional sundering of Mind and Matter, and a certain freedom from conventional phrases. Meanwhile, as I must remind you, the real reasons why I hold that some such hypothesis must be near the truth are general philosophical reasons. For here at length you have a first statement of the way in which the Nature empirically known to us can be so in general conceived as to reconcile its principal features with our Fourth Conception of Being.

This hypothesis may naturally be contrasted, as we close, with two or three somewhat related hypotheses.

In the first place, as you see, our hypothesis differs strongly from the view of Nature which is due to Bishop Berkeley. Berkeley was, with regard to the material world, an idealist, although he viewed the existence and the relations of individual minds in a fashion which seems to me to be essentially realistic, since the Spirits of his world are entities apparently conceived as, in their essence, logically independent of

[1] See his series of papers in the *Monist* for 1891 and the immediately subsequent years. The marked differences between the two hypotheses I have here no space to point out.

one another, and as linked merely through laws of causation, and through Over-ruling Providence. But Berkeley agrees with the general view of Idealism in asserting that Material substance exists not independently of minds. In particular, however, Berkeley holds that Matter appears to Minds only in and through the order of their ideas, as God ordains this order. And, as a consequence, Berkeley's hypothesis reduces Matter to an appearance having no basis except (1) the experiences and ideas of men; and (2) the direct influence of the power and providence of God upon these human experiences and ideas. Were men otherwise organized, and were the direct influence of God's Will upon men's minds other than it is, what we now call the material world would simply cease to be. As it is, according to Berkeley, you can say that Matter has a valid reality of the type of our own Third Conception of Being, and has, in addition, a more concrete foundation merely in what men experience and what God intends to have them experience. There is, then, for Berkeley, first the valid fact that the experience of approaching too near the seen fire, is inevitably followed by the experience of a burn. But, in the second place, the basis of this validity is Divine Providence, as evidenced in the actual occurrence which men observe.

Now our hypothesis agrees with Berkeley's view in asserting that no substance, and especially no material substance, exists independently of all Mind. But just as we ascribe some sort of Being beyond our own individual minds, to the minds of our fellow-men, so the hypothesis here in question ascribes an existence, beyond that of man's mind, to the finite mental life which we here suppose to be indicated to us by our experience of Nature. And we do not suppose with Berkeley that Nature has existence solely in our human experience, in the valid laws of succession which govern our experiences, and in the purpose of a Providence which is directly producing in us the experience in question. We suppose that there is a vast range of extra-human life, limited in its nature, like the life of man, and identical with the Absolute Life only in that universal sense in which, according to our theory, every life, however minute or however vast, is in relation to the whole organism of the Absolute. To this life, whose presence is hinted to us by our experience of Nature, our theory assigns an existence as concrete and essentially conscious as that of man himself. And we suppose that our human life is itself a differentiation from this larger life of Nature. Our deeper relations with the Nature-life we suppose to be, despite all the vast differences, essentially similar to the relations upon which our human social life is founded. They are relations of communication, and of an intimate linkage between the happenings that occur in various realms and provinces of the whole life of Nature. Hence, unlike Berkeley, we do not reduce our experience of Nature to anything that could plausibly be called illusory, or unfounded, or founded only in an arbitrary divine intervention. Nature for us is real in precisely the sense in which our fellow-men are real. Only we, of course, maintain that our present experience gives us very imperfect hints as to what the inner life of Nature contains; just as, even in case of men, our social experience of the doings of people whose language is not ours, and whose customs are very remote, leaves us long in ignorance of what they mean.

In the second place, our hypothesis stands in a strong contrast to the one associated with the name of Leibniz. Leibniz conceived the natural world as an infinite multitude of mutually independent Monads. While, even in case of Leibniz, many genuinely idealistic motives enter into his conception of the organism of this realm of the Monads, the primary character ascribed by him to this realm depends upon an essentially realistic conception of Being. The Monads are souls. Each one of them, to be sure, is in a preëstablished harmony with all the others. But they do not communicate. Their relations are wholly ideal. Each, in idea, mirrors the reality of all the other Monads, but this ideal link is not a genuine tie. For what happens within each Monad is determined solely by its own nature, and by nothing external. The creation of the Monads is indeed asserted to have been a fact. But it is a fact wholly inexpressible in terms of any links or ties such as now bind the various states of each Monad to the inner nature of that individual soul itself. Taken in itself, a Monad is an ultimate fact of Being, whose nature needs not the real nature of any other Monad to explain it, and whose essential independence of all that is external to itself is the first and the central fact about its form of Being. In strong contrast to this view of the Monads as real beings, stands, indeed, the assumed and preëstablished harmony of all the Monads. And when Leibniz emphasizes this aspect, his theory tends to lose its realistic hardness of outlines, and to lapse into a view for which the ideal relationships of the Monads, their significant unity as members of the one City of God, becomes the innermost truth of the universe. If Leibniz had given this aspect of his doctrine due emphasis, he would have recognized his own latent Idealism. As a fact, however, he remains on the whole a realist, whose Monads are in essence sundered and self-centred, and whose world is in fact shattered into a spray of infinitely numerous Independent Beings, while their asserted unity, as merely ideal, remains an appearance, manifest only to an external observer.

Our theory, I say, is in strong contrast to this Monadology of Leibniz. In Nature, as in man, we find individuality linked in the closest fashion with intercommunication, with the mutual interdependence of individuals, and with a genuine identity of meaning and of Being in various individuals. For us, as we shall later more fully see, it is perfectly possible that an ethical individual should have, in time, a natural origin, should result from processes that have previously taken place in other individuals, and should exist subject to a constant support received from other individuals. For us, a soul is no Monad, but a life individuated solely by its purpose, *i.e.* by the significant and unique meaning which its experience may embody. Our whole theory presupposes that individuals may be included within other individuals; that one life, despite its unique ethical significance, may form part of a larger life; and that the ties which bind various finite individuals together are but hints of the unity of all individuals in the Absolute

Individual. Hence we do not assume the variety of individuals within the natural world to be a wholly original fact, temporally predetermined by a single creative act. Nor do we suppose that, from its creation, Nature is thenceforth to be regarded as a realm whose harmony is preëstablished. For us no natural fact is more obvious than that every individual life is temporally dependent for its every act and state upon relations of direct communication with other individuals. And individuals are not kept asunder by chasms, but are made distinct through their various meanings, *i.e.* through the variety of the purposes of which their lives are the expression.

In another direction, our theory differs very deeply from all hypotheses of the type of Clifford's "Mind Stuff" doctrine. It is customary, in recent thought, for many who appreciate the importance of the natural processes summed up in the word Evolution, to attempt to conceive that inorganic Nature consists of a vast collection of elements of the type of our own sensations, or of our simplest feelings. The process of Evolution itself is regarded by such views as a gradual coming together and organization of such originally atomic elements of feeling into complex unities, which, viewed externally, appear as more and more organized bodies, while the same masses of content, internally viewed, come to take on, more and more, the character of conscious and, in the end, of rational lives. Our hypothesis, by virtue of its idealistic basis, rejects altogether the possibility of any such separate elements of Mind-Stuff. Nor do we admit that such elements, through any process of Evolution, could come to be interrelated after they had once separately existed. An element of physical life, a simple sensation of feeling, can neither be nor be conceived in isolation. Our very definition of Being forces upon us this result. And, if an isolated physical element could once exist, it would be like any other realistic entity. As an Independent Being, it could never come to be linked to any other Being. It would remain forever in the darkness of its atomic separation from all real life. For us, however, if all Nature is an expression of mental life, all mental life has Internal Meaning, and therefore conscious unity of purpose in every pulse of its existence.

And for the same reason, we reject every form of doctrine that regards Nature as in any sense a realm of the genuinely Unconscious, or that supposes the Absolute to come to self-consciousness first in man, or that conceives the process of Evolution as one wherein the life of the natural world, as a whole, grows from the darkness of obscure and unconscious purpose to the daylight of self-possessed Reason. Our general Theory of Being simply forbids every such interpretation of Nature. All life, everywhere, in so far as it is life, has conscious meaning, and accomplishes a rational end. This is the necessary consequence of our Idealism. Where we see inorganic Nature seemingly dead, there is, in fact, conscious life, just as surely as there is any Being present in Nature at all. And I insist, meanwhile, that no empirical warrant can be found for affirming the existence of dead material substance anywhere. What we find, in inorganic Nature, are processes whose time-rate is slower or faster than those which our consciousness is adapted to read or to appreciate. And we have no empirical evidence of the existence of any, relatively whole, conscious process, which is less intelligent or less rational than our own human processes are. For the psychical life which we refer to the lower animals is, according to my interpretation, merely a fragment and a hint of a larger rationality which gets its fuller individual expression in the evolution of a species or genus or order, or other relative whole of animal existence. And of this whole life, what we chance to view as the individual animal constitutes a mere fragment, brought within our observation by conditions whose relation to the innermost facts of Nature is doubtless very arbitrary.

As all these comments and comparisons indicate, the general character of our hypothesis about Nature is determined for us by our Fourth Conception of Being, and stands or falls therewith. It is the detail of our hypothesis, and its special adaptation to our experience of Nature, which we regard as tentative, and so as subject to correction. But in rejecting the Mind-Stuff theory of Clifford, our grounds are general and positive. That theory implies an essentially realistic conception of Being, and falls with Realism. The same is true of Leibniz's Monadology. The Unconscious we reject, because our Fourth Conception of Being forbids all recognition of unconscious realities. It follows that any hypothesis about Nature, which is just to the demands of a sound Metaphysic, must, like ours, conceive the natural world as directly bound up with the experiences of actually conscious beings. That, in addition to all these considerations, we should be led to reject Berkeley's cosmological hypothesis, is due, in part, to our own special form of

Idealism; but, in part, also to the fact that our theory about Nature ought to be just to the empirical inductions which have now been summed up in the modern Doctrine of Evolution. The essence of this Doctrine of Evolution lies in the fact that it recognizes the continuity of man's life with that of an extra-human realm, whose existence is hinted to us by our experience of Nature. Accepting, as we are obliged to do, the objective significance of this modern doctrine, we find ourselves forced to interpret Nature, not as an arbitrarily determined realm of valid experiences founded only in God's creative will and man's sensory life, but as an orderly realm of genuine conscious life, one of whose products, expressions, and examples we find in the mind of Man.

LECTURE VI

LECTURE VI

THE HUMAN SELF

THE contrast between Matter and Mind is usually regarded as a serious obstacle in the way of any interpretation of the world of experience in terms of a philosophical Idealism. In the last two lectures we have seen that this contrast is not empirically known to be as absolute as our customary fashions of conception often make it seem. The hypothesis concerning Nature which we suggested was partly intended to illustrate precisely this possibility of reconciling Idealism with the generalizations of our ordinary study of Nature. The hypothesis itself, like any other effort towards a Cosmology, is, in its details, provisional and tentative. Only its general type, as an idealistic hypothesis about Nature, seems to me to be a sure representative of the truth. In its special features it is to be subject to the control of further experience. But it provides in its very terms for such further control. The hypothesis asserts, in fact, that all the theories of the special sciences, together with the general theory of Nature suggested by this very hypothesis itself, must be viewed as incidents in the history of man's effort gradually to comprehend the organization of a realm of Mind, of which man himself is a member. Now every idealist holds that there is no dead matter anywhere in the world, and that all that is is the expression of the Spirit. But in what way this thesis is to be applied to the detailed interpretation of Nature, cannot be decided in advance of a careful scrutiny of the facts. And the special way suggested at the last time is the one which to me personally seems to promise most. I am sure that in its most general outlines, this hypothesis is sound. But all its details are subject to correction.

I

Herewith, however, we are led to the threshold of a new enterprise. We have so far stated a general hypothesis regarding Nature. But in forming this hypothesis, I myself have been especially interested in its bearing upon the conception of the place in Nature that is occupied by Man. Now as we know Man, he first of all appears to us as a being whose inner life is that of an individual Self. The Self of each man apparently has had an origin in time, and a development such as makes it dependent, for its contents and its character, upon natural conditions. In its turn, our self-consciousness, when once it has developed, furnishes to us the sort of insight by means of which we may hope for a comprehension of some of the mysteries of Nature. Any deeper criticism of our hypothesis about Nature must therefore depend upon a more exact account of what we mean by the human Self. We must know how we are able, both to conceive this Self as in any sense the outcome of the processes of Nature, and to apply our view of the Self to an explanation of Nature.

My next task must therefore be to state, in outline, a theory of the human Self.

What a man means by himself is notoriously a question to which common sense gives various and ambiguous answers. That by the Self one means a real being, common sense indeed insists. But the nature of this real being forms the topic of the greatest vacillation in all popular metaphysics. The most frequently mentioned doubt is that as to whether the Self is, or at least essentially includes, the bodily organism, or whether the Self is essentially an incorporeal entity. But this is but a single instance of the doubts and hesitancies of the popular doctrine concerning the Ego. And this indefiniteness of customary opinion regarding our problem most of all appears in the practical aspect of the current notions of the Self. If we ask, What is the value of the Self, and what do we gain by cultivating, by knowing, by observing, and by satisfying the Self? — common sense gives contradictory answers which at once show that the very idea of what the Self is, is subject to the most momentous changes as we alter our point of view. Ask the teacher of the people about the value and dignity of the Self at a moment when he is insisting upon the significance and the rights of individuality, and upon the duty of conscious reasonableness, and of moral independence. He will reply, perhaps, in the terms that Burns has made so familiar. "The man of independent mind" knows, asserts, expresses, preserves, glorifies the true Self, the moral individual. And the Self which he thus makes central in his moral world is an essentially honorable

Self, the determiner of all true values, the despiser of mere externals, the freeman to whom fortune is nothing compared with inner dignity. When one views the moral Self thus, one conceives that the root of all evil and of all baseness must always lie without and beyond the Self. The Self sins not through self-assertion but through self-abandonment. The lost soul is the man who is the slave of fortune. Pleasure, worldly honor, external good, — these may harm the Self, just because they are foreign to its true independence. The ideal lies where the Stoics sought it, in casting off the external bondage. For such a view, every man's Self, if you could only get at the heart of it, and get it to express itself, would appear as essentially good. What corrupts and enchains men is not their innermost selfhood, but the power of an external world of temptations. To assert the true Self, is to be saved.

But even more familiar than this ethical individualism, which so often thrills the hearts of noble youth, and which inspires so many to heroism, is another ancient and, as its history shows, profoundly religious doctrine. This latter doctrine equally appeals to the moral common sense of mankind; it is crystallized, so to speak, in some of the most familiar of our customary phrases; it inspires numerous effective moral appeals; it comes to us with all the weight of the authority of the faith of the fathers. This view is that the Self of man is precisely that which in its original nature is evil, so that it is just our salvation which must to us come from without, and be won through self-abnegation. "By grace ye are saved, and that *not* of yourselves." Self-denial is, for this view, the cardinal virtue. Self-consciousness is even a vice. A man ought to think little of himself, and much of God, of the world, and of his own external business. The central evil of our life is selfishness. Virtue is definable as altruism, *i.e.* as forgetting ourselves in the thought of others. The best eulogy that one can make over the grave of the departed saint is: "He had no thought of Self; he served; he sacrificed himself; he gave himself as an offering for the good of mankind; he lived for others; he never even observed his own virtues; he forsook himself; he asked for nothing but bondage to his duty." And George Eliot sings in praise of the "scorn for miserable aims that end in Self."

Now the opposition just suggested between two views of the value of Self, is so familiar that common sense not only uses these apparently conflicting phrases, but has its own lore regarding various devices by which they are to be reconciled. A man has, as we sometimes learn, two Selves, — the inner and the outer, the nobler and the baser. There is the natural man, who is by his very essence evil; and the spiritual man, who is by nature good. It is to the natural man that the advice about self-abnegation is given; it is to the spiritual Self that the well-known words of Burns make their stirring appeal. The fleshly Self is the root of all evil. The spiritual Self belongs, by origin and by destiny, to a higher realm.

This dualistic way of stating the case, and of attempting to solve the practical problem here at issue, would be more nearly final were it not that in the very effort to carry it out to its consequences, the former ambiguity only arises afresh, in a slightly altered form. The higher Self, the deeper spiritual nature, the individuality which ought to be, — to whom does it originally belong? To the man who finally wins a consciousness that this has become to him his true Self? Or does this higher Self come, as Aristotle said of the Nous, *θύραθεν*, from without, into the natural man? Does it create for him or in him a new selfhood, so that before the higher selfhood appears in this man, it exists perhaps merely as the intent of God to save this man, or as a selfhood embodied in other men, the teachers, inspirers, guides, of the man who is to be thus brought to the possession of the higher Self in his own person? This question may indeed at first appear an idle subtlety. But as a fact, both common sense and religion, both the teacher's art and the inner consciousness of those who have in any sense passed from death unto life, give this question a very living and practical significance. Our models and our inspirations, the mysterious grace that saves us and the visible social order that moulds us, — these lie at first without the Self. Yet they in such wise determine whatever is best about us that we are all accustomed to nourish the higher selfhood by means of what we find as no creation of the original Self, but as the free gift of the world. And the two doctrines which, in European history, have most insisted upon the duality of our higher and our lower selfhood, viz. the ethical teaching of Plato and the Gospel of the Christian Church, have agreed in insisting that the higher Self is a resultant of influences which belong to the eternal world, and which the individual man himself is powerless to initiate. In Plato's account of the process of the soul's release from its own lower nature, the eternal Ideas appear as the supernatural source of truth and of goodness. In the mythical state of preëxistence, the Ideas guided the soul by their visible presence; and the soul's higher nature meant nothing but the contemplation of their uncreated perfection. In this foreign authority the soul found all that was good. And in the present life our higher nature means only our memory of the former presence of the all-powerful truth. This memory guides our awakening reason, controls our irrational passions, binds the lower Self with the might of the eternal, and conducts us back towards that renewed and direct intercourse with the ideal world wherein consists our only higher Selfhood. Christianity, in all its essential teachings, has emphasized a similar source and meaning in speaking of the higher Self. The Divine Spirit enters a man in ways that its own wisdom predetermines, and without the work of God in preparing and accomplishing the plan of salvation, in revealing the truth to man by outward means, and in preparing the heart within for the reception of the truth, the nobler Self of each man not only is unable to win control of the baser Self, but never could come effectively to exist at all. In this sense, then, it is not I who win salvation, but it is God who works in me. The higher Self is originally not myself at all, but the Spirit warring against the Flesh. This spirit is essentially from God. It comes *into* the man like Aristotle's Creative Nous, and is precisely so much of a man as is not his own, but God's.

Now this well-known ambiguity of the traditional doctrines concerning the source and meaning of the higher Self in man, is not, as some have unwisely maintained, a mere consequence of theological and philosophical speculation. On the contrary, it is an expression, in terms of faith, of empirical facts about the Self which common sense everywhere recognizes. The same problems, in other formulation, exist in Hindoo philosophy as well as in Plato's; and they are recognized by Buddhism as well as by Christianity. Every watchful parent, and every conscientious teacher, is perfectly well acquainted with facts that illustrate the doctrines of saving grace and of the apparently external source of the higher selfhood, in case of every plastic child. We all of us know, or ought to recognize, how powerless we are, or should have been, to win any higher selfhood, unless influences from without, — whether you know them as mother love, or conceive them as the promptings of the divine Spirit, or view them as the influences of friends and of country, — have brought into us a truth and an ideality that is in no ordinary sense our own private creation. And every man who knows what the wiser humility is, has sometime said: "Of myself I am nothing. It is the truth alone that, coming from without, works in me."

But if you lay aside the problem as to the source of the higher Self, and consider merely the supposed duality of the lower and the higher Self as a given fact, have you in that case even begun to solve the problem as to what the Self of a man actually is? For the Self was to be something unique and individual. But the account here in question makes of it something disintegrated and internally manifold, and threatens to cause the name Self to mean, in case of every individual, a mere general term, applicable to various groups of different facts. For by the same principle whereby you distinguish the lower and the higher Self of a man, you might distinguish, and upon occasion, even in common life, do distinguish, many various selves, all clustered together in what we call the life of a single individual.

For if we are internally in any sense more than one Self, then we consist not merely of the lower and the higher self, but have, in some sense, as many selves as we have decidedly various offices, duties, types of training and of intellectual activity, or momentous variations of mood and condition. Of the man who is once seriously ill, common sense often says that he is no longer himself. If you ask, who then is he, if not himself, you may get the answer that he is another, — a deeply changed, — a strange Self. And if the change has at all the character of a mental derangement, common sense, ever since the savage stage of our social life, has been disposed to conceive the alteration in question as the appearance of an actually foreign and other Self, a new and invading individuality, which the superstitious view as a possession of the man's body by an evil spirit. Such instances are extreme ; but health furnishes to us similar, if less unhappy variations, with whose mystery the popular imagination is constantly busy. Deep emotional experiences give the sense of a new or of a wavering selfhood. There are many people, of a fine social sensibility, who are conscious of a strong tendency to assume, temporarily, the behavior, the moods, and in a measure, both the bearing and the accent, both the customs and the opinions of people in whose company they spend any considerable time. I have known amongst such people those who were oppressed by a sense of insincerity in consequence of their own social plasticity. "I almost seem to have no true Self at all," such a sensitive person may say. "I am involuntarily compelled to change my whole attitude towards the most important things whenever I change my company. I find myself helplessly thinking and believing and speaking as the present company want me to do. I feel humiliated by my own lack of moral independence. But I cannot help this fickleness. And the saddest is that I do not know where my true Self lies, or what one amongst all these various selves is the genuine one."

Now such confessions stand again for rather extreme types of variability of the mere sense of selfhood. Yet the experiences of which such less stable souls complain, exist in various degrees in many of us who are merely not sensitive enough, or perhaps not reflective enough, to notice our own actual variations of self-consciousness. I have known very obstinate men, who were full of a consciousness of their own independence and absolute stability of will and character. Yet, as a fact, they were people of very various and complex selfhood, who were, far more than they themselves supposed, the slaves of circumstances and of social influences. Only they regarded themselves as both independent and resolutely fixed in their individuality, merely because their one type of reaction in presence of any other man's opinion was to disagree with that opinion, and their one way of asserting their independence was to insist that their neighbors were wrong, while their fixed device for preserving their independence was to refuse to do whatever external authority desired them to do. But now such resolute opponents of their fellows are as much without a fixed and rational conscious principle of selfhood as their brothers, the self-accused slaves of the passing social situation. For it is as fickle to disagree with everybody as to agree with everybody. And the man who always opposes is as much the slave of external fortune as the man who always agrees. The simply obstinate man, who is said to be set in his own way, but who, in fact, is always set in the way that is opposed to the ways of whoever is just now his fellow, — such a man changes his doctrine whenever his opponent changes; and his teachings, his ideals, and his selfhood play, as it were, puss-in-the-corner with those of his neighbors.

But enough of familiar illustrations of how the mere sense of selfhood may vary, or of how its outer and inner expression may seem dual or multiple. What these facts give us, is not any decision as to the true nature of the Self, but some specification of our problem, and some explanation of the reason why common sense is so uncertain about how to define the true unity of the Self. The inconsistencies of common sense in regard to the Self are, upon their practical side, well summed up in the familiar advice which we are accustomed to give the young. "Forget yourself," we say, "all true success depends upon freedom from yourself." But to the careless youth we sternly say, "What! you *have* forgotten yourself." One sees, it is hard for the poor Self to please common sense. And the reason is that common sense does not in the least know, when it appeals to the Self, whom it is addressing, nor, when it talks of the Self, what object it is meaning.

II

Such considerations ought once for all to give pause to those who have regarded the problem of the true nature of the Self as a matter of direct inner knowledge, or as something to be settled by an appeal to the plain man. But of course these considerations merely indicate a problem, and are by no means decisive as against any metaphysical view which insists upon a true and deeper unity of Selfhood at the basis of all these variations of the apparent Self. But wherein shall our own metaphysical doctrine seek for guidance in this world of complexities?

I reply, The concept of the human Self, like the concept of Nature, comes to us, first, as an empirical concept, founded upon a certain class of experiences. But like the concept of Nature, the concept of the human Self tends far to outrun any directly observable present facts of human experience, and to assume forms which define the Self as having a nature and destiny which no man directly observes or as yet can himself verify. If we consider first the empirical basis of the conception of the Self, and then the motives which lead us beyond our direct experience in our efforts to interpret the Self, we find, as a result of a general survey, three different kinds of conceptions of what it is that one means or ought to mean by the term Self as applied to the individual man. Each of these sorts of conception of the human Self is once more capable of a wide range of variation. Each can be used as a basis of different and, on occasion, of conflicting notions of what the Self is. But the three have their strong contrasts with one another, and each lays stress upon its own aspect of the facts.

First then, there is the more directly empirical way of conceiving the Self. In this sense, by a man's Self, you mean a certain totality of facts, viewed as more or less immediately given, and as distinguished from the rest of the world of Being. These facts may be predominantly corporeal facts, such as not only the man himself but also his neighbors may observe and comment upon. In this sense my countenance and my physical deeds, my body and my clothing, — all these may be regarded as more or less a part of myself. My neighbor so views them. I may and very generally do so view them myself. If you changed or wholly removed such facts, my view of what I am would unquestionably alter. For to my neighbor as to myself, I am this man with these acts, this body, this presence. I cannot see these facts as my neighbor does, nor can he take my view of them. But we all regard such facts, not only as belonging to the Self, but as constituting, in a measure, what we regard as the Self of the present life. In addition to the external or corporeal Self of the phenomenal world, there is the equally empirical and phenomenal Self of the inner life, the series of states of consciousness, the feelings, thoughts, desires, memories, emotions, moods. These, again, both my neighbor and myself regard as belonging to me, and as going to make up what I am. To be sure, within this inner empirical Self, we all make distinctions, now so freely illustrated, between what does and what does not essentially belong to the Self. When a man tells me a piece of interesting news, or expounds to me his opinions, I naturally regard the ideas which then arise in my mind as his and not as mine. I have to reflect in order to observe the somewhat recondite fact that the ideas which he seems to convey to me are in one sense ideas of my own, aroused in me according to laws of association. On the other hand, when I think alone by myself, the ideas which occur to me seem to be primarily mine. I have to reflect in order to remember how largely they have been derived from books, from nature, or from conversation, and how little I can call originally my own. And everywhere in the inner life, as it flits by, I observe a constantly shifting play of what I distinguish as more truly myself, from what I regard as relatively foreign. This feeling or purpose, this mood or this choice, is my own. That other emotion or idea is alien to me. It belongs to another. I do not recognize it as mine. The distinctions, thus empirically made, have no one rational principle. They are often founded upon the most arbitrary and unstable motives. The vacillation of common sense regarding the Self is endlessly repeated in my own inner life. I am constantly sure that there exists a Self, and that there I am, present to my own consciousness as the one whose experiences all these are, and who set myself over against the foreign non-Ego at every moment. But in distinguishing my empirical non-Ego from the Ego, I follow no stateable rule in my inner life from moment to moment. I even voluntarily play with the distinctions of Self and not-Self,— dramatically address myself as if I were another, criticise and condemn myself, and upon occasion observe myself in a relatively impersonal fashion, as if I were a wholly alien personality. On the other hand, there are countless automatic processes that alter or that diminish the immediately given distinctions between Ego and non-Ego. The lover in Locksley Hall somewhat unobservantly tells us how:—

> "Love took up the harp of life, and smote on all the chords with might;
> Smote the chord of Self that trembling, passed in music out of sight."

The lover admits that in the state which he thus describes, the Self, if invisible in the inner experience, was still able, most decidedly, to make itself heard. And, as a fact, one may well question whether, in view of what the lover in Locksley Hall tells us, the Self of this lover ever passed beyond his own range of vision at all, or was in the least out of sight. But the happy emotional confusion of self-consciousness here in question is familiar indeed to all who know joyous emotion. And in the sadder emotions one also has endless varieties in the intensity, clearness, and outlines which in our empirical consciousness characterize, from moment to moment, the relations of Self and not-Self.

III

But one may now ask, still dwelling upon the empirical Self, what manner of unity is left, in the midst of all these variations, as the unity that the concept of the Self can still be said to possess in our ordinary experience? And by what marks is the Self to be distinguished from the rest of the world? I reply, by pointing out a fact of central importance for the whole understanding of the empirical Ego. The variations of our experience and of our opinion concerning the empirical Self are countless in number. And no purely rational principle guides us in defining the Self from moment to moment in the world of common sense, or in distinguishing it from the not-Self. But there still does remain *one psychological principle* running through all these countless facts, and explaining, in general, both why they vary, and why yet we always suppose, despite the chaos of experiences, that the Self of our inner and outer life preserves a genuine, although to us hidden unity. This psychological principle is the simple one that, in us men, the distinction between Self and not-Self has a predominantly *Social origin*, and implies a more or less obviously present contrast between what we at any moment view as the life of another person, a fellow-being, or, as you may for short in general call him, an Alter, and the life, which, by contrast with that of the Alter, is just then viewed as the life of the present Ego. To state the case more briefly, I affirm that our empirical self-consciousness, from moment to moment, depends upon a series of contrast-effects, whose psychological origin lies in our literal social life, and whose continuance in our present conscious life, whenever we are alone, is due to habit, to our memory of literal social relations, and to an imaginative idealization of these relations. Herein lies a large part of the explanation of those ambiguities of common sense upon which I have so far insisted.

My proof for this view I cannot here give at length. I have stated the psychological aspects of the whole case pretty extensively elsewhere.[1] My friend, Professor Baldwin of Princeton University, has independently worked out a theory of the psychological origin of Self-Consciousness, and a doctrine about the evolution of the relations of Ego and Alter, — a theory which I am on the whole prepared to accept, and which agrees with the considerations that I myself have been led to develope, and, in the places now referred to, to set forth. Here there is time only for a brief indication of what I mean by this theory of the empirical Ego, of its unity in variety, and of its distinction from the world of the non-Ego.

Nobody amongst us men comes to self-consciousness, so far as I know, except under the persistent influence of his social fellows. A child in the earlier stages of his social development, — say from the end of the first to the beginning of the fifth year of life, — shows you, as you observe him, a process of the development of self-consciousness in which, at every stage, the Self of the child grows and forms itself through Imitation, and through functions that cluster about the Imitation of others, and that are secondary thereto. In consequence, the child is in general conscious of what expresses the life of somebody else, before he is conscious of himself. And his self-consciousness, as it grows, feeds upon social models, so that at every stage of his awakening life

[1] See my *Studies of Good and Evil*, especially the essay on the Anomalies of Self-consciousness, *op. cit.*, pp. 169–197. Professor Baldwin's very complete treatment of the topic is to be found in the second volume of his well-known work: *Mental Development in the Child and the Race*, where it dominates the entire discussion.

his consciousness of the Alter is a step in advance of his consciousness of the Ego. His playmates, his nurse, or mother, or the workmen whose occupations he sees, and whose power fascinates him, appeal to his imitativeness, and set him the copies for his activities. He learns his little arts, and as he does so, he contrasts his own deeds with those of his models, and of other children. Now contrast is, in our conscious life, the mother of clearness. What the child does instinctively, and without comparison with the deeds of others, may never come to his clear consciousness as his own deed at all. What he learns imitatively, and then reproduces, perhaps in joyous obstinacy, as an act that enables him to display himself over against others, — this constitutes the beginning of his self-conscious life. And in general, thenceforth, social situations, social emotions, the process of peering into the contents of other minds during the child's questioning period, the conflicts of childish sport, the social devices for winning approval, — in brief, the whole life of social harmony and rivalry, — all these things mean an endless series of contrasts between two sets of contents, which retain, amidst all their varieties, *one* psychologically important character. Upon this character the empirical unity and the general continuity of our adult self-consciousness depend.

In any literal social situation, namely, one is aware of ideas, designs, interests, beliefs, or judgments, whose expression is observed in the form of acts, words, looks, and the like, belonging to the perceived organisms of one's fellow-men. In strong contrast, both in the way in which they appear in the field of our sense-perceptions, and in the current interests and feelings with which they are accompanied and blended, are the acts, words, and other expressions, of our own organism, together with the ideas, designs, and beliefs which accompany these acts. Now these two contrasting masses of mental contents simply constitute the Alter and the Ego, the neighbor and the Self, of any empirical instant of our literal social life together. That these sets of contents stand in strong contrast to each other is, for the first, a mere fact of sense and of feeling. One does not reason about this fact from instant to instant. One finds it so. Nor does one appeal to any intuition of an ultimate or of a spiritual Ego, in order to observe the presented fact that my neighbor's words, as he speaks to me, do not sound or feel as my words do when I speak to him, and that the ideas which my neighbor's words at once bring to my consciousness, stand in a strong and presented contrast to the ideas which receive expression in my words as I reply to him. Alter and Ego, in such cases, are found as facts of our direct observation. Were no difference observed between the contents which constitute the observed presence of my neighbor, and the contents which constitute my own life in the same moment, then my sense of my neighbor's presence, and my idea of myself, would blend in my consciousness, and there would be so far neither Alter nor Ego observed.

Now just such social contrast-effects have been occurring in our experience since childhood. The contrasts in question have always retained a certain general similarity, despite wide and countless differences. Just as all color contrasts are in a measure alike, so too are all social contrasts. Always the contents which constitute the Ego, at the very moment of their contrast with the remaining contents present during the social contrast-effect, have been associated with certain relatively warm and enduring organic sensations, viz. sensations coming from within our own bodies. Always the contents belonging to our consciousness of our neighbors have been relatively free from these accompaniments, and have had the characters belonging to external sense-perceptions. And there are still other empirical similarities present in all social relations. Hence, despite all other changes, the Ego and the Alter have tended to keep apart, as facts of our empirical observation, and each of the two has tended towards its own sort of organization as a mass of observed and remembered empirical facts. The Alter, viewed as a mass of experienced facts, — the words, looks, and deeds and ideas of other people, — differentiates and integrates into all that I call my experience of mankind; the Ego, centred about the relatively constant organic sensations, but receiving its type of unity especially through the social contrast-effects, stands as that totality of inner and outer experience which I recognize as my own, just because it sharply differs from my experience of any of the rest of mankind, and stands in a certain permanent sort of contrast thereto.

In origin, then, the empirical Ego is secondary to our social experience. In literal social life, the Ego is always known as in contrast to the Alter. And while the permanent character of our organic sensations aids us in identifying the empirical Ego, this character becomes of importance mainly because hereby we find ourselves always in a certain inwardly observable type of contrast to the whole of our social world.

Now what literal social life thus trains us to observe, the inner psychological processes of memory and imagination enable us indefinitely to extend and to diversify. The child soon carries over his plays into more or less ideal realms, lives in the company of imaginary persons, and thus, idealizing his social relations, idealizes also the type of his self-consciousness. In my inner life, I in the end learn ideally to repeat, to vary, to reorganize, and to epitomize in countless ways, the situations which I first learned to observe and estimate in literal social relations. Hereby the contrast between Ego and Alter, no longer confined to the relations between my literal neighbor and myself, can be refined into the conscious contrasts between present and past Self, between my self-critical and my naïve Self, between my higher and lower Self, or between my Conscience and my impulses. My reflective life, as it empirically occurs in me from moment to moment, is a sort of abstract and epitome of my whole social life, viewed as to those aspects which I find peculiarly significant. And thus my experience of myself gets a certain provisional unity. But never do I observe my Self as any single and unambiguous fact of consciousness.

IV

The empirical Ego has now been, in outline, characterized. The source of its endless varieties has been sketched. Its unity has been found to be not, in our present form of existence, a fact that gets anywhere fully presented, as a rationally determined whole of life or of meaning. The empirical unity of the Ego depends merely upon a certain continuity of our social and of our inner life of experience and memory. The most stable feature about the empirical Ego, is that *sort of contrast in which it stands to the social world, literal and ideal, in which we live.* But precisely as here upon earth we have no abiding city, just so, in our present human form of consciousness, the Self is never presented except as a more or less imperfectly organized series of experiences, whose contrast with those of all other men fascinates us intensely, but whose final meaning can simply never be expressed in the type of experience which we men now have at our disposal. Were our life not hid in an infinitely richer and more significant life behind the veil, we who have once observed the essential fragmentariness of the empirical Ego would indeed have parted with our hope of a true Selfhood.

But the two other types of conception of the Self remain to be characterized. The one of these types, the second in our list of three, need detain us at this stage but little. The third type we shall at once so sketch as to define the momentous task that yet lies before us in our later lectures.

The second type of the conceptions of the Ego consists of all those views which regard the Self as in some metaphysical sense a real being, without defining the true Being of this Self in strictly idealistic terms. Such conceptions of the human Self as an entity are numerous in the history of philosophy. Their classification and further characterization will receive attention in the next lecture. For the moment I may exemplify them by mentioning as their most familiar examples, those views which conceive the human Self as, in some realistic sense, a distinct and independent entity. For such views the true Self is often essentially a Substance. Its individuality means that in essence it is separable, not only from the body, but from other souls. It preserves its unity despite the chaos of our experiences, just because in itself, and apart from all experience, it *is* One. It lies at the basis of our psychical life; and it must be sharply distinguished from the series of the states of consciousness, and even from their empirical organization. It is the source of all the order of our mental life; and all our self-consciousness is a more or less imperfect indication of its nature.

Such realistic views are well known to you. And you also know now why, without showing the least disrespect to their historical dignity, I can and must simply decline to follow them into their details in these lectures. They are all founded upon the realistic conception of Being. They must therefore all fall with that conception. Their true spirit indeed is often of far deeper moment than their mere letter. What doctrines of Soul-Substance have often meant to express, namely, a respect for human individuality, and an appreciation of its eternal worth in the life of the Universe, our own theory of the human individual will erelong develope in its own fashion. But taken literally, the doctrine that beneath or behind our conscious life there is a permanent substance, itself never either presented or presentable in consciousness, but real, and real in such wise that its Being is independent of any knowledge that from without refers to it, — this whole doctrine, I say, simply perishes, for the purposes of our argument, together with Realism, and only its revised and purified inner meaning can reappear, in quite another guise, in the world of Idealism. Whatever the Self is, it is not a Thing. It is not, in Aristotle's or in Des Cartes' sense, a Substance. It is not a realistic entity of any type. Whether we men ever rightly come to know it or not, it exists only as somewhere known, and as a part of the fulfilment of meaning in the divine life. We are spared the trouble of proving this thesis here in detail, simply because our general proof of Idealism has discounted the entire issue. We are not comdemning Realism unheard; but only after the most careful analysis of its claims. But with Realism passes away every view which regards the real Self as anything but what every real fact in the universe is: A Meaning embodied in a conscious life, present as a relative whole within the unity of the Absolute life.

Well, there remains the third type of conception of the Self, namely, the strictly idealistic type. And precisely this type it was that I exemplified before, when I spoke of the way in which the Self has been distinguished, even by common sense, into a higher and a lower, a nobler and a baser Self. As stated in ordinary fashion, such concepts, as we saw, remain crude, and lead to frequent inconsistency. Revised with reference to the demands of our Idealism, the concept of the

Self will assume a form which will reduce to unity these apparent inconsistencies of ethical common sense, and will also escape from bondage to those empirical complexities forced upon us by the Ego of the passing moment. We shall then see that the concept of the individual Self is, in its higher forms, in large measure an essentially Ethical Conception. And the third type of conceptions of the Ego consists of definitions which have always laid stress upon just this aspect. From this point of view, the Self is not a Thing, but a Meaning embodied in a conscious life. Its individuality, in case of any human being, implies the essential uniqueness of this life. Its unity, transcending as it does what we ever find presented in our present type of consciousness, implies that the true individual Self of any man gets its final expression in some form of consciousness different from that which we men now possess. The empirical variety, complexity, ambiguity, and inconsistency of our present consciousness of the Self, is to be explained as due to the fact that, in the moral order of the universe, no individual Self is or can be isolated, or in any sense sundered from other Selves, or from the whole realm of the inner life of Nature itself. Consequently, even what is most individual about the Self never appears except in the closest connection with what transcends both the meaning and the life of the finite individual. Now, in our present form of conscious existence, we catch mere glimpses of the true meaning of the individual Self, as this meaning gets expressed in our deeds and in our ideals, and we also obtain equally fragmentary glimpses of the way in which this Self is linked to the lives of its fellows, or is dependent for its expression upon its relations to Nature, or is subject to the general moral order of the universe. These various transient flashes of insight constitute our present type of human experience. And it is their variety, their manifoldness, and their fragmentariness, which together are responsible for all those inconsistencies in our accounts of the Self, — inconsistencies which our present discussion has been illustrating. But if you want to free yourself from hopeless bondage to such inconsistencies, you must look, not to some realistic conception of a Soul-Substance, but to some deeper account of the ethical meaning of our present life than we have yet formulated. And from this point of view we get a notion of Selfhood and of individuality which may be summarized at the present stage much as follows.

Our general idealistic theory asserts that the universe in its wholeness is the expression of a meaning in a life. What this view implies about every fragment and aspect of life that your attention may chance to select, or that your human experience may bring before you as the topic of inquiry, we have in former lectures repeatedly pointed out. Any instant of finite consciousness partially embodies a purpose, and so possesses its own Internal Meaning. Any such instant of finite consciousness also seeks, however, for other expression, for other objects, than are now present to just that instant, and so possesses what we have called its External Meaning. Our Idealism has depended, from the first, upon the thesis that the Internal and the External meaning of any finite process of experience are dependent each upon the other, so that if the whole meaning and intent of any finite instant of life is fully developed, and perfectly embodied, this Whole Meaning of the instant becomes identical with the Universe, with the Absolute, with the life of God. Even now, whatever you are or seek, the implied whole meaning of even your blindest striving is identical with the entire expression of the divine Will. And it is in this aspect of the world that we have found the unity of Being. On the other hand, as we have also seen, this unity of the world-life is no simple unity, such as the mystic sought. It is an infinitely complex unity. And of this complexity, of this wealth of life that the complete expression of even your most transient and finite glimpses of meaning implies, — the foregoing facts about the Self are merely instances. If you are in company with a friend, the whole meaning of your thoughts and of your interests while you speak with him, not only requires for its complete expression his inner life as well as yours, and not only requires the genuine and conscious unity of his life and of yours by virtue of the ties of your friendship; but this same meaning also demands that, despite this unity of your life as friends, — yes, even because of this unity, your friend and yourself shall remain also contrasted lives, whose unity includes and presupposes your variety as these two friends. For a friendship is not a simple unity of conscious life, but the unity of two conscious lives each of which contrasts itself with the other, and feels in the other's relative independence the fulfilment of its own purpose. And just so, when your meaning is not friendly but hostile, and when you stand in presence of your opponent, your rival, your enemy, your finite conscious meaning still implies, even in the midst of all its confused illusions, the demand that the very life of your enemy shall exist as the expression of your hostile intent to hold him as your real enemy, while nevertheless this life of his, other than your present conscious experience, and linked with your experience through the ties of meaning, is contrasted with your own life as the life that yours opposes and in so far seeks either to win over to your purposes, or to annul. Finite love and finite hate, and human experience of life in any form, always imply, therefore, that the will now present, but imperfectly expressed, in this passing instant, is genuinely expressed through other conscious life that, from the Absolute point of view, is at once in conscious unity with this instant's purpose, and also in conscious contrast with this instant's purpose.

Primarily then, the contrast of Self and not-Self comes to us as the contrast between the Internal and the External meaning of this present moment's purpose. In the narrowest sense, the Self is just your own present imperfectly expressed pulsation of meaning and purpose, — this striving, this love, this hate, this hope, this fear, this inquiry, this inner speech of the instant's will, this thought, this deed, this desire, — in brief, this idea taken as an Internal Meaning. In the widest sense, the not-Self is all the rest of the divine whole of conscious life, — the Other, the outer World of expressed meaning taken as in contrast with what, just at this instant of our human form of consciousness, is observed, and, relatively speaking, possessed. Any finite idea is so far a Self; and I can, if you please, contrast my present Self with my past or my future Self, with yesterday's hopes or with to-morrow's deeds, quite as genuinely as with your inner life or with the whole society of which I am a member, or with the whole life of which our experience of Nature is a hint, or, finally, with the life of God in its entirety. In every such case, I take account of a true contrast between Self and not-Self. All such contrasts have a common character, namely, that in them an imperfectly expressed will is set over against its own richer expression, while stress is laid upon the fact, — a perfectly genuine fact of Being, — the fact that the whole expression always retains, and does not merely absorb or transmute, the very contrast between the finite Self and its desired or presupposed Other, — its world of External Meanings. But if you ask how many such contrasts can be made, I reply, An infinite number. In countless ways can the Self of this instant's glimpse of conscious meaning be set into contrast with the not-Self, whose content may be the life of past and future, of friends and of enemies, of the social order and of Nature, of finite life in general, and of God's life in its wholeness.

But if the contrast of Self and not-Self can thus be defined with an infinite variety of emphasis, the unity of each of the two, Self and not-Self, can be emphasized in an equally infinite number of ways, whose depth and whose extent of meaning will vary with the range of life of which one takes account, and with the sort of contrast between Self and not-Self which one leaves still prominent over against the unity. Thus, in the familiar case of our ordinary social self-consciousness, I first view a certain realm of past and future experience as so bound up with the internal meaning of this instant's conscious experience, that I call this temporal whole of life the life of my own human Self, while I contrast this private existence of mine with that of my friends, my opponents, or of my other fellows, or with that of human society in general. The motives that lead to such an identification of the Self of the instant with a certain portion of that which is the instant's not-Self, namely, with a certain portion of past and future experience, are, as we have seen, extremely various, and in our empirical existence, both fickle and transitory. Whoever believes that he has any one rational principle for his usual identification of his past and future with the Self of this instant, has only to consider the psychological variations of self-consciousness before enumerated to discover his error. What will remain, after such an examination of the Self of common sense, will be the really deep and important persuasion that he *ought to possess* or to create for himself, despite this chaos, some one principle, some finally significant contrast, whereby he should be able, with an united and permanent meaning, to identify that portion of the world's life which is to be, in the larger sense, his own, and whereby he should become able to contrast with this, his larger Self, all the rest of the world of life.

And now this very consideration, this fact that one *ought to be able* to select from all the universe a certain portion of remembered and expected, of conceived and of intended life as that of his own true and individual Self, and that one ought to contrast with this whole of life, with this one's larger or truer individuality, the life of all other individual Selves, and the life of the Absolute in its wholeness, — this consideration, I say, shows us at once the sense in which the Self is an Ethical Category. At this instant, as I have said, you can indeed identify the Self, if you please, with just the instant's passing glimpse of Internal Meaning; and in that case you can call all else the not-Self. To do this is to leave the Self a mere thrill of transient life, — a fragment whose deeper meaning is wholly external to itself. But you can, and in general you do, first identify a remembered past, and an intended future, with the Self whose individuality is just now hinted to you; and this enlarged self of memory and purpose you then oppose to a not-Self whose content is first the world of your fellow-men, and then the world of Nature and of the Absolute in its wholeness. Now what justification have you for this view of your larger Self? Apart from the capricious and shifting views of common sense, you can have, I reply, but one justification, namely this: You regard this present moment's life and striving as a glimpse of a certain task now assigned to you, the task of your life as friend, as worker, as loyal citizen, or in general as man, *i.e.* as one of God's expressions in human form. You conceive that, however far you might proceed towards the fulfilment of this task, however rich this individual life of yours might become, it would always remain, despite its unity with the world-life, in some true sense contrasted with the lives of your fellows, and with the life of God, just as now you stand in contrast to both. While your whole meaning is now, and will always remain one with the entire life of God, you conceive that this whole meaning expresses itself in the form of an articulate system of contrasting and coöperating lives, of which one, namely your own individual life, is more closely linked, in purpose, in task, in meaning, with the life of this instant, than is the life of any other individual. Or as you can say: "At this instant I am indeed one with God, in the sense that in him my own absolute Selfhood is expressed. But God's will is expressed in a manifold life. And this life is a system of contrasted lives that are various even by virtue of their significant union. For true unity of meaning is best manifested in variety, just as the most intimate and wealthy friendship is that of strongly contrasting friends. And in the manifold lives that the world in its unity embodies, there is one, and only one, whose task is here hinted to me as my task, my life-plan, — an ideal whose expression needs indeed the coöperation of countless other Selves, of a social order, of Nature, and of the whole universe, but whose individual significance remains contrasted with all other individual significance. If this is my task, if this is what my past life has meant, if this is what my future is to fulfil, if it is in this way that I do God's work, if my true relation to the Absolute is only to be won through the realization of this life-plan, and through the accomplishment of this unique task, then indeed I am a Self, and a Self who is nobody else, just precisely in so far as my life has this purpose and no other. *By this meaning of my life-plan, by this possession of an ideal, by this Intent always to remain another than my fellows despite my divinely planned unity with them, — by this, and not by the possession of any Soul-Substance, I am defined and created a Self.*"

Such, I say, will be your confession, if once you come

to define the Self in the only genuine terms, — namely, in ethical terms. If once you choose this definition, then the endless empirical varieties of self-consciousness, and the caprices of common sense, will not confuse you. You will know that since now we see through a glass darkly, you cannot expect at present to experience your human selfhood in any one consistent and final expression. But, too, you will know that you are a Self precisely in so far as you intend to accomplish God's will by becoming one; and that you are an individual precisely in so far as you purpose to do your Father's business in unique fashion, so that in this instant shall begin a work that can be finished only in eternity, — a work that, however closely bound up it may be with all the rest of the divine life, still remains in its expression distinguishable from all this other life. You will indeed recognize that at every moment you receive from without, and from other Selves, the very experiences that give your Selfhood a chance to possess its meaning. You will know that of yourself alone you would be nothing. You will also know that as co-worker with your fellows, and as servant of God, you have a destiny of which our present life gives us but the dimmest hint.

This is in outline, the doctrine of the ethical Self, to whose development and defence our later lectures shall be devoted.

LECTURE VII

LECTURE VII

THE PLACE OF THE SELF IN BEING

IN the last lecture, after a study of the various forms which our empirical self-consciousness assumes, we reached an idealistic definition of what we mean by an individual human Self, regarded as a Real Being. During the present lecture I shall, by the term Self, denote, unless I expressly declare to the contrary, the human Self, as thus defined, and not the Absolute Self as the Absolute.

In the present lecture I propose, first, to make some further comparison of our theory of the Self with doctrines that have been maintained in the history of thought, and in this connection to develope our own thesis more fully. Secondly, I shall undertake to consider the relation of our theory of the individual to that Interpretation of Nature which we expounded in our Fourth Lecture, and to discuss the sense in which, from our point of view, new individuals can appear in the course of natural evolution. Thirdly, I intend to consider briefly the question as to the degree to which the Self is causally determined, as to its experience and its will, by its relations to the natural order. Finally, I shall discuss the sense in which the individual Self can possess ethical Freedom, in view of its relation to the divine Will.

I

Historically, there are theories of the Self which correspond to each of the four conceptions of Being. And in the first place, ever since the doctrine of the Sânkhya, that classic instance of early Realism, realistic Metaphysic has been an especially wealthy source of various theories of the Self. Not always has Realism taken the form of the Soul-Substance theory, although, as we saw at the last time, that theory itself is a typical instance of Realism, and is an especially frequent instance of the realistic view of the Self. But any theory of the Self uses the realist's conception of Being, in case this theory views the Self as logically or essentially independent, in its innermost nature, of the fact that other Selves exist, so that you could conceive other Selves vanishing, while this Self still remained, in some innermost core of its Being, unaltered. Leibniz's Monads are realistic selves; and very frequently the extremer forms of ethical individualism, in order to preserve the dignity, or the freedom, or the rights of the Self, have chosen to use a realistic formulation. When thus defined by the more ethical types of individualistic Realism, the Self seems to stand, within its own realm, as a sort of absolute authority, over against any external will or knowledge that pretends to determine its nature, or its precise limits, or its meaning. It is merely what its own substantial nature determines it to be. It is thus a separate entity, in its essence unapproachable, in some sense, by God or man, unconquerable, possessing perhaps its own inalienable rights, the unit of all ethical order, the centre of its own universe. From this point of view, the principal problem, for any such realistic Individualism, always becomes the question how this Self, whose interests are essentially its own, can rationally come to recognize any responsibility to other Selves or to God, or to any absolute Ought, beyond its own caprice. Just because, within its own realm, it is whatever it is in entire indifference to whether you from without know it or not; or to whether your external will approves it or not; the problem at once arises as to why this Self should, in its turn, recognize any authority. In its knowledge of Being, the independent Self of any theoretical form of Realism, when once the independence of this individual Self has come to be recognized, tends to become, in extreme cases, solipsistic. But in its morality, this same Self, in equally extreme forms of ethical Realism, tends to become an anarchist.[1] If, in such extreme and less common forms, Realism, untrue to its usual historical tendencies, throws off its usual and respectable conservatism, that is merely because, in general, extremes easily meet, and because, in the special case of the theory of the Self, Realism deals with a test problem which is peculiarly apt to bring out its deeper inconsistencies. About the world external to all our human Selves, Realism, as it appears

[1] Max Stirner's *Der Einzige und Sein Eigenthum* is in the main an example of this type of treatment of the Self. Nietzsche's conception, however, cannot properly be placed here in view of the idealistic element which, as I think, can justly be recognized in his conception of the individual.

in history, is typically submissive, respectable, and conservative, just because it is dealing unreflectively with an unapproachable and absolute Reality beyond our own life. But so soon as Realism attempts to apply its categories to the realm within, where its unreflective methods are decidedly not at home, it does not, indeed, become less dogmatic than usual, and not the less disposed to cite tradition, and to hurl its customary pathological epithets at its opponents, but it becomes more manifestly unable, when once it has defined any one of its Independent Beings, to say what link or tie, what law or reason, what obligation or responsibility, can ever bind this Independent Being to any other. Hence the dogmatic anarchists of the history of ethics are often realists in their theory of the Self.

As to the Mystical theory of the Self, we have already followed to the end its account of the problem of life. The Self is the Absolute, the Absolute is simple, and there is neither variety of individuals, nor form nor law of life left. The only word as to the true Self is the Hindoo's *Neti*, *Neti*. Consequently Mysticism simply condemns all finite individuality as an evil dream.

Modern Critical Rationalism also has its own accounts of the Self. These again are manifold. But the Third Conception of Being in general, as we have all along seen, is both reflective and widely observant; and its theories of the Self have, in most cases, their large measure of truth. For Critical Rationalism the Self is no independent entity, nor any mere experience, but a being whose reality involves the validity of a system of laws and relationships. These laws may be viewed in their psychological aspect. In this sense my Self extends as far as my possible memories, or expectations, or definable plans hold valid for the empirical region called my human life. And my existence as a Self means merely that these laws of my memory, of my will, and of my personal experience are valid as long as I live. Or the laws in question may be viewed as those of an ethical interpretation of life. In this case, by the Self, Critical Rationalism means a being defined in the terms of a certain valid system of laws about the rights and the duties of persons. The Self, in the view of such theories, does not first exist as an Independent Being and then either originate, or else acquire, as an external addition, its system of rights and of duties. But, for Critical Rationalism, the ethical Self is defined and exists only through the prior recognition of these valid rights and duties themselves. Whoever has not learned to recognize his office in the world, as a subject of the moral law, or as a member of a social order, is therefore no ethical Self at all. But whoever is a Self, is such by virtue of this recognized validity of law. In the history of recent thought the Kantian conception of the Self, apart from its realistic elements, is, in its consequences, essentially of this third type. Kant's knowing Self exists, from our human point of view, precisely in so far as the Categories, which express its unity in the realm of experience, are valid. Its existence as the Subject of Knowledge, so far as we can know it, thus becomes coextensive with the range of such validity. Kant's ethical Self exists as the free recognizer of the Moral Law. And in Fichte, who purged Kant's doctrine of its realistic elements, this view of the Self especially comes to light, and contends with the purely idealistic tendencies of Fichte. For Fichte, the Self, although the very principle of Being, rather ought to be than is.

Now the truth, and the practical value of every such doctrine, lies in the fact that it recognizes the valid relations of the Self, and the laws which bind the Self to its fellows, as conditions without which the Self can neither exist nor be conceived. The defect of Critical Rationalism lies in the consequences of its essentially abstract and impersonal view of Being. The Self, in this sense, is a law rather than a life; and a type of existence rather than an Individual. It is precisely the restoration of individuality to the Self which constitutes the essential deed of our Idealism. For us the Self has indeed no Independent Being; but it is a life, and not a mere valid law. It gains its very individuality through its relation to God; but in God it still dwells as an individual; for it is an unique expression of the divine purpose. And since the Self is precisely, in its wholeness, the conscious and intentional fulfilment of this divine purpose, in its own unique way, the individual will of the Self is not wholly determined by a power that fashions it as clay is fashioned and that is called God's will; but, on the contrary, what the Self in its wholeness wills is, just in so far, God's will, and is identical with one of the many expressions implied by a single divine purpose, so that, for the reasons already set forth, in general, in the closing lecture of the foregoing series, the Self is in its innermost individuality, not an independent, but still a Free Will, which in so far owns no external Master, despite its unity with the whole life of God, and despite its dependence in countless ways upon Nature and upon its fellows, for everything except the individuality and uniqueness of its life.

Meanwhile, I cannot too strongly insist that, in our present form of human consciousness, the true Self of any individual man is not a datum, but an ideal. It is true that people at first very naturally, and often very resentfully, reject this interpretation. "Do I not directly know," one insists, "that I am and who I am?" I answer: You indeed know, although never in a merely direct way, *that* you exist. But in the present life you never find out, in terms of any direct experience, *what* you are. I know that I am, as this individual human Self, only in so far as every Internal Meaning, that of my present experience included, sends me elsewhere, or to some Other, for its complete interpretation, while this particular sort of Internal Meaning, such as gets expressed in the Cartesian *cogito ergo sum*, the meaning whereby I come to be aware of myself as this individual different from the rest of the world, implies and demands, for its complete embodiment, some sort of contrast between Self and not-Self. I am assured of myself, then, only in so far as I am assured of the Nature of Being in general. I am indeed right in thus contrasting Self and not-Self; but my certainty regarding the Being of this contrast depends upon the same general assurances that lead to my whole metaphysical view of the nature of Reality.

And now as to the finding out *what* I am, the answer to this question involves, upon its empirical side, all the complications and inconsistencies of common sense which we set forth at the last time. If you take me merely as common sense views me, I am, from moment to moment, whatever social experience or lonely reflection makes me seem. I am, so far, whatever my empirical contrast with you, with society in general, with those whom I love, or with those against whom I contend, — I am, in brief, whatever my remembered or anticipated powers, fortunes, and plans, cause me to regard with emphasis as myself in contrast with the rest of the world. There is no instant in our human experience when I can say, Here I have not merely assumed, or presupposed, or conceived, but actually found in experience the Self, so that I here observe what I finally am.

In what way then can I just now rationally define myself as this actually unique and real person? Already we have seen, in general, the answer to this question. The Self can be defined in terms of an Ideal. If we ask a man to observe once for all what he now is, we call his attention to various empirical accidents of his life, — to his bodily presence, to his organic sensations, to his name, to his social status, and to his memories of the past. But none of these are of any uniquely determined significance; and not thus can we show a man what he is. But when, in vexation at the moral ineffectiveness of a man, we significantly use the imperative mood and say, "Whatever you know or do not know about yourself, at all events *be somebody*," — we lay stress upon what is, after all, the essential point. What we mean by our words is the exhortation: "Have a plan; give unity to your aims; intend something definite by your life; set before yourself one ideal." We conceive, in such cases, that the

Self is definable in terms of purpose, of continuity of life-plan, and of voluntary subordination of chance experiences to a persistently emphasized ideal. If this ideal keeps the individual contrasted with other individuals, as the servant of these masters, or again as the servant, in some unique fashion, of God, — as the friend of these friends, as the teacher of these pupils, as the fellow-worker with these comrades, then the Self which we have defined is the Self of an individual man. It is in so far not to be confounded with their selves just because the ideal, if expressed in a life, would be expressed in constant contrast with these other lives. Our idealistic theory teaches that all individual lives and plans and experiences win their unity in God, in such wise that there is, indeed, but one absolutely final and integrated Self, that of the Absolute. But our idealism also recognizes that in the one life of the divine there is, indeed, articulation, contrast, and variety. So that, while it is, indeed, true that for every one of us the Absolute Self is God, we still retain our individuality, and our distinction from one another, *just in so far as our life-plans, by the very necessity of their social basis, are mutually contrasting life-plans, each one of which can reach its own fulfilment only by recognizing other life-plans as different from its own.* And if from the Absolute point of view, as well as from our own, every individual life that has the unity of a plan, takes its own unique place in the world's life, then for God, as for ourselves, we various human beings live related lives, but still contrasting and various lives, each one of which is an individual life, connected within itself, but distinguishable from all the other lives, precisely as our normal social consciousness makes us seem.

But now, if my human Self can be defined in a single and connected fashion only in terms of such an ideal, we see at once that, in our present human life, no one life-plan ever gets both a precise definition and a complete embodiment; and, therefore, we can say, Never in the present life do we find the Self as a given and realized fact. It is for us an ideal. Its true place is in the eternal world, where all plans are fulfilled. In God alone do we fully come to ourselves. There alone do we know even as we are known.

The conception of the Self thus sketched involves difficulties, and leaves special questions still to be answered, such as I should be the last to ignore. It was for the sake of meeting just such difficulties that our whole previous discussion of the Theory of Being was required as a beginning of our enterprise; and that our Theory of Nature has also been needed as a preliminary to the study of the Self. In general we stated both these difficulties and their answers in dealing with the general problems of Being. But in defining the Self we have already recognized these general problems in a case where, owing to the complex natural relations of the Self, they possess peculiar significance. Nobody can deal with the problem of the Self upon the basis of the empirical facts about human selfhood without seeing, as we saw at the last time, that the Self is in the most intimate relation of dependence upon both natural and social conditions, for every one amongst its attributes that can be defined in general terms. It has an origin in time. It has an hereditary temperament. It is helpless to become anything apart from social training. And, if you remove from its inner consciousness the recognition of its relations of contrast to its literal and to its more or less ideally conceived comrades, rivals, and authorities, it loses at any moment all that makes self-consciousness either worth having, or conceivable. Its whole ethical significance thus depends upon relations to God and to man which, in its capacity as finite being, it can only accept and cannot create. In all these senses the Self temporally appears as a product, a result, a determined creature of destiny. Remove from it the support of the world, and it instantly becomes nothing. Moreover, you in vain endeavor to save the independence of the Self by defining it as a Substance. For all the independence that it ever can even desire to have is a conscious independence, and to this a Soul-Substance contributes nothing. And if your consciousness is merely based upon an existence which lies beneath the consciousness, and which never comes to light as your own present will and meaning, you gain nothing but a name when this unobserved substratum of your personality is called your Soul. The Cartesian *res cogitans* is significant precisely in so far as it is the name for a rational thinking process, but not in so far as it is a *res*. What you want, however, for your Self, is conscious meaning, conscious individuality, and conscious freedom. And the problem is, in view of your unquestionable dependence upon the world for all your endowments, How shall you win this conscious meaning and freedom and individuality; and how is it possible that in any sense you should possess them? Now it is precisely these questions that our Idealism undertakes to answer.

From our point of view, your distinction from the rest of the universe, your contrast with other selves, your uniqueness, your freedom, your individuality, all depend upon one essential principle. This world that we live in is, in its wholeness, the expression of one determinate and absolute purpose, the fulfilment of the divine will. This fulfilment is unique, just because, in the world as a whole, the divine accomplishes its purpose, attains its goal, finds in absolute dominateness what it seeks, and therefore will have no other world than this. Now for this very reason, since the world in its wholeness is unique, every portion of this whole life, every fragment of experience, every pulsation of will in the universe, every intent anywhere partially embodied, is, by virtue of its relation to this unique whole, also unique, — but unique precisely in so far as it is related to the whole, and not in so far as you abstract its various features and endowments from their relation to God, and view them in finite relations. Taken apart from its relation to the whole, the finite fragment appears as something more or less incomprehensible, and therefore as something more or less vaguely general, — a mere case of a type, a member of a series — a temporal expression of dissatisfied will, — a fact that seeks for other facts to explain it, — a bit of experience subject to various psychological laws, — a sort of life that can be interpreted now in this way, and now in that, just as, at the last time, we found the Self subject to the most varying interpretations and estimates.

Yet fear not to find in what manifold ways your life depends upon Nature and Society. It depends upon them for absolutely all of its *general* characters. That is, whatever character it shares with others, implies dependence upon others. If it did not so depend, it would have no intimate share in the common life. But its dependence means precisely that it derives from the other lives everything *except* its uniqueness, — everything *except* its *individual fashion of acknowledging and taking interest in this its very dependence, and of responding thereto by its deeds.* When, as man, you take your place amongst men, you thus derive all of your life from elsewhere, *except* in so far as your life becomes for you your own way of viewing your relation to the whole, and of actively expressing your own ideal regarding this relation. This *your own way of expressing God's will* is not derived. It is yourself. And it is yours because God worketh in you. The Spirit of God in its wholeness compels you, — the individual, the Self, the unique personality, in the sense that it compels you to be an individual, and to be free. Or it compels your individual will only in so far as you consciously compel yourself.

You indeed find then, as Goethe found in his well-known verses about heredity, that your dependence on the rest of the world extends to every character of your nature, precisely in so far as you can define such a character in general terms. Your temperament you derived from your ancestors, your training from your social order. Your opinions, as definable ideas, belong to many of your neighbors also. Your consciousness of yourself, from moment to moment, depends upon social contrast effects, and varies with them. But your purpose, your life-plan, just so far as it possesses true rationality of aim, is the purpose to find for yourself just your own place in God's world, and to fill that place, as nobody else can fill it. Now this purpose, I maintain, is indeed your own. As nobody else can share it, so nobody else can create it; and from no source external to yourself have you derived it. And this I say on the sole ground that in you, *precisely in so far as you know the world as one world, and intend your place in that one world to be unique, God's will is consciously expressed.* And his will is one, and in that will every life finds its own unique meaning. Hence our theory of the Self assigns to it the character of the Free Individual but maintains that this character belongs to it in its true relation to God, and cannot be observed, at any one instant of time, as an obvious and independent fact.

II

But herewith, having defined what general Form of Being the Self possesses, we come to a question that in the former lecture was kept in the background, although it lay very near to us. This is the question as to the precise relation of our present doctrine about the individual human Self to our general theory of the process of Evolution in Nature. If the individual is, within the range of our experience, already known as a product of Nature, and of his social relations, by so much the more must his temporal origin, in those aspects of it which escape our direct observation, be viewed as a portion of the vast activities that are hinted to us by our experience of Nature in general. Therefore an effort to bring our theory of the Self into closer relation to our former interpretation of the process of evolution, must form at once the culmination of our doctrine about Nature and a sort of test of our views as to the Self. To such an effort we are now ready to proceed.

As has now been sufficiently shown, a frank admission of the natural origin of the Self, and a study of its relations to the physical world, in no sense involves an abandonment of the idealistic point of view. That the world is the expression of my will, and that nevertheless there has been an infinite past time in which I, the human individual, did not exist — may indeed seem at first a hard saying. But our discussion of the general Categories of Experience, our idealistic theory of Time, and our portrayal of the contrast between the private Self of the human individual and the Absolute Self in its wholeness, — all these preliminaries have cleared the way for an understanding of every such difficulty. In dealing with the categories of the Ought, we saw how and why it is always my will as this human being to acknowledge what is other than the present temporal expression of my will. In our doctrine of Time, we reconciled the fact of our acknowledgment of a remote past time with our assurance that all temporal facts are at once present to the Absolute. In our development of the concept of the human Self, we have shown that we ourselves demand the other individuals, as the very condition of our existence in the Absolute, and that through a wealth of individuality other than our own, and *only* through such variety, is our own life-purpose to be attained. Just as my opponent in a game embodies my will to play with him by opposing me, and gives me an opportunity to be myself through the very fact that he expresses my will in the form of a selfhood whose particular plans are uncontrolled by my private will, while mine are in part uncontrolled by his, — so in general, the private Self is this Self only through contrast with and dependence upon others; and finds its complete Selfhood embodied in other individual life than its own. Moreover, in order that my private will should at this temporal instant form a definite plan, I must always presuppose some world of completed fact as the basis of my present deed; and the realm of that which is viewed as the so far completed expression of the Will, is the temporally Past. The Past too, in its own way, embodies my present will, but embodies it by virtue of the very fact that the Past is the realm of the irrevocable, which I am therefore able to presuppose as a fixed starting-point in forming every new plan. The manifold dependence of my present will upon the social, natural, and temporal order, is thus not only matter of fact, but also a requirement of our idealism.

III

Meanwhile, in order to give full expression to our hypothesis regarding the temporal evolution of new forms of individual selfhood, it will be necessary first to recall some features of our doctrine of the sense in which the Absolute includes a variety of lives, and possesses a temporal expression at all. Only then can we see in detail how what we call novel forms of life can arise in time.

In our criticism of Mysticism, in the former Series of these lectures,[1] we pointed out that a goal which is "a goal of no real process, has as little value as it has content, as little Being as it has finitude." Ever since, in defining the Absolute from our own point of view, we have indeed declared it to be a goal, — *i.e.* a fulfilment of purpose, but have also insisted that, corresponding to each result that is attained in the Absolute, there must also be, in the real world of the Absolute itself, a corresponding purpose or intent, which, just because it is fulfilled in the whole, is at the same time consciously distinguished, as a longing, — a pursuit, a finite idea, — from its own fulfilment. This consideration has constituted, throughout, the ground of our deduction of finitude, — our means of conceiving the union of the One and the Many in the unity of the Absolute Consciousness. For, as a consequence of this principle, the Absolute Life is definable, in the terms of our Supplementary Essay, as a Self-Representative System. Every fact in this system, namely, fulfils a purpose. The consciousness of this purpose is, however, a fact distinct from the fulfilment, and yet correspondent thereto; while, on the other hand, this consciousness itself, as a fact, belonging to the system of the Absolute, is in its own turn the fulfilment of another purpose, which is the consequence, in some degree, of another act that has led up to it; and so on *ad infinitum*. A consciousness of purpose, distinct from fulfilment, is, how-

[1] Lecture V, p. 193.

ever, when viewed by itself, a longing, a dissatisfaction, an incompleteness. Hence the Absolute Life includes an infinity of longings, each one of which, in so far as it is taken in itself, is a consciousness of imperfection and finitude seeking its relative fulfilment in some other finite act or state. Only through such consciousness is perfection attainable. The only alternative here is Mysticism, and that is Nothingness. But, as our Supplementary Essay also showed,[1] any system that is self-representative in one way, is self-representative in countless other ways, and the consciousness of the system involved in each one of these ways of self-representation is therefore distinct from the consciousness involved in any of the others, since each way involves a series of voluntary strivings after a goal. In consequence, as the Supplementary Essay [2] also pointed out, whoever conceives the Absolute as a Self, conceives it as in its form inclusive of an infinity of various, but interwoven and so of intercommunicating Selves, each one of which represents the totality of the Absolute in its own way, and with its own unity, so that the simplest conceivable structure of the Absolute Life would be stateable only in terms of an infinitely great variety of types of purpose and of fulfilment, intertwined in the most complex fashions. Apart from any doctrine of evolution, then, we have to regard the Absolute in its wholeness as comprising many Selves, in the most various interrelations.

Now we must urgently insist that, when once we have recognized this variety of finite purposes, and of infinite sys-

[1] See the former Series of these lectures, p. 515, *sqq.*

[2] p. 546.

tems consisting of finite purposes, *within* the Absolute, we are not at all obliged to assume, as many more or less idealistic systems have done, some *further* principle of blind self-differentiation within the Absolute as the ground of the separation or falling away of the finite beings *from* their divine source. Longing, considered as a fact *other than* fulfilment, is, indeed, in its own already distinguished nature, to any extent blind. But, by our hypothesis, longing exists *in* the Absolute Life, and as a significant portion thereof. Any temporal present, taking that word in the "inclusive" sense that was defined in our Third lecture of the present Series, contains, as we saw in discussing Time, just such an experience of finitude and of dissatisfaction. Now longing, in itself, means *non*-possession of the goal; and the temporal instance shows us that the proposition: "To-day the ideal is sought for and *not* found," is perfectly consistent with the proposition: "In eternity the ideal *is* found." Nor is it necessary in the least to suppose that if the Absolute is possessed of the eternal point of view, and so is acquainted with the finding of the ideal which *to-day* is sought in vain, the Absolute is therefore *not* directly acquainted with the vain seeking of to-day, or is no sharer therein. Rather, from our point of view, is the very reverse the necessary conclusion. *In order to be possessed of the eternal knowledge of the attainment of the goal, the Absolute insight will actually include all that we experience when to-day we seek the goal in vain.* For the Absolute insight then, as for our own, the seeking of the goal *to-day* will *not* be successful. Just this ill-success of the temporal instant will be the very condition of the success of the eternally expressed Will. For, as we have insisted, without longing, no attainment. Therefore the larger consciousness does not lose the conscious incompleteness of the lesser, but gives that, just as it is, its place in the completed whole.

The unity of consciousness, even in our own narrow experience, gives us many instances where consciousness either spans in one moment the conflict between two opposing internal tendencies, or embraces in one act the contrasts of longing and fulfilment, of ignorance and knowledge, of defeat and victory. One who, to take a trivial instance, "expects the unexpected" (as a sensible man should in dealing with fortune), combines in one consciousness, at the moment when the surprising event occurs, the shock of knowing that event as surprising, and the little triumph of observing that, just because of its surprising character, it meets, in one aspect, his expectations, because he had expected a surprise. Just such expectation of surprises constitutes one of the most cherished joys of the Christmas holidays; and the children, as they fall upon the parcels which contain their presents and open these, have also an instant wherein their temporal span of consciousness, brief as it is, is long enough to embrace "at once" (in the sense discussed in our third lecture) the contrast between ignorant suspense and delighted discovery. Now for them, just that is the supreme moment. And it is so because consciousness spans at once the suspense and the solution. Or again, if I have wandered long, thirsty, in a dry land, and find the spring, the most perfect experience is that in which, even while I still am full of thirst, I *also* drink the water for which I have so agonized and wandered. Or still again, a recent psychologist[1] has extensively illustrated the well-known thesis that part of the joy of play lies in the "*bewusste Selbsttäuschung*," the "conscious self-deception" of the player. The delights of the theatre are of this sort; the plays of children and even of puppies and kittens, either exhibit, or at least suggest, the same state of mind. Now "conscious self-deception" is a state of mind that more or less definitely spans and includes ignorance and knowledge, blind belief and proud disbelief, in one act. It is only a petty bondage to conventional formulas, and in particular a purely formal and thoughtless use of the phraseology of the principle of contradiction, which makes some of us unwilling to recognize these normal complications that find place in the unity of even our own little consciousness. As a dramatic spectator, I can at once feel with Othello his own strong delusion, and also see with Iago the precise devices that are employed to deceive, and meanwhile, as spectator, can take my critical view of the whole situation. As reasoner, I can (in following the course of an indirect demonstration) appreciate the force of an argument even while I refute it; or can at once hold an opinion, viewed in its unreflective meaning, before my consciousness, even while I also reflect upon it, and so give it a new and a deeper import; or can think the meaning of the separate assertions contained in the antecedent and consequent of a hypothetical judgment, even while I hold in mind the

[1] Groos, in discussing the psychology of Play in his *Spiele der Thiere* and *Spiele des Menschen*. The term "*bewusste Selbsttäuschung*" Groos borrows from K. Lange. See *Spiele der Thiere*, p. 308; *Spiele des Menschen*, p. 164, *sqq*., p. 499, *sqq*.

decidedly different meaning involved in their combination in the judgment itself.

Now what these instances illustrate in our own narrow sort of consciousness, I apply, in universal terms, to the Absolute. I hold that all finite consciousness, *just as it is in us,* — ignorance, striving, defeat, error, temporality, narrowness, — *is all present from the Absolute point of view, but is also seen in unity with the solution of problems, the attainment of goals, the overcoming of defeats, the correction of errors, the final wholeness of temporal processes, the supplementing of all narrowness.*

Consequently, I see no reason, after once we have found that the Absolute, in order to be complete, must include finitude, to ask yet further, "How then in us does the finitude come to seem to be sundered from the Absolute?" Finitude *means* a sense of sundering, but of a sundering that from the Absolute point of view, also involves union. We, by hypothesis, *are* aware of the longings and of the ignorance. The Absolute, which is our own very selfhood in fulfilment, is aware of all that we are aware of (*i.e.* of the longings and of the ignorance) *and* of the supplement also. If one persists in asking, "But what has sundered us from the Absolute, and narrowed our consciousness as it is narrowed?" my only general answer is, Such narrowness must find its place *within* the Absolute life, in order that the Absolute should be complete. One needs then no new principle to explain why, as Plotinus asked, the souls fell away from God.[1] *From the point of view of the Absolute, the finite beings never fall away.* They are where they are, namely in and of

[1] Plotinus, *Enn.*, V, 1, at the beginning.

the Absolute Unity. *From their own point of view, they seem to have fallen away*, because (as finite) they are the longing aspect, and *not* the final fulfilment of longing; because they are partial ignorance, and not the fulfilment of knowledge; because they are the expression of an attention to *this* and *this*, and not of that attention to the whole which, in the Absolute, is the corrective and the includer of their inattention; and finally, because they are stages of a temporal process, while the Absolute is possessed of the inclusive eternal insight. The only *general* deduction of their existence is furnished by the fact that, unless they existed, the Absolute Will, which is also their own, could not be expressed.

What we have said of the relation of the Absolute to the various included Individuals, applies also, *within* the world of the various Selves, to the relation in which any larger or including Individual Self stands to the lives of the Individuals which, from our point of view, are included within it. Thus, according to our account, every new Self that arises in time must find its place *within* the life of a larger and inclusive Selfhood. This larger Selfhood indeed permits the included Self, in some aspect of its nature, to become an Individual, — an image of the Absolute, — a will that takes its own individual attitude towards the world. Yet the including Self also in some measure predetermines the character of that which it includes, and limits the latter to a particular place in Being. In our Supplementary Essay we suggested, very inadequately, the variety of internally differentiated structure which any Self-Representative System involves. As a fact, any Self except the Absolute is included within the life of a richer Self, and in turn includes the lives of partial Selves within its own. The consciousness of the included Selves is indeed hereby limited to a particular place in Being, and so constitutes only a particular type of consciousness. At any moment of time the consciousness that embodies a particular stage in the life and self-expression of any Individual, may therefore be limited to an explicit attention to certain facts only, — the "rest of the world" being known to this Individual, just then, only as the undifferentiated background of its consciousness. All such limitations will be expressible in the same general terms. The larger Selfhood involves the inclusion of the partial Selfhood. Therefore the partial Selfhood exists ; and one has not to explain by new principles why its consciousness at any temporal instant appears, from its own point of view, as cut off from that which includes it. It is cut off only in so far as it is indeed a partial form of consciousness, which, as this partial form, knows at any time so much of the whole world as just then expresses its stage of life-purpose.

An explanation of the particular existence of *this* finite consciousness can be given therefore, only in one of two forms: first, in terms of universal principles, in so far as without just this finitude, the eternal purpose would not obtain the wealth of individual expression that it actually possesses; or, secondly, in terms of the particular relations of each finite being, in so far as it is what it is in consequence of the presence in the world, and especially in the temporal Past, of other finite beings, whose nature and acts required some aspect of its own life as their resultant.

Consequently, any effort to give an account of the temporal origin and evolution of any particular finite being, such as one of ourselves, must follow the *second* of these forms of explanation, and cannot undertake to give an account of the origin of all finitude. The question about the evolution of new forms of finite life then becomes this: What conditions of the previous finite life of the world explain why, just at this point, a new Self should begin to appear? Or again, to put the question a little more generally, our former theory as to evolution accepted the thesis that humanity, as a whole, has sprung from some non-human process of experience which, before our special type of selfhood appeared, was taking place in the natural world. This previous process, we have said, was no doubt in itself a conscious process, perhaps possessing a type of consciousness whose "temporal span" was more or less different from our own, just because its present interest was always expressed by a longer or shorter series of facts than we now at present take into account. But in any case it was not what we should have called a human process. How came it to give origin to a process of our type? This is the sole question that any philosophical theory of the evolution of the Self can undertake to deal with.

Our answer will take some such form as the following, — a form inevitably hypothetical, but consistent with the facts and theories which we now have at our disposal.

IV

Any form of finite selfhood, just in so far as it is definitely conscious of explicit relations to the divine plan, tends, *ipso facto*, to express itself in an activity that accords with this plan, and that in consequence is one of the stages in that temporal process whereby the divine self-consciousness directly gets its own temporal embodiment.[1] Now since the divine plan of life, in its wholeness, is a self-representative system of longings and attainments, where each act expresses some particular purpose, and accomplishes that purpose, and where to every particular fact there corresponds just the purpose that wins embodiment in this fact, the conscious temporal life of any being who is explicitly aware of his relations to God, who acts accordingly, and who sees his act attaining its goal, must be a Well-Ordered series of deeds and successes, where each step leads to the *next*, where there is so far no wandering or wavering, where novelty results only from recurrent processes, and where plans, as a whole, do not change. We have already seen, especially in our Supplementary Essay, that the process of *counting*, dry and barren as it often seems, is for us, in our ignorance, an admirable example of the mere Form of such a recurrent activity as a being in full control of his own rational processes and of his experience would carry out. For counting produces an endless and, for our reflective investigation, an endlessly baffling wealth of novelties, as the Theory of Numbers proves. And yet this divine wealth of truth is the product of the seemingly so uniform, the unquestionably recurrent process, of counting *again and again*. Give to such a process the concrete

[1] The relation of this thesis to the problem of Free Will, and especially to the question whether the finite being is free to act counter to the divine plan, *i.e.* is free to sin, will find its place in the next lecture.

content of a life of action in accordance with a principle, and in pursuit of ideals, — and *then* you would have, in the will that expressed itself in this life, a boundlessly wealthy source of constantly novel experience. Such would be the grade of life that we sometimes ascribe to an angel, — a life wherein one is always serving God, unswervingly, and wherein one is nevertheless always doing something new, because at every stage (as in our own number-series) all that has gone before is presupposed in every new deed, and so secures the individuality of that deed.

But now such a finite life as this is, from our point of view, indeed an ideal. We are not such finite beings as this. Nor do we concretely know of any such. The finite beings whom we acknowledge in the concrete, are always, at any temporal moment, such as they are by virtue of an *inattention* which at present blinds them to their actual relations to God and to one another. Their acts are limited by reason of this inattention. They are indeed, as finite beings, aware of the world as a whole, as that which they acknowledge, and as that to which they ought to react thus or thus. But neither their own will nor their plans of action are at the present temporal instant clear to them. They are also conscious, although imperfectly, of themselves. And their imperfect self-consciousness does indeed show itself in the form of activities which tend to become recurrent, but in a somewhat tentative way. Such partially recurrent activities constitute intelligent habits. Examples of such are: a planful searching after plans, a rational striving to become more concretely rational, and so on. But in such processes these beings are seeking further definition of their own life and powers. They are seeking themselves, — their own purposes, and the means to the execution of these purposes. Now that such imperfect finite beings should be found in God's world at all, is explicable solely on the foregoing general grounds. Ignorance, error, striving after selfhood, — these are significant, even if, when taken by themselves alone, unintelligible forms of experience. They are, however, intelligible in their relation to the whole. If the divine life did not include them, it could not win the completion of their incompleteness, and so could not attain absolute perfection in the eternal world. We have here then to *presuppose* the occurrence of some such processes of a finite, that is of a longing, dissatisfied, incomplete type. What interests us here is simply the problem: given such forms of finite striving, how could new forms, new Selves, arise from them? What about their nature makes them fruitful of new types of individuality?

To this question, one may next respond with another, viz. What *constitutes* a new form of finite life and experience, — a new sort of selfhood? And the answer here is: A new form of selfhood means simply the appearance (as in our own case), of a *new type of interest in the world, in God, and in finding the way to self-expression.* A new individual is thus never a new *thing*, but a new kind of life-purpose, finding unique individual embodiment in experience by means of definite acts. Now already, in following the development of the empirical Ego *within* the range of our human experience, we have seen how a new sort of selfhood *can* arise. We have now only to generalize in order to see how a similar process can occur universally, and can lead to a transformation of finite consciousness in the direction of the evolution of new types.

V

It will be remembered that, in our second lecture, we saw how a finite consciousness is led to take a *twofold* view of its relations to the world. In the case of our human interpretation of the nature of things, it was this twofold view that gave us the conception of the contrast between the World of Description and the World of Appreciation. We are at present no longer concerned with the doctrines or theories about the universe which may result, in any finite mind, from the emphasizing now of this and now of that aspect of the contrast here in question; but we are much interested in dwelling, for a moment, upon the fact that this double view of things, which the ignorance of a finite being may lead it to take, has, or tends to have, a very important influence upon the differentiation of new *kinds of activity*. We may remember how the idleness of the cat watching the squirrels reminded us of the contemplative absorption of the men of science in describing phenomena. We easily see how vast an indirect influence upon human life and conduct such absorption in the study of the World of Description has possessed. But there is still another aspect of the tendency here in question which we must at this point emphasize.

In so far as a finite being conceives himself as already knowing enough, in general, for his purposes, he sets about attaining his goal by direct self-expression. That is, he proceeds to react upon his world in a definite way. In so far, however, as although intelligent, he still feels his inability to act in such a more direct way, he falls into that state of watchful discrimination, which looks, as we saw, *for some new object between any pair of objects that has already attracted attention.*[1] Now this search for the *between* is itself a kind of activity, with a recurrent plan. It differs from what we usually call a definite course of action by virtue of the way in which it deals with experience. And, as we saw, it is an activity directed by nothing so much as by *an attention to the contents of experience when once they chance to have been discriminated.* Therefore it is indeed on the whole opposed, by virtue of this attitude, to the more direct plans of action already present in the life which this love of discriminating novelties interrupts. It emphasizes, in a relatively random way, now this and now that special fact. It tries experiments in the forming of new series of linked contents. Now, in our last lecture, when we followed the genesis of the Empirical Ego, what did we find as the chief source of the new ideas that led to its gradual organization? Imitation. But upon what does all Imitation depend? First, upon an interest *in discriminating between the doings of some other individual and the present deeds of one's own organism;* and, secondly, upon an interest in seeking, through a per-

[1] The word *between*, be it noticed, is used here, and in what follows, in the generalized technical sense explained in Lecture II of this series.

sistent process of trial and error, to find a new course of action which, when discovered, shall constitute *a modification of the former deeds of one's own organism in the direction of the deeds of one's model.*

It will be seen at once that the accomplishment of an act of imitation, whereby I modify what I formerly could do, so as to be able to conform to my fellow's act, is essentially a construction of something that lies, in a technical sense, *between* the acts of my model, and what were formerly my own acts. Apart from my model, I already tended to act thus or thus. Under the influence of my model, I tend to approach his way of acting. *But I never merely repeat his act.* Imitation is a kind of experimental origination, a trial of a new plan, the initiation of a trial series of acts. The result of imitative efforts is that the world comes to contain a sort of action which lies *between* two former ways of action, in such wise that, if you regarded these two former ways of acting as equivalent to each other, the new way would be equivalent to both. Meanwhile, by being interested in the new act as in something different from both its predecessors, you define for your own consciousness, in a clearer way, the difference of these predecessors from one another. The result is, that the world of your consciousness wins a new expression of the relation of the One and the Many. For here, as in our former discussion of the relation of *between*, it appears that the original, and puzzling, diversity between the imitator and the model has, by the interposition of the imitative act between these prior courses of action, come to appear as a *diversity of stages in the same series.* The triad, formed of the three terms, — (1) the original activities of the imitative being, (2) the activities of the model, and (3) the imitative act itself, — is now a triad of connected members whereof the third lies between the two others. The finite world has hereby won a new consciousness of the unity of its own life.

Any individual Self grows, however, by means of very numerous imitations of many models. Every new act of imitation has this character of interposing a new intermediary between a pair of facts that, apart from the imitation, would have appeared less related. The result is that the new Individual, the life of the empirical human Self, comes to be, in one aspect, *a series of results of intermediation*, a more or less systematic establishment of new terms whereby triads are constituted. Every *result* of imitation tends, however, to the establishment of recurrent processes, whereby the new sort of action, once discovered, tends to repeat itself indefinitely in new acts of the same sort. For the mark of the will that has once discovered its own purpose is that its activities assume the recurrent form. Hence, in initiating new acts, the imitative activity tends to the establishment of new forms of recurrent self-expression.

In addition to this more definite experimental search for new forms of activity by means of imitative adjustments to the social environment, and in addition also to the recurrent activities whereby a growing individual shows that he has discovered *what to do*, and so seeks novelty only in the form of the new terms of a self-representative series, we find, indeed, in the life of any growing self, a still vaguer process of *growth through mere trial and error.* And in the early life of any mind, as well as in our maturer life whenever we are in the midst of very novel conditions, this process plays a large part. In this case, a being, as yet unconscious of a plan, and too ignorant or too unfortunate to find the right social models to guide him, acts *at random* in accordance with his instincts, until by mere happy accident he discovers a plan, which he then begins to pursue in recurrent fashion. This is in a great measure what happens when a child gradually learns to creep, stand, walk. This way of acquiring new habits by a wholly or partly non-imitative adjustment to the environment, has been studied by psychologists even more than the more complex processes of imitation. It is in this way that we vaguely look for new ideas, find our way in new places, help ourselves in learning new arts such as bicycling, and so on. Yet we always prefer the imitation of social models to this vaguer sort of wandering whenever social guidance is possible.

It is to be noted, however, that even here the new adjustment is learned by a process of finding constantly something new that stands *between* our former course of action and our vaguely appreciated goal. We are dissatisfied. That means, so far as we are conscious, that we find ourselves doing something, and conceive vaguely, in the yet unknown future, a way of acting that would satisfy if we could find it. Our course, hereupon, is to seek something *between* that unknown goal, and ourselves as we are. This something, as soon as found, tends to satisfy the will as an effort, even if it leaves us disappointed with the result.

All our finite striving thus includes a creation of new intermediaries between the starting-point and the goal, by imitation where that is possible, by random attention to new facts where such is our only course.

The evolution of a new Self, in the realm of our own conscious life, thus involves, at every step, just the contrast between the two finite ways of viewing the world, and between the two sorts of resulting series, — just the contrast, I say, which we studied so extensively when we compared the structure of the World of Description and the World of Appreciation. *Either*, namely, one has already found out, according to one's lights, what to do, *or else* one is vaguely trying to discriminate, in the vast background which constitutes the world, the facts whose union into series, through the establishment of intermediaries, will give one a comprehension of what one's environment is, a sense of how the One and the Many are related, and so an insight into what one has to do. In the *first* of these two ways of dealing with one's world, one is already, as far as one's consciousness goes, possessed of one's plan as a Self. One's life then consists in *doing again and again* what, according to one's conscious plans, one has to do, and in thereby winning new stages of self-representative life. But in the *second* case, one is receptive, rather than freely constructive; is searching; and succeeds, if at all, only by an experimental interpolation of new terms in given series of discriminated facts. The union of these two tendencies leads to a constant differentiation of new stages of self-consciousness. The principal source of the novel forms of self-expression is the *second* of the two tendencies.

The first tendency leads to the sort of novelty in results that the number-series has illustrated.

So much for the two processes, so far as we can observe them within the limits of our human consciousness. I now make the wholly tentative hypothesis that *the process of the evolution of new forms of consciousness in Nature is throughout of the same general type as that which we observe when we follow the evolution of new sorts of plans, of ideas, and of selfhood in our own life.* And, as the general evidence for the worth of such an hypothesis, I point out the following facts.

The types of life that are phenomenally known to us in Nature, form series such as indicate a gradual evolution of new forms from old. A new individual life, so far as we observe, in the outer world, the signs of its presence, is a new way of behavior appearing amongst natural phenomena. This new collection of functions comes to be manifested to us gradually. In the process of heredity, its generation involves, in a vast number of cases, the phenomena which our science interprets as the sexual union of cells that represent previously living individuals. As a result of this union of sexual elements, tho cell from which the new organism developes has, in all this class of cases, characters that lie *between* those represented by the parent cells. The resulting organism consequently has characters, and accordingly developes functions, that lie *between* those of formerly existing organisms; and so the new living individual is at once a new link in the series of the possible forms of its type, and an individual variation of its species. In these respects, *sexual generation is analogous to the process of conscious imitation.* For imitation (not, to be sure, in the case of a whole organism, but in the case of a single voluntary function) means that a new process results from the conscious union of the influence of *two* previous processes; and in case of imitation, as we have just seen, the new process lies *between* the original processes. Thus the conscious union of former types of activity, in the very act that, while uniting, discriminates them, results in a new sort of intermediate activity. A corresponding union of *two* elements, with a resultant that lies *between* formerly existent beings, characterizes sexual generation.

But in another class of cases, new living individuals, as they are phenomenally known to us, result *asexually.* Here the processes involved are sufficiently typified, for our present purposes, by the very process of *cell-multiplication* from which any new organism always results. All such processes are, in form, relatively recurrent. Novelty, where it becomes notable at all in the course of such processes, depends upon the massing of the results of former stages of this same recurrent process. So it is, in part, when the multiplying cells of a new organism undergo differentiation just because the newer cells find their places in a whole which is formed of all the previous cells, and so adjust themselves to an environment different from that in which the earlier cells grew. *But this whole process is analogous, in structure and in result, to the recurrent processes of the conscious will that has found what it has to do,* that does it again and again, and that reaches novel results in a way which the counting process has most clearly illustrated for us. Whether such novel results are significant, depends on the grade of significance that the special will, whose expression we observe, has reached. But such recurrent processes are, as we have seen, the normal ones of the World of Appreciation. They are known to us, in our own consciousness, as the source of a particular sort of novelty in the *results* of conduct. They lead to Well-Ordered series of self-expressions.

But further, the new living individuals, in their development, largely illustrate what we call the process of gradual *adaptation to the environment* by novel forms of structure and function. Here again the character of the enormously complicated organic processes involved is still analogous to a process that we observe in consciousness, viz. *to our conscious process of learning new arts through trial and error.* The series of facts that we observe in the living beings are, in this type of instances, on the whole, non-recurrent. The process is one of interpolating new terms in a series of stages that lie between the original condition of the organism, and a certain ideal goal of perfect adjustment to the environment which the individual organism never reaches.

So far then, for certain analogies between the evolution of new living beings in the phenomenal world, and the evolution of new forms of selfhood in conscious life. But now for one more analogy, and one that relates to that most critical phenomenon, the death of an organism, and to the temporal cessation of a given process of conscious striving.

The discriminating tendency that, in our consciousness,

gives rise to the conceptions of the World of Description, is always, as we have seen, one of *two* contrasting tendencies that our finite relation to our world determines. Of these two tendencies, this is the subordinate one, which yields to the tendency to recurrent expression of our already established Purpose, whenever we know what to do. So far as we conceive our world in terms of the will that is now explicit in us, we do not need to give ourselves over to the discrimination of new phenomena, and we do not do so. Descriptive Science is secondary to life, and the scrutiny of that world "in the background," in search of novelties, ceases whenever we are absorbed in what seems to us triumphant self-expression. This is true even when the will which seems to itself clearly conscious of what it has to do, and of how to do it, is in fact of what we have to call a relatively low grade. For in us the will can be base in content, even when it is in form to a great extent of the higher type.

Consequently, our discriminative activities, and also our imitations, our processes of trial and error, and all our tentative seekings after greater clearness, are subject to *the often rigid selection exerted by our already established conscious plans of recurrent action*. Or, as they say, *practical* motives predominate in our life. We make these tentative efforts for the sake of establishing new plans of action wherever we lack plans. But when we have plans, already accepted, the tentative establishment of new courses of action *between* stages already existing, is permitted only in so far as it does not run counter to these already established plans.

Well, just so, in Nature, the variations of organic life

that get established by means of the processes analogous (as we have just seen) to those of trial and error, and to those of imitation, are subject to a rigid selection on the part of the "environment." But the "environment," according to our own interpretation of Nature, stands, as an environment with already established characters, *for the expression of such portions of the Nature-life as have already won the habitual, that is, the more or less definitely and permanently recurrent form*, wherein a relatively persistent will to act repeatedly in the same way has become characteristic of the finite consciousness that we suppose to be represented by the natural phenomena in question.

In view of this analogy, I suggest that the evolution of new Selfhood in our own conscious case, and of new forms of life in Nature, is a process subject everywhere to the same sort of selection, whereby new tendencies are accepted or rejected according to their relation to preëxistent tendencies. The evolution of new Selfhood, as I conceive the matter, is rendered possible *by the fact that a finite form of conscious life may have a twofold relation to the Absolute*, and so may seek the truth and its own self-expression in a twofold way,—a more active and definite course of self-expression, or a more tentative one of discovery. That is, it may grow *either* by performing, in recurrent fashion, over and over, the type of action that it has already come to regard as its own form of Selfhood, *or else* by adopting the discriminating attitude that gives us, in our own conscious life, our conceptions that together make up our view of the World of Description. When a consciousness adopts the latter of these two attitudes, what happens within the unity of its sphere of experience is the appearance of new contents that lie *between* previously recognized contents, or that lie, as tentative expressions of its will, between itself and the goal. *These new expressions of purpose are tentative, like our trials and errors, or like our imitations.* When they are successful, they so mass themselves as to form definite centres of new experience. By emphasizing the contrast between the Self that has created or discovered them, and the rest of the world, they then suggest plans of action, which become recurrent, so long as they survive. But when they suggest nothing that permanently accords with the established habits of the Self within which they arise, *they are unadapted to their environment, and so pass away.* A rigid selection presides over their persistence. It is the selection established by the more persistent habits, and conscious intents, of the finite Self to which they belong. The portion of Nature where these tentatively adopted new forms of life phenomenally appear to us, we call the Organic World.

But now these new creations, if they survive, are not the mere contents of another and larger consciousness. They are also processes occupying time, and embodying will; they are themselves finite conscious purposes, having an inner unity, a relation to the Absolute, of which they also are *ipso facto* partial expressions, and a tendency to adjust themselves to the goal in their own way. If, as in case of the conscious Self of any one of us, they become aware of this their own relation to the Absolute, then they no longer survive or pass away *merely* in so far as they serve the larger purpose that originally invented them as tentative devices of its own. They then, like all finite purposes of self-conscious grade, *define their own lives as individually significant, conceive their goal as the Absolute, and their relations to their natural sources as relations that mean something to themselves also.* Their destiny thus becomes relatively free from that of the finite Self within which they first grew up.

Thus indeed the natural generation of an organism would be the mere phenomenon of a process of creating new stages *within* the life of previously existing Selves. But the new stages might become significant *for* themselves, with their own time-span, their own relations to the Absolute, and their own sort of selfhood. Originally I, as this Individual, coming into existence at this point of time, might result from an organic process that phenomenally represents how a finite Selfhood, much vaster than mine (let us say the Selfhood of the human race as a whole) established in a tentative and experimental way, within its own conscious life, a new process that was serially interpolated *between* the processes represented by the reproductive cells of my parents. This was, for the race, merely a tentative variation in its life-series, due to the same sort of interest that, in our imitative life, makes us interested in trying the effect of creating a new sort of function intermediate between two previous ones, or to the same sort of scrutiny of the world that leads us to make new experimental discriminations in our scientific thinking. Had this variation been inconsistent with the habits of action already established in Nature, I should not have survived. Just so, a useless imitation, or a new idea inconsistent with established ideas, is erelong abandoned. But having survived, I have entered, with all the instincts of my race, into the social order. On one side of my nature I am thus a resultant. My conscious interests were originally narrowed by the act that determined my place in the series. Hence I am primarily constituted by a series of interests in a small group of facts, and am relatively inattentive to all the rest of the universe. But *within* my narrow span I can still learn about universal truth, because, after all, I am a conscious process, and every such process is really linked to all the world. But when once I become *aware* that my little form of willing also is a hint of an Absolute truth, I know myself as in intent this Individual in the World. And now I have indeed a character that may well survive, that in fact *will* survive, all the organic processes which were originally expressed in my life as this variation of the human stock. For in God, I am this seeker after God, so soon as I know myself as a Self at all, and, as such a seeker after God, I no longer wholly depend on the finite Self *within* which I came into being, just as my organism, even in its physical functions, no longer depends on the parent organisms.

By precisely such processes, the evolution of new life everywhere in Nature would be, upon this hypothesis, explicable. Selves would always originate within Selves, but, as related to the Absolute, would be capable of surviving the finite experimental purposes for which they were originated. Their natural origin would be perfectly consistent with an immortal destiny, just because all facts in the world, however originated, have teleological relations with the Absolute, and because, whatever life includes an explicit seeking for its own selfhood is in *conscious* relations with the Absolute.

The appearance of *new* Individual Selves would be, however, when temporally considered, a genuine fact. And their source would be the one that in ourselves enables us to vary the plans of our Will through the tentative play of the Discriminating Attention. And thus, in completing the sketch of our hypothesis regarding the interpretation of Nature and Evolution, we have brought this hypothesis into definite relation to our former contrast between the World of Description and World of Appreciation. This contrast appears, not merely as a fact of our own consciousness, but as a consequence of a tendency that is responsible, in Nature, for the whole process of Evolution. What in us appears as the conflict between science and practical life, is an example of the struggle for existence in Nature.

VI

That the Self whose natural relations have been so definitely admitted, is, like any other phenomenon in Nature, a proper object for the investigations of any external observer who is interested in explaining the occurrences of his life in terms of Causation, is now plain enough. An external observer of a human Self, as expressed in the behavior of the phenomena of its organism, may be a psychologist. If so, he will be interested in explaining how any human Self appears as a resultant of temperament, heredity, training, and the rest, and how his life is subject to law. To treat the Self thus, is to make its life an object in the psychologist's own World of Description. The undertaking will be as much justified as any other undertaking of science. To an external observer who seeks to win his purposes as a student of science, the individual Self, and all its temporal deeds, must be viewed as facts to be explained, in so far as that is logically possible, through their causal connections with previous facts, and with the whole of Nature. Such an observer, in so far as he deals with the World of Description, can recognize no deed of the Self as a mere outcome of free will. Every describable character of the Self, its temperament, its motives, its impulses, its training, its knowledge, its deeds, will appear to this observer as causally explicable by heredity and by environment. In so far as these aspects of the Self are not yet explained by science, they will still be inevitable and proper *problems* for causal explanation. Science, whether physical or physiological or psychological, will remorselessly and unceasingly pursue the end of making man, the natural being, comprehensible to the understanding of man, the observer of Nature. And this undertaking will be strictly rational. When we admit all this, do we not endanger our own doctrine of the freedom of the Individual Self?

I answer: No, for this very undertaking will have as its sole justification the fact that the teleological structure of Being gives warrant for holding that the true purposes of our descriptive science are, as far as that is logically possible, actually expressed by the universe. Man, as the observer of Nature and of man, has a purpose, and a very profound purpose, in trying thus to comprehend in causal terms his relation to Nature and to his fellows. We know from earlier lectures what this purpose is. This purpose, according to our view, must be capable of some relatively final expression, viz. of the very expression, which our science now begins and unweariedly prosecutes, but which no merely mortal toil will ever finish. Hence it is true that human nature, down to the least externally describable detail of its temporal fashion of expressing itself, is a natural phenomenon, a part of universal Nature, and is as much capable of some kind of explanation in causal terms as is any natural fact. But, on the other hand, this very way of viewing man sets to itself its own limits, viz. the limits of the World of Description. For, in the first place, thus to view man is not to view him as he consciously views his own inner life, that is, as possessing Internal Meaning. To explain man in causal terms is to view him as an external observer sees or might see him; and not as he himself means to be when he expresses his will in his deeds. Hence what you never causally explain about a man is precisely his primary character as a Self, namely, his conscious meaning itself, in so far as it is his. And secondly, all causal explanation has to do with the types and the describable general characters of events, and never with whatever is individual about events. For the individual, as we saw in our foregoing series of lectures, is the indefinable aspect of Being. But what you cannot define, you cannot explain in causal terms.

And so, to sum up, — that I now have this character, and this environment, and that I am subject to these or these consequences of my past experience, you can undertake to explain causally. Yes, whatever about my words, my deeds, my manner, my mood, my feelings, or my plans, is describable as a feature common to me and to any other being in the world, — whatever then there is about me which is expressible in general terms, or which is capable of being externally observed, you can and must undertake, with rationality, to explain causally as due to my ancestry, training, circumstances, environment, and dependence upon Nature in general. But what remains causally inexplicable is precisely my Being as this individual, who am nobody else in God's world. Now my individuality is not in the least separable from what the Scholastics would have called my "common nature." My individuality means simply, that my innumerable common traits are teleologically expressed in this internally determinate but externally undetermined unique life which is now mine, and which, if I have a personal ideal, is to be mine until I have come to my full and final embodiment as this one of God's individuals. And so once more, if you ask me what, in my present consciousness, expresses not the separable portion, but that inseparable *aspect* of my nature which neither God nor man can causally explain, then I answer: *Just my conscious intent to be, in God's world, myself and nobody else.* In this sense alone my life, not as that of an Independent Being, but as the life expressing a rational purpose to win an unique relation to all the universe, an unique contrast with all other Selves, or if you will, an unique instance of dependence upon all the rest, is now, and will always continue to be causally inexplicable and irreducible. For the unique as the unique is not the common nature as such; and only the common nature of things can be causally explicable.

VII

So much then for the causal relations of my Selfhood. "But," you may insist, "is not my unique and individual nature, if not causally determined, still teleologically determined by that very relation to the whole upon which my existence as this individual depends? How can our doctrine speak of the will and of the individuality of the Self as in any sense free, and still recognize that unity of the world and of the divine plan upon which our whole theory depends?"

To answer this objection I must indeed still further repeat considerations sketched in our former series of lectures, and must afresh apply them to the Self. Let us return therefore, as we close, to our former teleological view of the universe, and to the relation between God's inclusive will and the various individual wills. Here I can only emphasize, in the form of replies to objections, a theory whose basis has been fully stated in our general Theory of Being.

In answer, then, to this whole view of mine, you still may say, "In so far as this my will is God's will, and is related to the whole, it is God and not my private Self that wills me to be what I am." I reply, The divine act whereby God wills your individuality to be what in purpose and meaning it is, is identical with your own individual will, and exists not except as thus identical.

"Yet has not the oneness of Being been so explained,

by our idealistic theory, as to imply that every life, *i.e.* every fact in the universe, is so related to every other, that no fact in the universe could be altered without some consequent alteration of every other fact? For this was the earliest generalization reached by our Idealism in our criticism of the realistic doctrine. Now if there are thus no Independent Beings, how can there be in any sense Free Beings? And if I am so related to the world that a change in the universe beyond me would alter whatever I am, then am I not dependent upon the rest of the universe for whatever I am? Upon this idealistic theory, is not the teleological determination of every fact in the universe by every other fact a reciprocal determination? But is not such reciprocal determination absolute? Is not then every individual fact in this idealistic world so determined in its purpose by the purpose of every other that nothing undetermined, nothing free, is anywhere left?" So the objector may state his case.

Hereupon I respond, In the very reciprocity of my relations to all else in the universe lies the very assurance that I possess a certain true and significant freedom. The world beyond me can say to me, "Were I to change, you would change, and become in some sense another, both in your experience and in your purpose." All this is true. But in turn I can reply, to the whole universe, natural and spiritual, Aye, but if my individual will changed, if I chose to be another than what I am, you, O world, just because of the universal teleology of your constitution, would be in some wise another, and that in every region of your Being. For you are no more truly independent of me and of my will than I am of you and of your might. However slight the change that I can make, I still do make a difference, by my will, to all beings in heaven and earth. And if I, in my individual capacity as this being, do not create the other beings, just as truly can one say that, in my individual character, they do not create me. Upon precisely such a consideration as this, our whole argument for Idealism itself was founded.

"Yes," you may insist, "but according to this doctrine, God's will creates us all alike, and in some sense (viz. from the Eternal point of view), all *at once*, so that we various beings of the world are equally creatures of the one plan." I respond once more, The very essence of our whole theory, as we already saw in the closing lecture of the foregoing series, is that the categories, whether of causation or of teleological dependence, however they are conceived, are inevitably secondary to the fact that the world exists, in its wholeness and in every fragment and aspect of its life, as the positive embodiment of conscious will and purpose. Now to say that another either causes or teleologically determines me, is to say, at bottom, that my life expresses a purpose that is in some sense different from my purpose, or that is in some sense *not* my own private or individual purpose. But to say this is to point out what indeed is true of every aspect of my life that can be reduced to my relations with Nature and with my fellows, and with whatever else the world beyond me contains. Now all this my dependence upon other beings is not only true, but is desired and intended by my own purpose itself whenever my purpose is rational. For, as our idealistic argument from the very outset has maintained,

I can purpose at all only by purposing that my will should find its expression in what is Other than myself, and consequently in what, in some sense, gives my will its own determination as a will that lives in this world of other life than my private life. That I depend for my life and meaning upon life not my own, is as true as that I am I at all. That this dependence involves a temporal origin, is due to the very nature of Time. The question is whether I *wholly* thus depend. And our answer has been that there is that about me which makes my will, as the will of an individual, not wholly the expression of other purposes than my private or individual purpose. This answer has been based upon our whole Theory of Being. If now I, the individual, exist, in one aspect, as the expression of nobody's will but my own, does this assertion in the least conflict with our other assertion that I and all beings exist as the expressions of the divine will? I answer: There is no conflict; for the Divine Will gets expressed in the existence of me the individual only in so far as this Divine Will first not merely recognizes from without, but includes within itself my own will, as one of its own purposes. And since God, for our view, is not an external cause of the world, but is the very existence of the world in its wholeness as the fulfilment of purpose, it follows once more that my existence has its place in the Divine Existence as the existence of an individual will, determined, just in so far as it is this individual will, by nothing except itself.

The problem then of my freedom is simply the problem of my individuality. If I am I and nobody else, and if I am I as an expression of purpose, then I am in so far free just because, as an individual, I express by my existence no will except my own. And that is precisely *how* my existence expresses, or results from, God's Will. That this same existence of mine also has, besides its individuality, its dependence, its natural relations, its temporal origin, means that I am not only I, but also the Self along with all other Selves. But that the One Will of God is expressed through the Many individual wills, — this results from that view of the relation of the One and the Many which our former series so extensively discussed. Simple unity is a mere impossibility. God cannot be One except by being Many. Nor can we various Selves be Many, unless in Him we are One. To know just this is to win the deepest truth that religion has been seeking to teach humanity.

LECTURE VIII

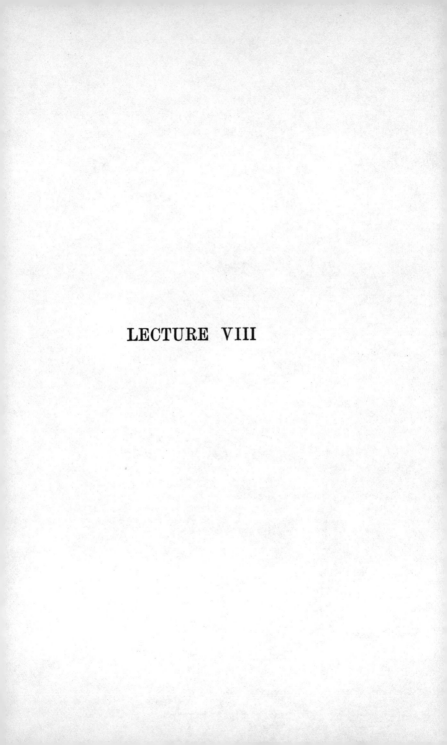

LECTURE VIII

THE MORAL ORDER

In dwelling at such length, in the third lecture of the present series, upon the contrast between the Temporal and the Eternal aspects of Reality, I was dealing not merely with one of the most frequently misunderstood issues of philosophy, but with one of the most practical of the concerns of life. For in this contrast, and in the unity which underlies it, is involved the solution of the most perplexing problem with which the ethical consciousness of humanity has to deal. I call this problem the general question concerning the sense in which the world is a Moral Order. Our Idealism has declined to accept the world as a real fact merely given, in advance of an analysis of the sense in which the world is to be real. When we therefore now assert that the real has this or that character, our undertaking depends upon a previous analysis of what it is *to be real*. *To be*, we have said, means *to fulfil a purpose*, in fact, to fulfil in final, individual expression, the *only* purpose, namely, the Absolute purpose. Our closer study has shown us that this Absolute purpose is not only One, but also infinitely complex, so that its unity is the unity of many Wills, each one of which finds its expression in an individual life, while these lives, as the lives of various Selves, have an aspect in which they are free, in so far as each, while in many aspects determined, is still in its own measure a determiner of all the rest. We have also further seen that, in so far as we mortals can undertake at all to conceive the expression of the Absolute Purpose, this expression is in one aspect Temporal, in so far as there is a process which has successive stages, such that some are *no longer*, and others *not yet*, *when* the present stage of the world-process is. In another aspect, as we have seen, the same world-process is Eternal, in so far as the whole of it is viewed at one glance by the Absolute, precisely as we view the whole of any brief rhythmic succession at a glance whenever we observe such successions. That the world has all these interrelated characters at once, we assert, yet not because we *first* recognize that all these characters are given as mere data in a realistic realm, so that only *then* we proceed to try to unify them after admitting their independent Being. No, we assert these various aspects of the world to be real only in so far as we can see that hereby purpose is fulfilled. Hereby each of these characters is deduced from our general concept of Being, as that concept is illustrated by our experience. *One* is the Absolute, because in *mere* multiplicity there would be no finality of insight. *Many* is the Absolute, because in the interrelationships of contrasted expressions of a single Will lies the only opportunity for the embodiment of wholeness of life, and for the possession of Self-consciousness by the Absolute. For the mystic long ago showed us that simple Oneness meant Nothingness. *Individuals* are all the various expressions of the Absolute, in so far as they are Many; just because, where the One is individual, every aspect and element of its self-expression is unique. *Free*, in its own degree, is every individual will amongst all the wills that the world-life expresses, because every such will, as unique, is in some respect underivable from all the others. *Temporal*, is the world order, because, so far as we can know, time is the universal form of the expression of Will. *Eternal* is this same world order, because past, present, and future time equally belong to the Real, and their Being implies, by definition, that they are present, in their wholeness, to the final insight. And Time, surveyed in its wholeness, is Eternity.

So far, then, we have merely developed our central concept of Being, and have attempted to interpret experience in the light of this concept. But now we assert that this world which we have been characterizing is a Moral Order. In what sense, and for what reason, do we assert this?

I

Despite the general exposition and defence that the ethical aspects of our conception of Being received in the former series of these lectures, and despite the frequent illustration that this same aspect has already received in the present series, it still seems necessary to face, more carefully than heretofore, familiar objections which, as experience shows, are sure to be directed against such a view as ours, whenever it is considered with reference to the moral consciousness of man. These objections, as I conceive, are founded upon a failure to grasp our doctrine of Being in its wholeness. Persistently dwelling, now too exclusively upon this and now too abstractly upon that aspect of our theory, and neglecting to regard the meaning of all its aspects together, an objector finds it easy to say, sometimes that the universe which we depict is not sufficiently fixed and final in its form of Being to meet the demands of common sense, and sometimes that it is far too fixed and moveless in its type of Being to leave room for any genuinely moral activity. We have defended ourselves against Realism. Have we found sufficient room for the demands of a strictly ethical Idealism? We have maintained the unity of Nature and of Mind. Have we escaped from the danger of making our moral activities the mere incidental phenomena that help to express our own predetermined individual nature? We have vindicated the uniqueness of every human Self. But have we given the Self any sufficiently significant moral task to perform in the universe? We have insisted upon the finality and perfection of the whole life of the Absolute Self? But have we succeeded as yet in rescuing the individual Selves from being mere expressions of a preëstablished harmony? We have assigned both to rigid and unchangeable natural law and to causal determination, a very subordinate place in the universe. But have we avoided a result equivalent to a sort of ethical fatalism? I conceive that, even after all that precedes, such objections will not infrequently be urged by some who may have followed so far our course. The answer, however, to every such objection lies at present extremely near. Our fuller statement, regarding the relations of the temporal and the eternal aspects of Being, has only to be applied to the present issues in order to lead at once to a recognition of the way in which all these ethical doubts are to be met.

For the moment, however, I must give the ethical objector the word. He shall undertake to show what he means by calling the world a Moral Order. He shall attempt to show that the world which we have been depicting is not a Moral Order, or is not a complete and sufficient Moral Order. We shall then see how, from our point of view, such objections are to be met. And first, then, what is a Moral Order? And secondly, has our Idealism place for such a Moral Order?

II

"A Moral Order," our objector may first maintain, "depends upon recognizing not only that Selves exist, but that they so exist that they can do good or evil of their own accord, and by means of their own free will. In a true Moral Order, there is indeed law and control present in the universe; but each Self has its own sphere. And within this sphere the Self is not merely an unique voice in a symphony whose divine perfection is preëstablished, but an agent in a realm where one not only can go right but also can err, and where perfections are attained, if at all, by means of the will of the individual. In a Moral Order there can be true progress. But progress, where it has an ethical meaning, involves the production of what never existed before, — of the novel, and not merely of the absolute, of the finite, and not merely of the divine. Moreover, in a Moral Order, any ethical agent can say, 'It is not yet foreordained what I shall accomplish. I must find that out by my own work.' The ethical agent must also be able to say, 'I am needed. Even God needs my help. Without my doing of the right, something would remain forever undone.' The salvation of the individual moral agent must depend in part upon his own free choice. However the divine will may coöperate in the moral world, it is open to the free agent to choose whom he will serve. Above all it is essential, for every moral view of the universe, to conceive that the world can be made better than it is. There is thus an essential opposition, for the moral, even if not for the metaphysical consciousness, between the predicate *ought to be*, and the predicate *is*. Perfection, in the moral sense, is something still to be sought, it cannot be merely found. *The best world for a moral agent is one that needs him to make it better.* The purely metaphysical consciousness in vain, therefore, says of the good, *It is*. The moral consciousness insists upon setting higher than every such assertion the resolve, *Let it be*.[1] The moral consciousness declines to accept, therefore, any metaphysical finality. It rejects every static world. It is dynamic. Nowhere could it say, 'I have found that what is is altogether good.' Its watchword is, 'Grow better and make better.'

"But now," the objector may continue, "this your idealistic world lacks these essential characteristics of a true Moral Order. In your world everything, including all of what you call the free acts of the moral agents, — everything is present at one glance to the Absolute. And, for the Absolute, no other world than

[1] See Mr. Wm. Salter's *Ethical Religion*, p. 13, for an eloquent expression of this attitude.

this one is, or in concrete truth can be. For in this world in its wholeness, the Absolute purpose, by your hypothesis, is embodied. Therefore, the whole, when viewed as a whole, is seen to be static, fixed, changeless. The individual agent knows at any instant, first, that what he really means, even in his blindness, is identical with the Absolute Will. He knows, then, that he can neither produce what ought not to be, nor create by his own deed a needed good that ought to be, and that, without his coöperation, would never come to be. For his deed, as your theory teaches, is never anything but one of the incidents in the process through which the Absolute wins the eternal perfection. The individual agent therefore does not find that the world needs him to make it better, except in the one sense, that, according to you, the world is indeed certain to have one of its own incidental finite perfections embodied in whatever the individual agent does. Your moral agent, so called, is therefore unable to sin, or to go wrong, or to be less, at any temporal moment, than he should be.

"Were he other than he is, then, as you maintain, the whole world would indeed also be other than it is. But, according to you, the world, as known to the Absolute, is known as a world that fulfils the Absolute purpose, and that, in so far, cannot be other than it is. Hence, once more, despite all that you have said about uniqueness and freedom, the individual is certain to be, in his own place, best as he is, whatever he is. And your Idealism is therefore, in its optimism, unable to give any genuine moral meaning to life. For in making *whatever is*, the final fulfilment of purpose, you have wholly lost sight of that contrast between *what is* and what *ought to be*, upon which all the moral consciousness depends. Your unique voices in the divine symphony are no more the voices of moral agents than are the stones in a mosaic. And if you relieve the individual from absolute causal determination, you do not relieve him from a fatalism none the less all embracing. You relieve him from absolute causal determination by saying that the purpose to explain him by taking account of his relationships to other beings, is always a purpose of somebody else, of some finite observer who is external to the being explained; and you say that this external purpose of the causal explainer of any agent's life is limited, as to its success, by the fact that this individual agent himself is unique, and that therefore, in some aspect, he is always incapable of being explained through any knowledge of his heredity, or of his environment, or of anything which is not himself. Now suppose that all this is granted. Still, by your idealistic hypothesis, any individual agent, if not explicable by means of anything external to himself, is still included in a perfect whole in such wise that he constitutes, despite his uniqueness, an organic part of that perfect whole. From this fate, according to you, he cannot escape. You have said, yourself, in a former discussion, in these lectures: 'In vain do we wander in darkness. We are eternally at home in God.' According to you, then, we please God, and are ourselves pleased, in our union with God — and pleased too even with ourselves, whatever we are. And this indeed is our fate. As for foreordination in general,—your doctrine of the temporal and the eternal has still to face the ancient difficulty concerning the reconciliation of the divine foreknowledge, and the free will of man."

I have allowed the objector, so far, to state his case as well as I am able to indicate, from my own experience of such arguments, what that case is likely to be. I can answer only by pointing out, what, to my mind, are the facts regarding the matter here at issue.

III

And first, whatever our ethical doctrine may be, we shall all agree that the moral *Ought*, in its primary sense, is a category of temporal application. However eternal the moral law may be, in its validity and in its relation to the knowledge of man or of the Absolute, it is a law whose reference is to acts, and to intended consequences of action, in so far as they follow one another in a time-sequence, or may be conceived as in such a sequence. Whoever says, "I ought to do thus or thus," stands in a present moment of time, and looks forward to a future. His present decision is to be followed by a course of action. And in a world where there were no succession, there would be no morality. Consequently, the metaphysic of conduct is subject to the same general conditions as govern the metaphysic of any time-process. But, from our point of view, as we have now seen, time has its perfectly definable place in Being. There is succession. And our view of the Eternal has place for just such real view of succession. When one asserts that the future is *not yet*, our view, equally with the view of common sense, maintains that this assertion has truth. When one also asserts that past and future, — what is *no longer* and what is *not yet*, have their place together in the *totum simul* of the eternal order as the Absolute sees it, — we have already observed how and why there is no conflict whatever between this assertion and the assertion that the past and the future are, temporally speaking, *not* present. Hence our view, in recognizing the true nature of the temporal order, and in showing the relation of this order to the eternal order, has already defined as real the general condition upon which all moral activity depends, and has asserted that this condition, namely, the temporal succession of the world's events, is as real a fact for the Absolute as for us. The difference between the human view and the Absolute's view of the temporal order is simply that, for men, only very brief series of successive events can be viewed *totum simul*, while for the Absolute, *all* events are thus viewed, while all events remain, for such an inclusive view, none the less successive than they are for us.

So far, then, as to the mere temporal form in which alone any moral activity can take place. And now, in the next place, as to the more special conditions of moral activity: Our objector has said that, in a moral world, any moral agent can either do right, or choose the wrong. We accept the statement. Let there be any moral agent, *A*. We agree with our opponent that *A* must perform any one of his moral acts at some temporal moment. The act, in order to be a moral act at all, must, despite all of the aspects in which it may be determined by the heredity, environment, etc., of the agent, still possess an aspect in which it is *not* deducible from any external conditions, but is the agent's own present deed. Moreover, in order to be a moral act, this deed must form part of a succession of intentions, and of deeds, in which the agent's own will is progressively expressed. And this individual will of the agent must be so expressed in the deeds that in some genuine respect it lies with the agent himself to determine what nothing else in the world wholly determines, namely, the right or wrong character of this deed, and its conformity or nonconformity to the standard which constitutes the Ought. All this our opponent asserts. All this, however, we too assert. And we have already in general indicated in former discussions why and how we assert just this to be true. Our present purpose is merely to develope and to apply, more specifically, the former results.

Yet now, when our opponent still insists that we have no right to assert that these characters of freedom and of relative self-determination, and of individual power to do right or wrong, belong to the moral agents of our world, we in reply might stubbornly insist, if we chose, that our opponent himself should explain in what sense he regards the freedom and the individual initiative of moral agents as real facts in his own world. We might ask him, in other words, to make articulate his view of the sense in which his Moral Order has any sort of Being whatever. In our former series of lectures, we exhaustively treated the possible meanings of the ontological predicate. Our opponent, if he is to present a rational view, must do likewise. When he asserts the moral agents to be in any sense free, or to have in any sense their individual power of initiative, he becomes responsible for an ontology. He is a realist, or a mystic, or a critical rationalist, or an idealist in his metaphysic, whatever may be the ethical contents whose Being he asserts. We long since saw, then, why he can be consistent in his ontology only in case he is an idealist. But, unless he can set aside our former argument as to the nature of Being, then, whatever his well-warranted enthusiasm for a Moral Order may be, he can assert the Being of that Moral Order only by declaring that it is real simply because the Absolute knows it to be whatever it is, and because the Absolute Will finds in just this individuality, freedom, and initiative of the moral agents, whose acts occur in time, the fulfilment of the highest purpose. Now this is precisely what we ourselves assert. And we assert it for precisely the reason that leads our opponent to assert it, — namely, because, to our view as to his, a world where the temporal succession of acts, despite all its causal connections and its countless general characters, has room for individuality and for initiative, is precisely the sort of world wherein, and wherein alone, the highest purpose can be fulfilled, and the most perfect life expressed.

Yet we shall indeed turn from this more polemic fashion of challenging our opponent to explain in what sense his Moral Order can express any Being at all; and we shall now explain, more fully, in what sense we declare that the temporal acts of individuals involve the power to go right or to go wrong, and in what sense, according to us, what *ought to be* and what *ought not to be*, can with equal possibility occur at any one temporal instant, despite, or in fact, just *because of* the eternal perfection of the whole. The true distinction, and the true connection, between the temporal and the eternal aspects of Being, furnish, in truth, the basis for a solution of this whole problem.

IV

Let us return to the individual moral agent. By his reality, as an individual being, at any moment of time, we now well know what we mean. We mean that just then there is a finite Internal Meaning, which seeks its own Other, and which, in any degree of blindness or of imperfection of insight that you please, is seeking, as this Other, the Absolute itself. We hold that this finite Internal Meaning is, furthermore, the meaning of a Self, which contrasts itself, more or less sharply, with the whole of the rest of the universe, even in seeking to find in this universe its own will expressed. So far we have, if you please so to call it, the fate of every finite Self. To seek anything but the Absolute itself is, indeed, even for the most perverse Self, simply impossible. All life is looking for God, however base the forms of idolatry beneath which the false love of the world may ignorantly hide its own meaning, at any one temporal instant. And now, however you define your moral philosophy, it is indeed true that by the Ought you mean, at any temporal instant, a rule that, if followed, would guide you so to express, at that instant, your will, that you should be thereby made nearer to union with the divine, nearer to a consciousness of the oneness of your will and the Absolute Will, than you would become if you acted counter to this Ought. Now it is enough for our present purpose that a consciousness of such a rule can arise in any Self, at the moment of a moral act. Hereupon, however, there also arises the familiar situation in which conduct counter to the consciousness of the Ought appears, to the temporal Self, to be possible.

This situation, so far as it here concerns us, in this extremely general sketch of the possibility of a Moral Order, is as follows: The Self, inevitably meaning the Absolute as that Other which it seeks to know as the Real, and inevitably seeking, also, to win union with that Absolute wherein its own final will is expressed, and to know the world as its own, and its own life as in harmony with the world, is still, as this present finite Self, conscious of its *contrast* with that world which it views as beyond its present range of experience, or as beyond the circle wherein its Internal Meaning is now consciously expressed. Common sense expresses this contrast by saying that I have one will; while the world seems to have another will, which may to any extent oppose mine. The Ought, under these conditions, comes to our finite consciousness in the form of some principle which, in general, however we may formulate it, says: "Harmonize thy will with the world's Will. Express thyself through obedience. Win thy victory by accepting thy task. The world is already thy Will absolutely expressed. Learn this truth by conforming thy deed to an absolute law." It is enough for us here that this consciousness of the Ought can and does arise; while the essence of it is that the Self is to accomplish the object of its search through obedience to an order which is not of its own momentary creation.

But, as we have said, the Self is known through a contrast-effect. Its own will, as it now is consciously present, is not yet known as in harmony with the Other wherein it inevitably seeks to find its own expression. It is always abstractly possible, therefore, for the Self to conceive its search for self-expression as simply an undertaking not to obey, but to subdue, to its own present purpose, the world which is beyond. Instead of developing its momentary Internal Meaning into harmony with its own External Meaning, it may, in its narrowness, seek to convert the latter into the former. Instead of assuming the attitude that Tennyson expresses by saying: —

> "Our wills are ours to make them thine,"

the Self may seek its self-expression explicitly in the form of rebellion. Nor is such a rebellious attitude by any means wholly evil. Conscious choice of a total evil is, indeed, impossible. For the Self, at its worst, seeks finality of self-expression, and seeks this self-expression through a life that is at once Other than its present Internal Meaning, and perfected in its form and content. Yet because the consciousness of the Self depends upon a contrast, the overcoming of the oppositions involved in that contrast, while never conceivable in an utterly evil shape, can be conceived, by the finite Self, as in conflict with what a clearer insight knows to be the Ought, since the consciousness of the Ought demands of the Self an overcoming of the opposition through a rational obedience to the law of the Absolute, while the consciousness opposed to the Ought seeks to master the world in the service of the mere caprice of the Self.

Or, to state the conflict in its simplest terms: I always will to become one with my world, and so, with God. But when I explicitly follow the Ought, I seek to transform myself as I now am into the likeness and the expression of God. And when I oppose what a clearer insight would see to be the Ought, I seek to fashion the truth after the image, and to make God the mere tool of myself as I now am. In both cases it is indeed impossible for me to avoid seeking a good, and expressing a truth as I act. For as a fact, I can only assert my finite Self by actively transforming myself; so that I actually obey, in some measure, even while I rebel. For the finite Self cannot seek its own, without passing over into new life. And there is self-sacrifice involved in even the most stubborn rebellion; and courage and endurance are exercised, unwillingly, even by the most cowardly of pleasure-seekers. The soul of goodness in things evil lies deeper than those admit who see not the tie that binds all Being in one. Even in the depths of hell the lost, if such there were, would still, despite themselves, serve God amidst their darkness. Nor can any being wander so far as to escape not only the presence, but the indwelling, of the Absolute. Moreover, even when the finite Self rebelliously seeks to subdue all Being to its own present conscious caprice, it actually expresses, in its own way, a truth. For there is indeed no life, however slight, which makes no difference to the rest of the world; nor is there any caprice, however perverse, that is not an aspect, however fragmentary, of God's perfect meaning. So that when the Self rebels, it can rebel only because the Spirit dwells in it; and when it would fashion all things to its own will, it utters a truth, viz. the truth that, in its own degree, it is the object and expression of the divine interest. But if the rebellious Self expresses thus unwillingly a truth that is already divine, the obedient Self, willingly seeking, even in what is Other, its own will, and surrendering in order that it may possess, acts willingly in accordance with a truth that is final, and is conscious of its own meaning in a form that is far more significant than the one in which the life of the rebellious Self is embodied.

Now it would belong to a system of ethical doctrine to develope what I thus only hint, namely, the positive content of the moral act, and the deeper nature of the contrast between what ought to be and what ought not to be. Here I am only interested in defining the alternative courses of action that are possible in a finite being sufficiently to show that a moral act, when once its content has been defined, can be conceived as occurring at any temporal instant, and in the life of any finite Self. But having defined the general situation which any moral agent faces, we again ask the question, Can our theory find room, in the temporal world, *for free moral choices that conform or do not conform to the Ought?* In other words, can a finite Self, knowing the Ought, in any sense freely choose to rebel or to obey? And is such free choice to do ill consistent with our theory of the perfection of the whole, and the finality of the eternal order?

V

Our question, as thus formulated, assumes several aspects, each of which must now be considered in its turn. Our own statement, in a former lecture, concerning the individuality and freedom of the finite Self, turned upon saying that in the unique whole of the Absolute life, every finite life, as related to that whole, and as one of the aspects of this whole, must be itself unique. Since this uniqueness of each finite life, in other words of each Self, is itself the embodiment of an aspect of the Absolute Will; this aspect in turn appeared as itself an unique will, not elsewhere precisely duplicated, and so as the individual will of this finite Self. As the unique cannot be wholly defined through its external relations, or deduced from them, or causally explained by means of them, we found each finite Self to be, in some aspect of its nature, free. And viewing the same facts in the light of the distinction between the temporal and the eternal, we now assert that each finite Self, in so far as it is an ethical individual, having a continuity of purpose in its life, expresses itself in a series of deeds, each one of which, as a deed that has an unique place in an unique life, is itself, in some measure and in some aspect, however slight,—free,—so that the individuality of every act sets a limit to the possibility of the causal explanation of this act by an external observer. We have now to see how this former theory of the general nature of finite and temporal freedom applies to the case of the moral act, as that act has here been defined. That every such finite freedom of action is a strictly limited freedom, we clearly see. Our question is whether such freedom is sufficient to give finite acts their needed character as a choice between what ought to be done, and what ought not to be done, by the individual agent at any moment.

Our objector may hereupon say: "What you have called the freedom of the finite Self certainly cannot be *moral* freedom. For, according to you, the Self always wills the same essential aim, namely its final union and harmony with its Other, or, in other words, its fulfilment through its oneness with the Absolute. As for the conflict between the Ought, on the one hand, and the rebellious attitude of the finite Self on the other hand, — a conflict whose decision, as you assert, constitutes the content of the moral act, — *such a conflict can depend solely upon ignorance.* The Self seeks its own realization. It *can* seek nothing else. This realization means oneness with God. No other aim is possible. But ignorance of how to reach the goal is possible in a finite being. And, according to you, the rebellious Self is thus ignorant of its own true good, and states its fragment of truth in a false form. The Self that follows what a higher insight sees to be the Ought, on the other hand, merely knows the truth, and knowing follows. Your so-called moral acts are thus *mere expressions of knowledge or of ignorance, — not of freedom.*"

To this objection I reply that, by our hypothesis, whenever an individual acts, his deed is at once, and inseparably, an act of knowledge and an expression of purpose, — an insight and a choice. And the sense in which it is both knowledge and will at once is just here best indicated by remembering the sense in which every act of will, and every process of knowledge, involves what the psychologist calls Attention. To attend, is to be at once guided in your momentary deed by what you know, and determined in your knowledge by what you do. And, as Professor James has so successfully pointed out, and as we ourselves have maintained from the outset of the present series, the central feature of every voluntary deed, the constitutive principle of every finite life, is a process of Attention. An idea arises in your mind. The idea already involves a nascent deed. Attend to that idea rather than to any other, and at once the idea, filling the whole circle of your consciousness, turns into its appropriate completed deed. In a moment of temptation, the man who has his opportunity to embezzle, begins to think of how he could misappropriate the funds intrusted to him. The idea, already possessed of its ominous Internal Meaning, comes to consciousness as already the nascent deed of a Self rebellious against what is, for a higher insight, the Ought, — against the law of honor that here binds the Self to the truth, and to the Absolute. Does the conceived deed win possession of the whole field of consciousness? Then, indeed, by what thenceforth appears to the externally observant psychologist as an altogether automatic process, the deed is carried out in the man's conduct. In other words, if the man thinks of nothing so much as of his opportunity to embezzle, then, if the opportunity also persists, and the physical power to accomplish the deed remains, he inevitably embezzles. On the other hand, if he thinks rather of the law of the obedient Self, of his honor, and of the tie that, when fully comprehended, is seen to be a tie that binds him to God, the deed remains undone, and the nascent evil Self is suppressed by the wiser Self. The only field of choice, in such a case, is therefore *the field of attention.*

But an act of attention, I repeat, is at once an act by which we come to know a truth, and an act by which we are led to an outward deed. Such outward deed may be (as in the case earlier dwelt upon in our discussion of the World of Description), a deed whereby we come to seem, to an external observer, inactive, and merely observant of our world. But such inactivity, if it be deliberately chosen, is itself a sort of activity. As a man attends, so is he, so he knows, and so too, he acts, or voluntarily refrains from action. Therefore it is vain, in case of any true choice, to separate, at just that instant, the knowledge which guides and the voluntary activity which then and there expresses this knowledge. What I potentially know, can indeed be, for any one abstract purpose, pretty sharply sundered from what I am able to do. Thus my memory has stores of possible knowledge that I do not now recall. And on the other hand, my acts could create outer objects that I have never yet made. And when one thus views the realm of what I can know, as for instance my storehouse of memories; and the realm of what I can do, namely, the possible new objects that my will could produce, knowledge and will seem far apart. But, in our present consciousness, knowledge and will are, as we long ago saw, merely two aspects of the present unity of conscious life. What we now know means whatever is at present a discriminated fact in the unity of consciousness. What we now do means whatever we win through the present expression of our purposes in knowing. But the process whereby our present knowledge alters to meet our purposes, and is known as thus altering, is the process of attention. This process involves, then, an alteration of present knowledge to suit our purpose. It also, and inevitably, involves an acting according to our present knowledge.

In the second lecture of the present series, we considered our discriminating attention in its theoretical aspect, as something relatively opposed to definite action. But this opposition, as we saw, comes to light in cases where we so far lack the knowledge that is sufficient to guide us in a definite course of action. Here, however, we have to consider attention in so far as it means *a deliberate and free dwelling upon, or ignoring of, plans of action which we are supposed already to possess.* In this case, our attention appears not in its theoretical, but in its practical aspect. This attention is our choice to narrow the field of our own consciousness in a particular way at a particular moment.

It is indeed true that, according as a man now views the relation of the Self to the world, so, just now, he acts. It is equally true that, since every conscious act is a present act of attention, which is directed to some aspect of the relation between the Self and the world, therefore, according as a man now consciously acts, so, at this instant, he comes to view this very relation between the world and his individual Self. A morally ignorant man, who has never learned the law, or conceived in some particular sense of his own higher good, we acquit of moral defect, just in so far as he acts in this so far invincible ignorance. He must first get knowledge, as we say, before he can choose the right course of acting. It does not, however, follow that his knowledge of the good, when it comes, will deprive his good deeds of their free character. For in performing any one good deed, if he acts voluntarily, he will act by virtue of his own conscious attention to the good. So long as he clearly thinks of nothing so much as of his already known relation to the world and to God, he will indeed inevitably act accordingly, and be not the rebellious, but the obedient Self; precisely as while the tempted man thinks of nothing so much as of his temptation to embezzle, he will inevitably steal whenever the opportunity offers. But, in both cases, knowledge will determine outer deed, precisely in so far as the inner deed of attention gets its purpose expressed in a particular kind of present knowledge.

To our objector we consequently here reply: According to our view, all beings, everywhere, serve the Absolute purpose precisely in so far as then and there they know that purpose. Nor can any, even the worst beings, act without in some measure relating their momentary deed to what, however blindly, they then and there know of that purpose. But, on the other hand, *all conscious beings, at any instant, know what they are conscious of, precisely in so far as they attend to an ideal.* But the act of attention of just this instant, taken together with the resulting knowledge, is peculiarly apt to be the expression of just this instant's unique, and accordingly free, will. In one aspect, as we saw before (in our second lecture), our consciousness at this instant is made narrow, our attention is centred upon just *these* facts, by virtue of conditions which we *cannot* now control. But in another aspect, our voluntary narrowing of the field of our attention, at this instant, *does* alter the range of what we now know. Now it is in *this* aspect that our attention, and so our will, can be, at any one instant, morally free. Hence when a being, by virtue of his training, and of the present grade of his consciousness, has at any instant present to him some form of the conflict between the Ought and the rebellious Self, *what he then does turns upon, and is the expression of, the way in which he then and there attends to one or to the other of the warring interests.* If he chooses to think of nothing so much as that it is just the private Self, as it now is, whose fulfilment, at any cost, he seeks, he comes to lack, in so far, the moralizing knowledge. His caprice, for himself, becomes then the only hint of the divine that tends to remain in sight. In so far as this tendency excludes everything else from sight, he forgets God as God, forgets the Ought as the Ought, and acts with a *viciously acquired naïveté.* Such a deed can never be wholly bad, simply because nothing absolutely evil exists, and because, as we metaphorically said, even in the depths of hell they still unwillingly serve God. But if, on the other hand, the attention *fixes* nothing so much as the truer relation of the present temporal Self to the Other, upon whose definition the Ought depends, then just such attention wins its expression in the obedient and self-surrendering deed. *What is in any such case done is, therefore, indeed the expression of present knowledge. But in this case the present state of knowledge is the expression of the present attention. And the attention is the will of the instant.* Our theory is, that, despite all the causal dependence of the Self upon its own past, and upon all its social and natural conditions, just this act of attention, at this temporal instant, never occurred before, and will never occur again, and is, in so far, unique, individual, incapable of any complete causal explanation, and is, in consequence, the free act of this self. And thus, despite all the objections, we vindicate for our theory the power to deduce the possibility of temporal acts that possess a true moral significance.

The sole possible free moral action is then a freedom that relates to the present fixing of attention upon the ideas of the Ought which are already present. To sin is *consciously to choose to forget*, through a narrowing of the field of attention, an Ought that one already recognizes. For while I cannot avoid acting in accordance with the Ought so long as I clearly know it, I can, through voluntary *inattention*, freely choose to forget it. And while, again, the truth as far as I know it compels my deed, I do the good freely in so far as I freely choose to *continue* my already existent attention to the already recognized truth concerning the good. All sin, then, is sin against the light by a free choice to be inattentive to the light already seen. Or again, all sin is a free choosing of the *sort* of narrowness which, in our second lecture, we found to be, in one aspect, the natural fate of the human being. That is, sin depends upon a *narrowing of consciousness*, so that a present ignorance of what one *ought to know* occurs. Now a certain narrowness of consciousness we before found to be our fate. But *freely chosen* and vicious narrowness, — a deliberate forgetting of what one already knows of God and the truth, this is of the very essence of sin. All free choice of the good, on the other hand, is voluntary persistence in attending to the good already known. Moral freedom is simply this freedom to hold by attention, or to forget by inattention, an Ought already present to one's finite consciousness. But such freedom is, upon our view, possible and actual.

VI

Yet the objector's strongest argument remains still insufficiently emphasized. "Not thus," he may say, "do you escape from the moral fatalism which was urged against you at the outset. What you have so far made out, if your argument be altogether granted, is, that, at any one point of time, a given moral agent, *A*, may freely so act, through his attentive process, as to emphasize either a false, or else a true view, of his relations to the Other that he seeks, namely, to the final expression of his whole will in the eternal order. The consequence may be a deed that a moralist will call an evil act or a good one, according as the agent decides by his choice in attending or not attending to the Ought as he knows it. But you have done well to admit that according to your metaphor, even in hell they unwillingly serve God. Those who make the hellish choice serve God ignorantly. But then, according to you, *God knows that they do so.* And in him even their own whole intent, together with the more conscious and obedient intent of those whom the moralist calls the good, is completely brought to light, and is eternally fulfilled, in an unique whole which, as you have repeatedly insisted, is such that no other fulfils or, speaking in terms of the concrete will, can fulfil, the one absolute purpose. In this unique whole, as you have also pointed out, every finite life and intent has its own individual place, a place that no other could take. And this place is, by hypothesis, a place in an absolutely perfect whole. The sinners, then, even by all their worst efforts to forget the good, cannot accomplish anything that makes the world less than perfect. Nor can the good do anything but express by their persistent attention their own consciousness that the whole is perfect. They cannot make the world better. Now where the world is such that the eternal perfection is predetermined, whatever the moral agent does, the situation is one of a moral fatalism."

I reply that here at last we reach the point where the distinction of the temporal and the eternal order becomes of most critical importance. Moral acts, as I have pointed out, occur in time. It is with reference to time, and in particular, to the time which any moral agent views as his future, that the agent himself, or any one who judges him, estimates any act as good or as ill. The free agent, whose temporal act (as an attentive choice between a persistence in knowing the Ought, and a free forgetting of Ought in favor of the evil), we have already characterized, is told by the moralist, that by his deed he can make his world better, or worse. The emphasis here is laid, and rightly laid, upon *his* world, upon the world *as he can view it in relation to his deed*, — upon an aspect of Reality as such, and not upon the eternal whole of Reality taken as a whole. The moral agent is explicitly this Self as contrasted with other Selves. He is this individual among other individuals. You cannot indeed separate him from other individuals; but you recognize him as this individual by contrasting what he intends and effects, with what other individuals intend and effect.

Now once considering the individual as acting in time, what you have a right to say to him is, that, if he intends evil results, — let us say, repeating our former example, — if he intends embezzlement, in a region of the temporal world where embezzlement is possible, and is accordingly an evil, — then, just in so far as he succeeds in carrying out his end, he produces what, at just that point of time, is indeed an actual evil. Now, in one of the lectures of our former Series, in speaking of death and similar evils, we already briefly considered how our Idealism has to view the general nature and the possibility of actual finite ills. Our examples of such ills were chosen, at that stage, not from the region of human conduct, but from our experiences of what seem to be natural ills, — ills whose source and true meaning are in large part unknown to us. Of such natural ills, death is a classic instance, and we used it, in the discussion to which I here refer, as our principal instance. Let us recall the main features of our view as there stated, reminding ourselves, for the moment, not so much of the sense in which moral ills or sins are possible, but rather of the general sense in which any evil can be said to have a place in Being.

A finite ill is a fact of experience whose fragmentariness makes our universal search for the Other, for what lies beyond, for the context, explanation, justification, and supplement of this fact, peculiarly pathetic and eager. In the most general sense of the word evil, *all* finite facts, viewed as such, are indeed evil, precisely in so far as, when taken in themselves, they have no complete meaning, and leave us in disquietude, searching still for the Other, *i.e.* for true Being in its wholeness. To this aspect of finite life we long since called attention. It is not satisfactory to be finite. On the other hand, for our view, no finite fact is a total evil, for taken in its eternal context, as aspect of the whole, it ultimately implies, demands, or, if you please, *means* all other finite facts, and forms together with them, the total life in which the Absolute Will is fulfilled. In the more special sense of the word, however, we apply the term *evil* to facts which are *so* disquieting that they especially emphasize, as it were, their own finitude and ours, in so far as our experience is confined to them. When we face such facts anywhere in the temporal order, and are conscious of them as evils, we very especially desire to change our own experience of them. This we desire, just because these facts send us so imperatively to some Other, wherein we hope to find the features by virtue of which the positive value of the world shall become plain to us. In the presence of such ills, as for instance, pain and death, we inevitably say, "If this were all, then indeed better no world at all than this one." And thus, in so far, an evil is a fact that very loudly proclaims, as it were, to our consciousness. "In me, Being in its wholeness and finality is not to be found. Elsewhere, elsewhere, lies the experience of the final truth."

Now how such ills can have any place in Being, we in a measure have seen from the very moment when, in refuting the abstractions of pure Mysticism, we first observed that unless the finite is real, the Absolute itself has no Reality. If Being is a final whole of experience, there must be that experience of which it is the whole, that striving of which it is the finality, that imperfection of which it is the completion. Or, to state the matter in less technical terms, unless the Absolute knows what we know when we endure and wait, when we love and struggle, when we long and suffer, the Absolute in so far is less and not more than we are. For all these states of ours mean something. The meaning of the world is the meaning of life, not of the lifeless; and attainment is not won except as the attainment of the goal of painful endeavors. And the more significant the endeavors, the deeper the experience of finitude, and so of evil, that they include. But nothing that is known to the finite is lost to the Absolute; and finitude is a condition for the attainment of perfection, in precisely the sense in which the temporal is a condition for the consciousness of the eternal, or, to use our former simile, precisely as the successive chords of the music are a condition of the beauty of the whole succession when it is viewed *as* a whole. What ills find their place in finite Being, and what place any particular evil finds, — these are topics for special consideration. But of ill in general, this is the idealistic theory.

But from such an indication as to the nature of ill in general, we return to the special case of moral evil. If evil in general can exist, in any finite and temporal region of our idealistic world, then evil can be the work of some finite moral agent. And this is as true for us as for our opponents. For when we call the evil the work of any agent, we mean that it expresses that agent's will, as he embodied his will at some temporal moment of his life. Now for us it is as true, as for our opponents, that the will of a finite being can win an actual temporal expression. And in consequence of what we have already said concerning the uniqueness and the individuality of the free agent's temporal act, it is quite as possible for us as it is for our opponents to conceive that a just observer, aware of the facts, could say to a given finite agent, regarding a particular ill: "This is what you have done. And but for you, and for you only, amongst all those who act in the world, this ill,—just this temporal fact that dissatisfies, never would have been."

"But," says our opponent, "according to you, the nature of Being, viewed in its wholeness, is fatally so constituted that this ill, which a given finite agent does, is so supplemented, so overcome, so included in a richer life, so taken up into the Other which this ill, even as it is, already means and implies,— that the whole is perfect despite the ill." Yes, I reply, but *how* is this ill included and reconciled within the perfect whole? Not, according to our hypothesis, by virtue of the fact that the evil deed expresses the finite agent's evil will, but *because his will is supplemented, is overcome, is thwarted, is overruled*, by what expresses some other will than his finite will was, in so far as he himself, at the moment of acting, consciously defined that will. For the supposition is that what he intended, just in so far as he opposed what he then viewed as his own interest to the world's interest, and just in so far as this deed expressed his will, was the ill, and not the Absolute life ; the finite rebellion, and not the final harmony, — the embezzlement, for instance, and not the Ought. If *per impossibile* he had won might over Being, as he did win in his own measure and time, a momentary self-expression, the whole universe would have been an ill, and in fact, since nothing finally ill can exist as a whole at all, the universe would have been destroyed. For, by the very nature of Being and of evil, every sin, in its intention is, in essence, world-destroying. For in conscious intent, as an act of choosing to narrow attention so as to ignore what ought to be known and then to act in accordance with this vicious ignorance, it is inconsistent with the very conditions which make Being as a whole possible. What the ill-doer accomplished, then, was an actual ill, and an ill that would not have been, and that need not have been, but for his individual choice in narrowing his attention as he did. And in so far as his will was effective, there was that in the universe that had to be atoned for, and thwarted. Only through the conquest over this evil-doer and his deed, is the final perfection won. His deed is related to the goodness of the whole, much as the dread that in itself is cowardly, and is destructive of courage, is related to the courage that consists in enduring and in overcoming this dread, and that in so far depends, for its very perfection, upon that dread.

In the temporal world, then, the evil-doer's will is, according to our hypothesis, possessed of a measure, both of individuality and of freedom. It is in its own time and degree morally effective. What it produces is, in its temporal reality as this act or series of finite acts, an evil. This evil is due to the evil-doer, and without his choice it need not have occurred at all. Therefore, any free moral agent, in so far as he is free, may either choose or avoid evil deeds by choosing to attend to the good that he now knows, or to narrow his attention and ignore this good. Consequently, such an agent's own world, that is, the world of the facts which express his finite will, precisely in so far as he himself distinguishes himself from all the rest of the Absolute life, — *his* world, I say, is, for our doctrine, as for our opponent's doctrine, a world which this finite agent can make worse or better if he chooses, and, within his own range of efficacy, *as* he chooses. The *means* by which he can freely do this we have seen, viz. his free attention or inattention to the good. As for the consequences of this free choice of his, they may, in a closely linked world, prove to be as grave, extended, and as lasting as temporal conditions may determine.

So much then for the possibility of free and significant moral choices of good and of ill. Consequently, as to the charge that our view is a moral fatalism, what *we* say to the moral agent is this: You act as you will, just in so far as you are free. And you are free in the before-defined sense. That is, you are free to attend or not attend to the Ought as you already, at any moment, have come to know it. If you do ill, the world-order will, indeed, in the end make good the ill you have done, and in *that* sense will make naught of your deed, — yet not because you are unable to do any ill at all, but because elsewhere, in the temporal order, other agents, seeking to overcome the disquieting ill which your will has chosen as its expression, will somewhere and somehow succeed. You yourself may, — yes, doubtless will, in the end, come to join in this self-conquering task. The moral order of your idealistic world means, then, not that no moral ill can be done, but that, in the temporal order, *every evil deed must somewhere and at some time be atoned for, by some other than the agent, if not by the agent himself*, and that this atonement, this overcoming of the evil deed, will in the end make possible that which in the eternal order is directly manifest, namely, the perfection of the whole.

Now it is decidedly the condition of a moral order that evil should be, in the end, overruled for good. And precisely this is the result that our own theory defines and necessitates. When we then say that, in the eternal order, the whole is good, we do not say that this evil-doer is wholly good, or that his deed has no ill effects, or that any fate predetermines how he shall take his place in the good order. We assert that he becomes a part of the perfect whole in so far as his evil deed is overruled for good, either by another, or later, by his individual Self.

VII

We have herewith in substance dealt with our opponent's case. We may return, however, in conclusion, to his original statements in their order as we stated them. "For the Absolute," our objector (referring to our own view of the Absolute) said, "no other world than this one is, or in concrete truth can be." Hence, as our opponent insisted, the whole, when viewed as a whole, is "static, fixed, changeless." And therefore the deed of any moral agent is powerless to change this perfect world for good or for ill. Our reply here runs that the world, seen from the eternal point of view, is indeed not *further* subject to change. Yet this is only because the eternal point of view includes in its single glance the whole of time, and therefore includes a knowledge and estimate of all the changes that finite agents, acting in time, really work in *their own world*, namely, in the temporal world that is future to their own deeds, and subject to their own will. The totality of temporal changes, forms indeed, in one sense, a static whole, namely, in so far as no *further* series of events succeeds the whole of the temporal order of succession. But in another sense our world is as full of morally significant novelties as the nature of any world in any wise permits. For at every instant of time, according to our hypothesis, something novel, significant, individual, and in its own measure free, occurs, and leads to new results for which the choices of finite moral agents are responsible.

Our objector further insisted that, for our view, "The individual knows at any instant that what he really means, even in his blindness, is identical with the Absolute Will." Our reply is that here all turns upon the sense in which the word *identical* is used. The identity of the finite and the Absolute meaning is, for us, no mere identity without difference. I now know that, however blindly I strive, I suffer, or sin, my meaning, when fully interpreted in the light of all other life, of all the events that I now ignore, of all the future through which I and my fellows are yet to pass, of all the atoning deeds that shall yet reconcile my stubborn will to God's will, and of all the acts that shall overrule for good my worst intent, — that my meaning, I say, when included in one whole with all these endless differences, is identical with God's will. But taken by myself, as now I am, I am, indeed, remote enough, in my passing consciousness, both from my own self-expression, and from my final conscious union with my Other, namely with the Absolute.

"But," said the objector, "the agent's deed, as your theory teaches, is never anything but one of the incidents in the process through which the Absolute wins the eternal perfection. Therefore your agent is unable to sin, or to go wrong, or to be less, at any temporal moment, than he should be." I respond, The conclusion does not follow. Whatever I do, in my finitude, at this point of time, is, indeed, an incident in a process. The moral question is, *What sort of incident?* Viewed in itself the incident may be an evil deed. In that case, by the very definition of evil, and because the process, in its eternal completion, is good, the incident will be one that is turned to the good only by a further temporal process of overcoming the consequences of this deed, and of atoning therefor. The agent, then, according to us, is able to go wrong and to sin. If he sins, the eternal perfection includes his condemnation and the overcoming of his evil will, just as the hero condemns and overcomes his own dread, and thereby attains the perfection of courage.

"Were the agent other than he is," urges the objector, "the whole world would, indeed, be other than it is. But according to you, the world as known to the Absolute, is known as a world that fulfils the Absolute purpose, and that in so far *cannot* be other than it is." Hence the individual, as our objector also urged, cannot, without a failure of the Absolute purpose, be other than he is, and "is certain to be, in his own place, best as he is, whatever he is."

Our answer here insists simply upon a closer examination of the situation before us. There is an agent, *A*, whose will is, in some aspect, determined by nothing external to or other than himself, as he, at some moment of time, consciously is and acts. Were he other than he is, all the rest of the universe would in some sense be altered. Now he is an element in a perfect whole. But he is so merely because, in so far as evil appears in any region of that whole, this evil, by its very nature, demands, and finds, some Other, which so supplements it that it is overruled for good. As an evil, it cannot exist in isolation. Its supplement appears in the form of deeds of atonement, reparation, control, condemnation, and in the end, fulfilment. Such deeds in general are made necessary, by the evil deed, although their actual accomplishment will involve, by our hypothesis, the expression of individuality that is in some sense or aspect other than the individuality that accomplishes the evil deed. These amending deeds will themselves, therefore, possess, in some measure, the character of free will acts. They will occur, in the temporal order, subsequently to the evil deed. They will, as common sense would word the situation, "make good" the evil done. Only by virtue of these deeds, and because in the end they not merely offer external palliations to the ill done, but so include and control the will of the evil-doer himself that he comes to be related to the whole much as the dread of the hero is to the hero's courage, — only *thus* does the evil-doer enter into and become one with the perfect whole. In himself considered, however, the evil-doer, as evil-doer, is not, for our view, "best as he is." And if he had done otherwise, just these amending, atoning, reconciling, and perfecting deeds need never have occurred. If the evil-doer replies, "Yes, but the Absolute Will wrought even in and through me when I did ill," we reply, The Absolute Will wrought in you, as Absolute Will, *in so far as it was indeed well that you, as temporal individual actor, should just then be, in your own measure, free* and individual. For freedom and individuality are aspects of every element in a perfect whole. But the Absolute Will, as such, was just what, in the evil deed, in so far as it was your free deed, you *denied* at the moment of your act; for, declining to attend to it, you made as if it were not. The amending and atoning deeds are not yours, in so far as you temporally chose the ill, but are acts either of your own Self at a later time, or of the other Selves. In brief, the Absolute Will wins through your condemnation and overcoming of your ill, and not through your coöperation, so long as, and whenever, your temporal act is not one of coöperation.

"But you lose sight," continues the objector, "of that contrast between what is and what ought to be, upon which all the moral consciousness depends." My reply here is that what ought to be and what is, can and do indeed fall asunder *at any one instant of the temporal order.*

For that is the very nature of time, viz. that what is just now, at this instant of time, is *not yet what ought to be*, but needs Another to supplement it. Therefore is time the very form of the restless, finite Will. But what ought to be at any or at every point of the temporal order, is real in the eternal order in its wholeness. The world is not *now* good, nor is Being at this instant a temporally present whole, nor does either God or man at this instant of time see what *now* is as a fulfilment, or as right. Hence the future is needed to supplement the present. Hence it is that hope springs eternal in every finite instant. Hence it also is that, as the pessimists so mournfully observe, every hope for temporal good brings always its measure of disappointment. Nowhere in time is the good finally found. It is found, as the final good, only in the eternal order.

"According to you," the objector had still insisted, "we please God, and are ourselves pleased, in our union with God, — and pleased too with ourselves, whatever we are." I respond, God is pleased, if so you wish to express the fact, and we too, in our union with God, are pleased, *with the eternal triumph of the good over the evil.* But this final satisfaction presupposes and includes just that dissatisfaction with evil, which requires that every temporal evil deed shall meet its true adjustment to the good order through the deeds of atoning efficacy, or, in general terms, through the presence of that Other which every evil deed, when once seen as evil, demands. We are indeed pleased, in our union with God, in the eternal order, to see that our own evil deeds have been overruled for good. But just herein lies the essence of the moral order of the universe, viz. in that we, too, however we wander, come in eternity freely to our home.

"Yet your doctrine," the objector finally urged, "has still to face the ancient difficulty concerning the reconciliation of the divine foreknowledge and the free will of man." My response to this last objection is that, for our Idealism this ancient difficulty simply does not exist. We do not conceive that God, first preëxisting and foreknowing, then in time creates a world that is real beyond himself, and that, in time, is subsequent in its events to his preëxistent foreknowledge. For us, *God does not temporally foreknow anything, excepting in so far as he is expressed in us finite beings.* The knowledge that exists in time is the knowledge that finite Selves possess, in so far as they are finite. And no such foreknowledge can predict the special features of individual deeds precisely in so far as they are unique. Foreknowledge in time is possible only of the general, and of the causally predetermined, and not of the unique and the free. Hence neither God nor man can perfectly foreknow, at any temporal moment, what a free-will agent is yet to do. On the other hand, the Absolute *possesses a perfect knowledge at one glance of the whole of the temporal order, present, past, and future.* This knowledge is ill-called foreknowledge. It is eternal knowledge. And as there is an eternal knowledge of all individuality, and of all freedom, free acts are known as occurring like the chords in the musical succession, precisely when and how they actually occur.

So much then for the detail of our objector's arguments, so far as we here need recall them. His general principles have before been duly met. We conclude then, that our idealistic realm is a moral order, wherein any moral agent has his place, his task, his effectiveness, his freedom, and his individual worth, and has all these just by virtue of his unity with all Being, and with God. His acts are his own, even because God's Will is in him as the very heart of his freedom. And his deeds are not indifferent to the whole universe, which wins through his free aid when he coöperates, and through the overruling of his caprice when he withstands. Yet it wins by regarding and including his freedom.

LECTURE IX

LECTURE IX

THE STRUGGLE WITH EVIL

ALL finite life is a struggle with evil. Yet from the final point of view the Whole is good. The Temporal Order contains at no one moment anything that can satisfy. Yet the Eternal Order is perfect. We have all sinned, and come short of the glory of God. Yet in just our life, viewed in its entirety, the glory of God is completely manifest. These hard sayings are the deepest expressions of the essence of true religion. They are also the most inevitable outcome of philosophy. We have by this time laid the foundation for an understanding of the sense in which all these propositions are true. In doing so we have offered our principal contribution to the interests of Natural Religion. In the bare assertion of just these truths, that appear to our ordinary consciousness a stumbling-block and foolishness, the wisest of humanity, in India, in Greece, and in the history of Christian thought, are agreed. But the philosophical problem has always been to reconcile these doctrines with reason. An idealistic philosophy, when once understood, gives to all of them its own peculiar interpretation, but then makes them seem almost commonplaces.

Yet we have still further to develope and to illustrate, in the final stage of our argument, the precise way in which these central truths are to be held and applied.

Nothing in philosophy appears more discouraging than any serious theoretical misstatement of the problem of evil. Yet nothing is more opposed to the interests of the awakened soul than to refuse every attempt to understand that problem in philosophical terms. In its purely ethical aspects this problem concerned us at the last time. In its more general relations we shall now finally consider its meaning and its bearing upon the great virtues of courage, endurance, resignation, and hope. Hereby we shall be led to the view of the Union of God and Man which shall form the topic of our concluding lecture.

I

In speaking of moral evil, at the last time, we assumed, without special analysis, and as a result of ethical doctrine, the meaning of the Ought, and the sense in which the conduct of a moral agent is to be judged as good or as evil according as it does or does not conform to the standard of the Ought. Upon the present occasion, where I shall have to deal with the general problem of evil, we shall less depend upon the special doctrines of Ethics. We shall use a more general and simpler definition of evil, in terms of our Theory of Being, — a definition which has repeatedly come to our notice. An evil is, in general, a fact that sends us to some Other for its own justification, and for the satisfaction of our will. This account of what it is to be an evil, we have now repeatedly illustrated. The account, when taken strictly, obviously applies, without exception, to every finite fact, *quâ* finite, and especially to every fact in the temporal order, when that fact is viewed in relation to its own future. Any temporal fact, as such, is essentially more or less dissatisfying, and so evil. The only question, in this regard, about any temporal event, is how great an evil it makes manifest to our experience. But that in Time there is, for the will, no conscious satisfaction, is a thesis that, according to our view, is the necessary correlative of the thesis that Time is the form of the will. The future of our experience is that region to which, in our finite dissatisfaction, we proceed, seeking therein our fuller expression. To say this is simply to affirm that Time possesses the idealistic type of Being, and no other type. If one rejects, as we do, any realistic account of Time, as of every other aspect of Being, one finds no other way than this to view the nature of Time, or to define the relations of the present to the future. For future time exists for me, in my finite capacity, either as that to which I have a conscious relation, or as that to which I have relations whereof I am just now unconscious. In the latter sense, the future time when, for instance, I shall be sleeping, or shall be dead, appears to me indeed at this moment, as a time whose order is to go on without any reference to my will; and in so far, the law that every present has its future, and that to every instant another succeeds, seems to be capable of a purely realistic interpretation. Time, when so viewed, is regarded as the fate of the world, — as the devourer, the destroyer, of whatever now is. But the reasons that led us to abandon Realism have long since led us to declare that our conscious and not our merely fatal relations to Time, are the ones that give us our only genuine glimpses of the true nature of the temporal order. And, thus interpreted, future time is that realm of Being in which my will is yet to be expressed, or in which the other finite wills that I view, through the social contrast, or through my knowledge of Nature, as contemporaneous with mine, are also yet to be expressed. But if our will is yet to be expressed, then it certainly is not yet fully expressed in our experience. And this means that our finite will is now dissatisfied. Our original idealistic formula here recurs. Were the will satisfied with its present expression in experience, the whole of Being would now be present. No Other would be or be conceived. There would be no future; for future time would have neither meaning nor place in Being. As it is, a brief abstract and epitome of every finite conscious life in the temporal world might be given in the words, "Dissatisfied with what now is, I press on towards what is yet to come."

It follows that dissatisfaction is the universal experience of every temporal being. How this dissatisfaction empirically appears, under what form, with what intensity, — this is a matter that the more concrete experience of life, taken in all its various aspects, has to decide. Vast ranges of finite ill, namely, those that are filled with physical suffering, have characters which we men are of course unable, at present, to explain in detail by any such abstract formula as the foregoing. Yet in those cases where our life is already largely under voluntary control, and where we are therefore more conscious of what life's meaning is, we are able ourselves more directly to observe that the conscious ills, which, in such cases, still beset our fortune, are in a large measure due to the very magnitude and ideality of our undertakings themselves, to the very loftiness of our purposes, and even to the very presence of our active control over our deeds. For all these more ideal aspects of our consciousness mean that we set our standard high, and strive beyond the present more ardently. And in such cases our ideals actually imply our present dissatisfaction, and so contribute to our consciousness of temporal ill. In such instances, too, we see that the principal defect of these higher regions of our life is a defect of the very form of our present consciousness, and of any consciousness which is limited to some temporal present. For the type of consciousness that we now possess, and any type of temporally limited consciousness, is too narrow for our higher purposes. It never can contain what shall adequately and finally express our present ideas. Hence the larger our ideals, the more we understand *why* it is that nothing temporal can satisfy us.

On the other hand, it is indeed true that the abstract formula just stated does not enable us to comprehend why, quite apart from our consciousness of our ideals, sometimes pain overwhelms, or sorrow besets, or fortune bears down heavily upon us, while at other times the conscious course of the time-stream appears relatively smooth, and we are even disposed, at some deluded moments, to say, with Othello, "My soul has found her rest so absolute." I have no intention of using our merely general formula about temporal evil as a means for predicting or for explaining in detail our special human experience of ill. I admit at once that man's Selfhood is bound by the most manifold ties to the life of universal Nature. In consequence, man constantly has fortunes that have no definite relations to his own conscious ideals. Man echoes, in his passing experiences of good and of ill, the fortunes, the interests, and the ideals of vast realms of other conscious and finite life, whose dissatisfactions become, as it were, *per accidens*, part of each individual man's life, even when the man concerned cannot himself, at present, see how or why his own ideals, or what he takes to be his own concerns, are directly such as to make these dissatisfactions his fate. And this is true, first, in so far as man, the social being, echoes the joys and sorrows of his fellow-men, without regard to whether he consciously knows how these joys and sorrows stand related to his own ideal interests. But this echoing of other finite life than ours extends, secondly, as my hypothesis about Nature supposes, to all those relations with the life of Nature upon which I earlier dwelt, when we were stating our cosmological theory. Thus, for instance, our organic pains, and our more instinctive emotions, have a depth and a manifoldness that I should hypothetically explain, in accordance with the theory of Nature earlier expounded, as due to the fact that vast strivings, — expressing the Will of the race rather than of the individual, and of Nature-Life in its wholeness rather than of the life of any one man, — strivings, that in themselves are conscious and ideal, are at any moment, in our narrow present consciousness, merely echoed and hinted, by many of our profounder, but less rational joys and sorrows, repugnances and attractions. According as these vaster interests that pervade the processes of Nature, and that constitute the various meanings of its temporal occurrences, become more or less indirectly represented in our conscious life, we have experiences of such joys, and of such griefs, of such successes and of such failures, as we ourselves cannot directly explain in ideal or conscious terms. In so far, our dissatisfactions are indeed not recognized by ourselves as due to the temporal non-fulfilment of our own plans; and, therefore, in precisely these cases, our fortunes seem unearned. And so, owing to the vast extent and to the complexity of these our relatively opaque relations to Nature, no one formula for the fortunes of life can possibly prove adequate to explain to ourselves, in our present form of consciousness, the wealth of our experiences of evil and of good, and the detail of these experiences.

And yet, apart from these endless complications, the abstract formula does hold good that all finite and temporal processes of will must inevitably involve dissatisfaction. And the truth is also verifiable that, in so far as we can consciously grasp the meaning of our own lives, we know why they not only are, but, in the temporal order, must be, and, I may add, *ought to be* unsatisfactory, just because our ideals are so much vaster than our present form of experience, with its brief present instants, can ever adequately express, and just because the realm of finite life to which we belong is full of ideal strivings, so that the whole creation, seeking its own fulfilment, groaneth and travaileth together in pain until now.

On the other hand, for our idealistic Theory of Being, this very presence of ill in the temporal order is the condition of the perfection of the eternal order. The most general reason why this is true we have now repeatedly stated. Simple Oneness is nothingness. Simple finality, apart from the process towards finality, is equally unintelligible. Attainment of a goal means a consciousness that a certain process wins its own completion. But this process is essentially a struggle towards the goal. Where there is the aim, there is also a consciousness that includes incompleteness, and that contrasts this with the completion of the very process which itself embodies the various stages of the aim. The only way to give our view of Being rationality is to see that we long for the Absolute only in so far as in us the Absolute also longs, and seeks, through our very temporal striving, the peace that is nowhere in Time, but only, and yet absolutely, in Eternity. Were there then no longing in Time, there would be no peace in Eternity. When the prayer is uttered that God's will may be done on earth as it is in heaven, we do well to remember that the meaning, which here appears in the form of a petition, is identical with what philosophy must report as a simple fact, directly implied by our Theory of Being. Were not God's Will in its totality, triumphant in the struggle that goes on upon the earth, it would never be done in heaven at all. For heaven, if taken as the name for a realm where the Absolute Will is directly expressed, means simply the Eternal Order in its wholeness. While earth, taken as a region where the same Will at each instant appears as yet struggling with evil, is nothing whatever but a portion or aspect of the Temporal Order. But, as we have seen, these two orders are not divided in their Being. Realism would have sundered them. We simply cannot. The Temporal Order, taken in its wholeness, is for us identical with the Eternal Order. There are, then, not two regions sundered in their Being, in one of which the divine Will reigns supreme, while in the other the success of the divine plan is essentially doubtful. These two realms of Being are merely the same realm, viewed in one aspect as a temporal succession, wherein the particular present Being of each passing instant is contrasted with the *no longer* and *not yet* of past and future, so that fulfilment never at one present instant is to be found; while, in the other aspect, this same realm is to be viewed, in its entirety, as one life-process completely present to the Absolute consciousness, precisely as the musical succession is present at a glance to whoever appreciates a phrase of the music.

II

Thus, in its most abstract aspect, we have before us our idealistic method of viewing the ills of fortune, just as, at the last time, in speaking of the Moral Order, we endeavored to set before ourselves the idealistic way of viewing the nature and place of moral ills. But herewith we are indeed led to dwell upon yet another aspect of the problem of evil. The two undertakings just mentioned are not to be sundered. Our former study here again concerns us. Every ill of human fortune, since for our view it must be regarded as the expression, in the temporal order, of some finite will, is not explicable merely in abstract terms as due to the general nature of temporal Being. For it is also, presumably, either directly due to the magnitude and ideality of our finite plans, or else is more or less directly the expression of the morally defective intent of some human or extra-human moral agent, or of the inadequacy of such an agent to his own ideals.

In regard to the question: Whence and by whose deed or defect came just this ill-fortune?—we have indeed seldom any right to venture upon any detailed speculations. For since the Internal Meaning of the processes of Nature is, in general, hidden from man, we do well, in considering our natural misfortunes, rather to observe how best to adjust our skill to the actual ways of Nature, than to waste our time in a practically vain blaming of unknown hostile agencies for their blind or intentional interference with the life of man. Man's practical business is with the direction of his own will to the service of God. And he does this most wholesomely when he least concerns himself with the misdeeds, if such there be, of extra-human finite agents. Not even in case of the consequences of human conduct is it wholesome to judge our fellows, except within the narrow range where the facts are inevitably known to us, or where our judgment can lead to the improvement of the conduct of our fellows. Still less is the search for the origin, and for the specific nature of what one might call, in traditional speech, the diabolical elements in the finite world at large, any profitable search for us mortals. The wise man contents himself, as far as possible, with the knowing, in general, that there is an indefinitely vast range of voluntary finite evil-doing which, in the temporal order, has to be endured, and for which atonement must be temporally rendered, in order that the divine will may be eternally accomplished.

On the other hand, it is indeed plain that the moral ill

of any agent, when once it has to be recognized as such, is thereby seen at once to become the source of ill fortune to other finite moral agents. For just because this world is a moral order, we suffer together. Nor can it be wholly indifferent to any righteous man that his neighbor sins. In a sense the sin of every evil-doer amongst us taints all of us. For if I am a man, and if nothing human is alien to me, then, however much my individual free will may be set against any direct consent to the evil-doer's particular purpose, this my free will, by virtue of our very definition of individuality, is in no sense absolutely independent of the common human nature that I share with the sinner. All human sin is therefore indeed in some sense my own. It is at least my ill fortune, even where it is not at all my own individual choice. And in this sense every wise man, in contemplating sin and its consequences, in all cases where he must needs know of them, hears the echo of the word, *That art thou*, sounding in his own heart in a tone which is as tragic, as the assertion itself is here one-sided, but in its own partial measure, true, even for the saintliest of men. No man amongst us is wholly free from the consequences, or from the degradation, involved in the crimes of his less enlightened or less devoted neighbors; and the solidarity of mankind links the crimes of each to the sorrows of all.

Morally evil deeds, and the ill fortune of mankind, are thus inseparably linked aspects of the temporal order. To know this in the right sense is not to be predisposed to a hasty moral judgment of our fellows, nor to the wanton imputation of blame to agencies either human or extra-human; but it is rather to learn to judge our own life-task more seriously. Let an ill fortune come, in such wise that I myself can impute to my own free will no conscious share in provoking this ill fortune. In general, I shall then be entering upon a vain search, if I try, in my finitude, to discover whose guilt or whose defect it is, whereof I now suffer the consequences. Yet since the whole temporal order is the expression of will, and since even the processes of external Nature, for our own view, embody the intent of finite agents, whose life is linked to ours by ties to us at present mysterious, I can indeed say, in general, that all ill fortune results from the defects, or at least from the defective expression, of some finite will. This finite will is in general unknown to me. I do well not to trouble myself to impute blame. Yet presumably every such defect of finite will has, like our own defects, a genuinely moral significance. I am therefore right in holding that, when I suffer an ill fortune due to external natural agencies (however meaningless that ill fortune may appear to me), I am enduring a part of the burden of the world's struggle with temporal finitude, or with sin and with its consequences. Hence my endurance becomes, to my wiser view, no merely self-centred Stoicism, intended only to show my own powers, but a willingness to coöperate, whenever I can, in the divine task of giving meaning even to the seeming chaos of our present temporal experience. My willingness to bear hardness, as a good soldier, when I possess such willingness, is therefore never content to be merely passive, or to remain a mere matter of personal pride. I shall undertake to atone for the ill that the unknown agent has done, and so to show how even the seemingly accidental natural ill can be made an element in a life of significant devotion and of positive meaning. The soul of goodness in things evil I shall not merely assume, but shall try actively to find out, through my very effort either to coöperate in removing this natural ill, or so to face it, that I shall come to work all the more serviceably and loyally because of its very presence in my life.

On the other hand, when I inevitably am obliged to know *whose* sin it is whereof I endure the consequences when I suffer, I shall then remember, once for all, that all men are brothers, and that no man's fault can really be wholly indifferent to my Being ; and I shall even rejoice, when I have the strength, that to me the opportunity is here given to join consciously in the common task of atoning for this sin.

Were I at this point a realist, I might no doubt rebel to find that my essentially independent moral entity had been, by ill fortune, somehow yoked by external and by arbitrary ties to my fellow's evil deeds, so that I seemed to myself to be dragging about with me the corpse of another man's crimes even while my deserts were wholly sundered from his. But I am no realist. I know that I have no Being whatever which can be sundered from the Being of my fellow-man. I know that I have moral individuality only in so far as I have my unique share in the identically common ideal task of endurance, and of seeking for the expression of the Eternal Will. My individuality is therefore parted by no chasm from my fellow's life. My responsibility, while not that of my fellow, is in no sense any absolutely independent fact in the universe, but is most intimately linked with my fellow's deeds and fortunes. I shall therefore indeed rejoice when, quite apart from any idle desire to impute blame, I become conscious of this, as of all other truth. And I do become conscious thereof whenever I am forced to observe that my sufferings are due to my fellow's misdeeds. I do not indeed rejoice that he did these evil deeds. But that wherein I rejoice is to have thus indicated to me the common human task of undertaking, in company with my fellows, to make good just this evil. I do not go out of my way to learn even this sort of truth. For it is, I repeat, not my human business to seek to impute blame, but to serve God however and whenever I can; and search for the source of an evil deed is in general an idle task, in a world where fortune constantly teaches me quite as much about such matters as I just now need to know. Yet to pry into the guilt of my neighbor is one matter; to rejoice that I have found a human office is quite another. And when the knowledge of my neighbor's fault is forced upon me through my own resulting misfortune, I rejoice, if I am wise, to discover at least one case where my share in the atoning work of our common humanity is clearly laid out before me.

But further, this knowledge of the intimate, although often to us so mysterious, relation of ill fortune and sin, renders especially serious my view of my own moral task. No sin of mine is wholly indifferent to my fellows. All future life is in some wise other because of my misdeeds, whether finite beings observe the fact or not. This our whole definition of Being necessarily implies. I constantly carry about with me a genuine, if in one sense strictly limited, responsibility for the whole world's fortunes; for what is deed to me is in some sense fortune for all other Selves. My visible sphere of action cannot then be so narrow that I am wholly without influence upon the whole realm of Being, and upon every region thereof. And thus the significance of my moral existence, however petty my apparent range of influence, and however limited in one sense my powers may be, extends, in another sense, without limit, through the whole range of the future temporal order. In brief, it is with your moral efficacy as with your physical efficacy when viewed in accordance with the ideal theory of gravitation. According to that theory, when you move, you move, however little, the whole earth and the sun and the stars.

And thus we have sketched, in general terms, our idealistic view of the solidarity of the moral order, and of the interrelation between evil doing and ill fortune. All that we have herewith asserted is in strict accord with the definite, but also limited, range that our foregoing lecture gave to the moral freedom of the Individual. Our doctrine of individuality demands that every Self shall be in some respect free. Our doctrine of the unity of Being implies that all Selves are known, without any true separation, in the organism of a single world life. And so far from there being any opposition between these two aspects of our idealistic realm, they are strictly reciprocal aspects. The one World and the free Individual imply each the other. For the proof and the significance of individuality are to be found, not in any independence and separateness of soul, but in the very fact that since the Absolute life is One, every region of this life has unique relations to the whole, while uniqueness of will and meaning imply everywhere a measure of finite freedom. On the other hand, the proof of the Absolute unity is statable only in terms of the principle that whatever is, is the final expression of the fully developed internal meaning of any finite idea; so that the Absolute is needed in order to give meaning to any Self, and no Self can be wholly independent of any other.

III

The most general formula whereby the presence of ill in the temporal order is to be explained and the general relations between moral defect and ill fortune, have now been severally considered. What happens in the temporal order is always more or less evil. And on the other hand, the content of any particular evil is due to some finite will. Meanwhile, we mortals have an extremely limited power to understand in detail the connections between sin and ill fortune. Yet we can very certainly say that ill fortune is by no means always, or even predominantly, due to the sins of the sufferer. On the contrary, the very solidarity of the moral world implies that when any individual sins, all beings, in a measure, endure the evil consequences; so that, in general, the greater part of any man's suffering is due to causes that are not in any wise identical with his own free will.

It next concerns us to consider the consequences of the

foregoing view in their relations to the problems of Theodicy, and in their further practical bearings upon the spirit in which the ills of life are to be met.[1]

The older forms of Theodicy were determined mainly either by realistic or by mystical motives. Such fashions of justifying the presence of evil in the world fall with the realistic and the mystical concepts of Being. Yet, even apart from the general metaphysical objections to such older solutions of our problem, their theoretical and practical defects, when viewed as ethically significant hypotheses, deserve here some brief attention. Let us simply summarize one or two of the principal forms of such hypotheses.

Mysticism, by its very nature as an ontological doctrine, involves a conscious effort to deal with the problems of evil. Such an effort is therefore an essential part of its undertaking, and every mystical theology is also a Theodicy. The mystical doctrine is, of course, that evil has no Being at all. And on the other hand, most of the numerous efforts, in the history of ethics and theology, to prove that evil is simply something illusory, rest upon a more or less explicitly mystical basis. Herein, however, lies a very sharp contrast between Mysticism and our own Idealism. For us, evil is certainly not an unreality. It is a temporal reality, and as such is included within, and present to, the eternal insight. What we have throughout asserted is that no evil is a whole or a complete instance of a being. In other words, evil, for us, is some-

[1] The following discussion follows, to some extent, the lines of my essay entitled "The Problem of Job," published in my *Studies of Good and Evil.*

thing explicitly finite; and the Absolute as such, in the individuality of its life, is not evil, while its life is unquestionably inclusive of evil, which it experiences, overcomes, and transcends.

But Mysticism, on the contrary, has always asserted that an experience of evil is an experience of unreality, or is, like every finite experience, an illusion, a dream, a deceit. Now, not only do such doctrines fall with the form of ontology upon which they depend; but taken in themselves, as comments upon life, and as ethical doctrines, they are at once self-contradictory and Antinomian. If evil is merely called finite error, this finite error remains none the less, as a fact of human experience, an evil. One has only changed the name. The reality remains what it was. And in escaping from such error, the mystic either escapes from nothing at all (and in that case, indeed, escapes not at all, since nothing has happened when he escapes); or else he escapes from a real ill, when he turns from error to the Absolute (and in that case, the reality of the evil from which he escapes is admitted). The whole dialectic of practical Mysticism thus depends upon condemning as worthless our finite illusions, while yet asserting that, as worthless, they have no Being whatever, and so cannot even be rightly condemned or transcended. For what you condemn or transcend has, for you, while you condemn or transcend it, a place in Being, even though, as our Idealism asserts, it is, indeed, never the whole of Being taken as a whole. But this dialectic of Mysticism, as thus stated, is obviously endless. The mystic first denies that evil is real. He is asked why then evil seems to exist. He replies that this is our finite error. The finite error itself hereupon becomes, as the source of all our woes, an evil. But no evil is real. Hence no error can be real. Hence we do not really err, even if we suppose that evil is real. Herewith we return to our starting-point, and can only hope to escape by asserting that it is an error to assert that we really err, or that we really believe error to be real. And of the dialectic process thus begun there is, indeed, no end, nor at any stage in this process is there consistency.

On the other hand, it is equally obvious that this simple denial of the reality of evil makes an end of every rational possibility of moral effort. Where there is nothing to escape, to transform, to transcend, or to make better, deeds become as illusory as the ills with which they contend. Meister Eckhart well said, of his Absolute, the Godhead "never looked upon deed," and knows nothing of good works or of evil-doers; while the Hindoo mystics with equal right pointed out that, to the Absolute Self, there is no difference between the murderer and the saint. And Angelus Silesius stated the mystical view with a like consistency when he declared that the prayer, *Thy will be done*, is fulfilled only in so far as the true God has no will at all that can be thwarted: —

> "Und sieh, er ist nicht Wille,
> Er ist ein' ewige Stille."

In consequence, the mystical Theodicy is, indeed, thoroughly Antinomian. You may do what you will. You can do no evil. For evil has no reality. How could you give to any evil deed true Being, even of the most fragmentary type?

It remains by way of comment upon the mystical Theodicy, to point out once more, and with emphasis, that our Idealism herein very sharply differs from Mysticism. For us God has and is a Will. And through all the struggles of the Temporal Order, just this will is winning its way; while, on the other hand, in the Eternal Order, just this will is finally and triumphantly expressed. Meanwhile, in the Temporal Order, there is, at every point and in every act, relative freedom. And for that very reason there is the possibility and the fact of a finite and conscious resistance of the will of the World by the will of the Individual. The consequences of such resistance are real evils, — evils that all finite beings and the whole world suffer. Such evils are justified only by the eternal worth of the life that endures and overcomes them. And they are temporally overcome through other finite wills, and not without moral conflict. The right eternally triumphs, yet not without temporal warfare. This warfare occurs, indeed, *within the divine life itself*, and not in an externally created world that is realistically an independent Being, other than God, and sundered from him. But this very view makes the conflict no less genuine, and the eternal victory no less a moral victory.

A modified form of the mystical Theodicy, in connection with the realistic elements, apears in the classic doctrine of evil in the Scholastic theology. Here evil has, as the Thomistic doctrine assures us, no positive entity; but involves imperfections whose only real basis lies in the perfections of the beings concerned. Yet this doctrine escapes from the direct consequences of Mysticism only through the addition of those realistic elements which characterize the scholastic doctrine of the created world.

IV

We may pass then, next, directly to the realistic forms of Theodicy. And of these, for the moment, we need especially mention but one, — a form especially familiar in popular theology, and by no means ignored in the classic statement of the just-mentioned scholastic theory of evil. According to this view real evil is entirely due to the free will of moral agents who are essentially Independent Beings, and who have their existence apart one from another, like all the entities of Realism. "The soul that sinneth it shall die." This is the central thesis emphasized by such a realistic Theodicy. Any moral agent with a free will is created by God. But God's will then leaves him quite free to choose for himself whether he will do well or ill. In so far as he chooses ill, evil enters the world. This evil is not in any sense in God, nor yet in the world by any divine consent; but is in a being who, in his freedom, is now wholly independent of God or of any other moral agent. The divine justice hereupon indeed demands that the moral order should be vindicated by requiring the sinner to reap the consequences of his deed. As usual with Realism, a primary sundering of entities is somehow to be made good by a secondary act that annuls the sundering. And the ills of the world, thus explained as the divinely determined penalty of sin, are such that the sufferers have only their own sinfulness to blame for their woes, while God's righteous government is vindicated by their inability to escape his judgment.

I call this view, in many of its popular forms, a realistic Theodicy, because its expounders usually and profoundly object to our foregoing account of the deeper unity of the Temporal and the Eternal Orders, and lay great stress upon sundering the moral agents of the universe. They do this, first, for the sake of making, as they often say, the responsibility of each moral agent something quite definite and unmistakable, and secondly, for the sake, as they often add, of entirely clearing the divine Will from any responsibility for the deeds of the finite agents, and finally, for the sake of assuring us that no true harm can come to the righteous. In its most consistent form this theory would be forced, as a consequence, to regard all the explicable and real sufferings of the world as the direct penalty of sin, and as visited upon the individual evil-doers themselves. For, as a well-known and highly realistic popular ethical view has often asserted, it would be unjust if God visited upon one moral agent the penalty of another moral agent's sins. For are not the Selves, one insists, essentially and mutally independent entities, whose salvation or damnation ought to be, and in a moral world is, their own doing? And how can God's ways be justified unless we suppose that he wishes all men, — these Independent Beings whom he has created, — to prosper and to win blessedness, if only they choose to be righteous? If they sin, theirs is the just penalty. But no ill can happen to the righteous in this justly governed world of the ethically Independent Beings.

Accordingly, in view of the complications of life, and because of the frequent appearance of ills that seem to fall upon the innocent, and because of the seeming delay of the divine justice in the visible affairs of men, this doctrine, ever since the days of Job's friends, or of the speculations of the more realistic of the early Hindoo sages regarding the source of evil, has been forced to make use of various supplementary hypotheses, which here, indeed, need not long detain us. A righteous man seems to suffer. Hereupon this realistic Theodicy appears endangered. Injustice appears to have come into the world. How shall one explain the facts? Well, with Job's friends, one may make the hypothesis that the righteous man has secretly sinned. Or, with the popular doctrine of the Hindoos, a doctrine occasionally imitated in Western thought, one may suppose that a sin done in some previous state of existence is visited upon the sufferer in the present life. Or, borrowing from the mystic as much of his lore as one needs, one may divide apparent ills into two sorts, — the one sort being merely illusory ills, blessings in disguise, or matters that the enlightened can see to be of no real moment whatever; while only the other sort of ills, namely those which are the penalties of sin, are genuine ills. To the former class are then referred those ills of mere fortune which seem to come both to the just and to the unjust. One supposes that only human illusion makes these appear to be ills at all. For God's will has wrought them, and, by hypothesis, not as penalties of sin. And God's will could mean naught but good to his righteous children. Hence of such ills we must make light. They may often seem grave. But this sort of Theodicy calls them mere appearances. On the other hand, there are, in the world, true evils. But they are the penalties of sin. And they are always visited upon the evil-doer himself.

Seldom has such a Theodicy as this been carried out with any very rigid consistency. On the other hand, as a general tendency in doctrine, this form of the explanation and justification of evil is very well and popularly known. Yet if it were ever expressed with a thoroughgoing consistency, I hold that its consequences would be as hopeless, when viewed with reference to the interests of any ethical interpretation of the universe, as the realistic ontology upon which it is based is helpless against the attacks of a sound metaphysical analysis. This view gives us in truth no intelligible Theodicy whatever.

For, as a fact, our ethical interest in the universe is quite as inseparable from a belief in the solidarity of all human life, and in fact in the solidarity of all finite life, as this same ethical interest is also inseparable from a belief in the relative freedom and the individuality of finite agents. Moral agents must indeed possess their measure of finite freedom, if the world is to be a moral order. But in no ethically significant sense can they be Independent Beings, of any realistic type, if this same world is to possess any moral unity of meaning whatever. For what gives the moral life its whole positive significance is the fact that individuals can and do suffer, and undeservedly suffer, and, in a measure, helplessly suffer, for the wrong-doing of other individuals, while for the very same reason, moral agents can do positive good in and for the lives of other moral agents. In a moral world I, as ethical agent, must indeed be free to choose my own measure of individual and moral good and ill. But I cannot be free to suffer only for the consequences of my own sins. For if this latter were the case, and if this freedom to suffer only for my own sins were the general rule that held for all moral agents, then everybody's true inner fortune would indeed be wholly independent of the deeds of his fellows. But in that case no moral agent would have any genuinely significant task to perform. For our genuinely significant moral tasks all involve helping our fellows. And the power positively to help my fellow is necessarily correlative with my power to harm him. Where I cannot harm, I cannot help. And in a world where I cannot genuinely help another, my whole moral life becomes limited to the task of cultivating a purely vain and formal piety, as empty as it is ineffectual. It follows that this form of realistic Theodicy, in joining to its theory of free will a conception that finite Selves are sundered in their true Being, and so in their fortunes, by chasms, has unwittingly destroyed the moral universe.

This consequence of this realistic Theodicy can easily be developed by any illustration of a case where a good deed appears possible. The stranger has fallen by the wayside. Can the good Samaritan do him any service? Yes,—but only upon the hypothesis that real evils are not solely the inevitable consequences that divine justice brings upon sufferers because of their own sins. For if the real evils of the world are all of them the just penalties of the sins of those who suffer, then, according to the realistic theodicy, yonder stranger's suffering is one of two things. Perhaps, namely, it is no real evil at all, but an illusory appearance of mishap. In that case no good need or can be done by giving the stranger succor. But perhaps, on the other hand, it is a well-earned penalty for his past misdeeds, — a penalty which divine justice inflicts. But in the latter case, by the hypothesis of the realistic Theodicy here in question, the penalty has come to this stranger solely because a righteous God knew that it was earned, and that it *must* come. How then can the good Samaritan hope to intervene between the just God and the righteous penalty? If he succeeded in relieving the sufferer, he could at best only postpone the day of God's just wrath, and of the inevitable penalty. Or, in other words, the relief would be a mere illusion. The priest and the Levite who pass the sufferer by, and who leave him to the punishments of God, are therefore following out the only consistent practice that our realistic Theodicy could counsel. At most, like Job's friends, they might have approached the sufferer to warn him of the necessity of making his peace with God. Even this warning could convey to him no real good. For the grace of repentance also he would possess, if he deserved it, and if it could avert any of the evil consequences of his deed. Meanwhile, the thieves amongst whom the stranger fell really did him no ill except just what he deserved. They too, then, were God's ministers, and in no wise evil-doers.

The result is here indeed a moral fatalism, of an unexpected, but none the less inevitable, sort. But what the illustration brings to light is, that the problem of evil indeed demands the presence of free will in the world; while, on the other hand, it is equally true that no moral world whatever can be made consistent with the realistic thesis according to which free will agents are, in fortune and in penalty, independent of the deeds of other moral agents. It follows that, in our moral world, the righteous can suffer without individually deserving their suffering, just because their lives have no independent Being, but are linked with all life.

Nor, in fact, can any realistic conception of the moral agents, as souls essentially independent, in their Being, of their creator, or of one another, be just to the solidarity upon which every explanation and justification of the ills of the world must rest. If the ills of the creatures are events external to the life of their creator, then the creator has fashioned suffering in which he himself has no share, and of which he is independent. In that case the ancient dilemma as to the limitation of his power upon the one hand, or of his benevolence upon the other, retains all its hopelessness of meaning. The ways of God cannot thus be justified.

V

I return afresh to our own idealistic view. I state again its theses and their consequences,—but this time in a directly practical form.

I suffer. Why? In general because I am an agent whose will is not now completely expressed in a present conscious life. I seek in the Beyond my fulfilment. The higher my ideals, the more far-reaching my plans, the more I am full of the longing for perfection, the more there is in me of one kind of sorrow,—namely, of sorrow that my present temporal life is not yet what I mean it to be. Moreover, the narrowness of my present form of consciousness not only limits my ideal search for the fulfilment that I conceive in the future. It also sets bounds to my conscious retention of my former attainments. What I have won, I too often forget and forsake. My past is no longer mine, just because my consciousness is of such narrow span. I lose my own past, just as I struggle in vain to win what is still my future. Thus I am beset with temporal ill behind and before. The *no longer* and the *not yet* equally baffle me.

Now is there any good in all this essential, and, nevertheless, ideally colored, misfortune that besets the best deeds and meanings of my present form of consciousness? Yes. There is, indeed, one very great good. For in respect of this better aspect of my life, I suffer because of the very magnitude and the depth of my meanings. I am in ideal larger than my human experience permits me, in present fact, to become. My evil is the result of this my highest present good. Can I improve this my state of temporal ill? Yes, by every serious effort to live in better accord with my ideal. To be sure, there is no infallible rule for winning temporal good fortune; for my fortunes, and my actual power to attain my temporal goals, depend upon my infinitely complex natural relations with other life. No act of my finite individuality has created, or can transform, my temperament, my heredity, my environment, or can free me from the burden that I must cheerfully accept, — the burden of being this man, weighted with the presence of this organism, this inheritance of human sorrow and sin, this task in a world of cares. But one thing lies in my power. And that is, to be devoted to my life's task, namely, to the Eternal. For me the readiness is all. But I can be ready, ready to accept the dear sorrow of possessing ideals, and of taking my share of the divine task.

But in all this my own struggle with evil, wherein lies my comfort? I answer—my true comfort can never lie in my temporal attainment of my goal. For it is my first business, as a moral agent, and as a servant of God, to set before myself a goal that, in time, simply cannot be attained. Woe unto them that are at ease in Zion. Yes, woe unto them, for they are essentially self-contradictory in the blindness of their self-assertion. They assert that they win peace in their temporal doings; but temporal peace is a contradiction in terms. We approach such peace nearest of all when we have least of ideal significance in our consciousness. We attain it only in deep sleep, while the restlessly beating heart suggests that nature is even then dissatisfied with and in every present state of what men call our organism; but while we, as mere finite human individuals, will nothing, think nothing, and for just that time are nothing. Whoever is awake, is content with the present precisely in so far as the world means little to him. The more the world means, at any moment, to our consciousness, the more we go onward towards some goal. The more then are we discontent with the instant.

Our comfort cannot, therefore, be at once significant, and yet a matter of purely temporal experience. Wherein, then, can comfort truly be found? I reply, In the consciousness, first, that the ideal sorrows of our finitude are identically God's own sorrows, and have their purpose and meaning in the divine life as such significant sorrows; and in the assurance, secondly, that God's fulfilment in the eternal order — a fulfilment in which we too, as finally and eternally fulfilled individuals, share, — is to be won, not as the mystic supposed, without finitude and sorrow, but through the very bitterness of tribulation, and through overcoming the world. In being faithful to our task we, too, are temporally expressing the triumph whereby God overcomes in eternity the temporal world and its tribulations.

I say, our sorrows are identically God's own sorrows. This consequence flows directly from our Idealism. And we accept this consequence heartily. It contains the only ground for a genuine Theodicy. The Absolute knows all that we know, and knows it just as we know it. For not one instant can we suppose our finite experience first "absorbed" or "transmuted" and then reduced, in an ineffable fashion, to its unity in the divine life. The eternal fulfilment is not won by ignoring what we find present to ourselves when we sorrow, but by including this our experience of sorrow in a richer life. And, on the other hand, nothing in our life is external to the divine life. As the Absolute is identically our whole Will expressed, our experience brought to finality, our life individuated, so, on the other hand, we are the divine as it expresses itself here and now; and no item of what we are is other than an occurrence within the whole of the divine existence. In our more ideal sorrows we may become more clearly aware *how* our intention, our plan, our meaning, is one with the divine intent, and *how* our experience is a part of the life through which God wins in eternity his own. And the comfort of this clearer insight lies precisely here: — I sorrow. But the sorrow is not only mine. This same sorrow, just as it is for me, is God's sorrow. And yet, since my will is here also, and consciously, one with the divine Will, God who here, in me, aims at what I now temporally miss, not only possesses, in the eternal world, the goal after which I strive, but comes to possess it even through and because of my sorrow. Through this my tribulation the Absolute triumph, then, is won. Moreover, this triumph is also eternally mine. In the Absolute I am fulfilled. Yet my very fulfilment, and God's, implies, includes, demands, and therefore can transcend, this very sorrow.

For now, secondly, I assert, even in all this, that the divine fulfilment in eternity can be won only through the sorrows of time. For, as a fact, we ourselves, even in our finitude, know that the most significant perfections include, as a part of themselves, struggle, whereby opposing elements, set by this very struggle into contrast with one another, become clearly conscious. Such perfections also include suffering, because in the conquest over suffering all the nobler gifts of the Spirit, all the richer experiences of life, consist. As there is no courage without a dread included and transcended, so in the life of endurance there is no conscious heroism without the present tribulations in whose overcoming heroism consists. There is no consciousness of strength without the presence of that resistance which strength alone can master. Even love shows its glory as love only by its conquest over the doubts and estrangements, the absences and the misunderstandings, the griefs and the loneliness, that love glorifies with its light amidst all their tragedy. In a world where there was no such consciousness as death suggests to us mortals, love would never consciously know the wealth and the faithfulness of its own deathless meaning. Whoever has not at some time profoundly despaired, knows not the blessed agony of rising from despair and of being more than the demonic powers that are wrecking his life. Art, which in its own way often gives us our brief glimpses of the eternal order, delights to display to us all this dignity of sorrow. The experience of life, amidst all the chaos of our present form of consciousness, brings home to us this great truth that the perfection of the Spirit is a perfection through the including and transcending of sorrow, — and brings it home in a form that leaves us no doubt that unless God knows sorrow, he knows not the highest good, which consists in the overcoming of sorrow.

So much then for our sorrows, so far as they have to us, as we are, a consciously ideal meaning. But, you may say, much of sorrow, such as mere physical pain, and such as our more degrading ill fortune, has not this quality. To us as we are such sorrow seems in no wise ennobling. What comfort have we for ills that seem not to have, for our present consciousness, any ideal meaning? Do they link us with the divine? Do they help us onwards in the task of life? Do they not rather tend to drive us to forget our goals, and to lose sight of life's meaning? Can such sorrows thus be justified?

I have already, in substance, replied to this objection. Man, as he is, lives not only his more consciously ideal human life. Linked as he is to countless processes of nature, and of his fellows, he echoes, in his passing experiences, the sorrows of the world. He cannot now know the ideal meaning of the vast realms of finite life in whose fortunes he is at present mysteriously doomed to share. His comfort here lies in knowing that in all this life ideals are sought, and meanings temporally expressed, — with incompleteness at every instant, with the sorrow of finitude in every movement of the natural world, but with the assurance of the divine triumph in Eternity lighting up the whole.

In brief, then, nowhere in Time is perfection to be found. Our comfort lies in the knowledge of the Eternal. Strengthened by that knowledge, we can win the most enduring of temporal joys, the consciousness that makes us delight to share the world's grave glories and to take part in its divine sorrows, — sure that these sorrows are the means of the eternal triumph, and that these glories are the treasures of the house of God. When once this comfort comes home to us, we can run and not be weary, and walk and not faint. For our temporal life is the very expression of the eternal triumph.

LECTURE X

LECTURE X

THE UNION OF GOD AND MAN

For better or for worse, the investigation to which our two series of lectures have been devoted now draws to its close. Our case has been presented. A theory of Being, itself founded upon an interpretation of human experience, has been applied to special problems, such as human life constantly offers to our notice. The result has been an outline of the basis of a Philosophy of Religion. We began our first series of lectures by stating our general problem as that of the World and the Individual, — of their nature and their relations. As we close, we are chiefly interested in that aspect of this problem which now, in view of the immediately preceding lectures, lies nearest to us; viz., the question as to the relations between God and Man.

I

Our account of the human Self has endeavored to be as just as our space permitted to the complexity, the temporal instability, and the natural dependence, of Man the finite being, when he is viewed in the context of the physical world. There is a sense in which man is a product of Nature, and in which his life is but one incident in a vast process of Evolution, — a process whose inner meaning in great part at present escapes us. We have tried to see the extent to which just this is true. There is also a sense in which man's life as a Self appears to be a mere series of relatively accidental experiences, and of shifting social contrast-effects. We have attempted to show how far this also is the case. There is a philosophical truth in saying, as tradition and common sense long ago said, that man is a prey of fortune,—that his life is a shadow, that all his essence seems insubstantial, transient, and uncertain, and that, so far as you find law governing his life, it appears to the external observer to be a merely natural law, indifferent to the meanings and ideals that man himself most prizes. And to such truth also we have endeavored to be just. But when we were led to emphasize all these limitations of human nature, our interpretation of them was from the outset determined by the inevitable consequences of our general theory of Being. None of these aspects of man's existence could appear to us startling or strange, or even disappointing, because we had long since learned in what sense, and in what sense only, these very facts could possess any Being whatever. For in thinking of this world, where his natural place in the temporal order is so insignificant, man finds that the very link which binds the whole universe to this instant's knowledge is a link that predetermines what meaning the whole must itself possess, and consequently what meaning man's life, despite its apparent pettiness, must illustrate.

To the individual man we have accordingly said: Conceive yourself, in the light of your science, as this seeming plaything of natural destiny. Know your frame. Remember not only that you are dust, in the ancient sense of that word, but also that you are in your inner life, in the way that psychological analysis has now rendered familiar, — an insubstantial series of psychical conditions, physically and socially determined, precisely in so far as such determination is possible, — a being whose nature has only such permanence as may prove to be involved in the permanent meaning of those fleeting conditions themselves, in case they indeed may possess any such meaning. View yourself as an incident, or at best an episode, in the world-embracing process of evolution. And then, when you have done all this, ask afresh this one question: How can I know all these things? And how can all these facts themselves possess any Being? You will find that the only possible answer to your questions will take the form of asserting, in the end, that you can know all this, and that all this can be real, only by reason of an ontological relation that, when rightly viewed, is seen to link yourself, even in all your weakness, to the very life of God, and the whole universe to the meaning of every Individual. In God you possess your individuality. Your very dependence is the condition of your freedom, and of your unique significance. The one lesson of our entire course has thus been the lesson of the unity of finite and of infinite, of temporal dependence, and of eternal significance, of the World and all its Individuals, of the One and the Many, of God and Man. Not only in spite, then, of our finite bondage, but because of what it means and implies, we are full of the presence and the freedom of God.

But now, emphasizing the especially human aspect of our ontology, and the especially ethical significance of our theoretical results, we must expound a little more fully some of these our characteristic theses. And the particular further task of this closing lecture must be to bring together the various threads of our argument, in so far as they bear upon the doctrine of the individual Self, and of the more practical aspects of this its union with God. We have laid our basis. Let us indicate some of the consequences of our theory.

II

And next, as to our whole definition of the nature of the Divine Life. If our foregoing argument has been sound, our Idealism especially undertakes to give a theory of the general place and of the significance of Personality in the Universe. Personality, to our view, is an essentially ethical category. A Person is a conscious being, whose life, temporally viewed, seeks its completion through deeds, while this same life, eternally viewed, consciously attains its perfection by means of the present knowledge of the whole of its temporal strivings. Now from our point of view, God is a Person. Temporally viewed, his life is that of the entire realm of consciousness in so far as, in its temporal efforts towards perfection, this consciousness of the universe passes from instant to instant of the temporal order, from act to act, from experience to experience, from stage to stage. Eternally viewed, however, God's life is the infinite whole that includes this endless temporal process, and that consciously surveys it as one life, God's own life. God is thus a Person, because, for our view, he is self-conscious, and because the Self of which he is conscious is a Self whose eternal perfection is attained through the totality of these ethically significant temporal strivings, these processes of evolution, these linked activities of finite Selves. We have long since ceased, indeed, to suppose that this theory means to view God's perfection, or his self-consciousness, as the temporal result of any process of evolution, or as an event occurring at the end of time, or at the end of any one process, however extended, that occurs in time. The melody does not come into existence contemporaneously with its own last note. Nor does the symphony come into full existence only when its last chord sounds. On the contrary, the melody is the whole, whereof the notes are but abstracted fragments; the symphony is the totality, to which the last chord contributes no more than does the first bar. And precisely so it is, as we have seen, with the relation between the temporal and the eternal order. God in his totality as the Absolute Being is conscious, not *in* time, but *of* time, and of all that infinite time contains. In time there follow, in their sequence, the chords of his endless symphony. For him is this whole symphony of life at once. Moreover there is indeed, for our doctrine, no temporal conclusion of the world's successive procesess, — no one temporal goal of evolution, — no single temporal event to which the whole creation moves. For as, even in the finite symphony, every chord restlessly strives after a musical perfection that in itself it only hints, and that it does not yet finally contain, but as nevertheless this very perfection is in the whole symphony itself, viewed as a whole, — so, in the universe, every temporal instant contains a seeking after God's perfection. Yet never, at any instant of time, is this perfection attained. It is present only to the consciousness that views the infinite totality of this very process of seeking.

Such has been our doctrine concerning the divine life, when taken in its character as the life of the Absolute. That a conception of an endless temporal process which nevertheless constitutes one whole, present to one consciousness, is a possible conception, and that this conception is free from the self-contradictions which have usually been ascribed to the idea of the Infinite, — all this I have endeavored to show at length. But in consequence of this endlessness which I ascribe to the temporal order, and in consequence of the fact that no last event, no final occurrence in the sequence of the world's life, is to my mind possible, and in consequence of the wholeness of meaning which I nevertheless attribute to the divine consciousness itself, I am led to add here a word as to the general significance of historical progress, and of the evolutionary processes of the universe, — a word that will prove necessary for the purposes of this our concluding lecture.

At every instant, in the temporal order, God's will is in process of expressing itself. Now since this is true of every instant of time, it follows that every stage of the world-process, viewed as God views it, stands in an immediate relation to God's whole purpose. Hence there is, indeed, always progress in the universe in so far as at any instant some specific finite end is nearing or is winning its temporal attainment. Yet those are wrong who lay such stress upon the conception of progress as to assert that, in order for the world to attain a divine meaning at all, it is necessary to suppose whatever comes later in time to be in all respects better, or to be in every way nearer to God's perfection, than is what comes earlier in time. To make this assertion is to declare that in the divine order of the universe there is a Law of Universal Progress in time, so that all temporal things grow, by God's will, in all respects better as the world goes on. But our view does not make this assertion. Unquestionably, in the temporal order, if this is indeed, as we have asserted, a Moral Order, there is always in some respects Progress, because there is always a seeking of some new form and partial expression of Being, and a passing on towards such new forms and expressions. Moreover, as we have seen, there are new Ethical Individuals originating in time, and thenceforth adding their significance to the world's process. But if the temporal world thus always contains progress, it none the less obviously always involves, for any temporally limited conscious view, decay. Temporal progress, then, is only one aspect of the temporal order. For, as we pass on into our own future, we lose closer conscious touch with our own past. The growth of the man involves the death of his own childhood, with its special suggestions of divine beauty. The maturity of age means the loss of youth. For us mortals, every new temporal possession includes the irrevocable loss of former conscious possessions. Now this same tendency, as we have earlier seen, seems to hold true of all the irreversible process of universal Nature. For in Nature, too, nothing recurs. The broken china will not mend. The withered flowers bloom no more. The sun parts forever with its heat. Tidal friction irrevocably retards the revolution of the earth. And all these things, while they include the very conditions of progress, also involve decay.

In brief, it is, with the occurrences of the successive movements of time, or with the stages of life, precisely as it is with whatever else in the universe you learn to conceive as an individual fact. One finite individual, taken as such, never possesses the precise and unique perfections of its fellow, *i.e.* of any other individual. Hence whenever you have to pass, in your finite experience, from a partial view of one individual fact to a similar view of another individual fact, you lose something as well as gain something; and of this truth you become more clearly aware the nearer you come to an insight into the true natures of the objects concerned. Nothing can really be spared from the whole, *i.e.* from the universe. Hence every transition, such as we make in our finite experience, is a loss as well as a gain. No progress therefore is mere progress. Every growth is also a decay. Every attainment of temporal good is also the suffering of a temporal ill. And just that is what every mother observes when she learns to mourn because her children win the very maturity that she has all the while longed and striven to help them win. Just such is our experience too when we listen to music. In hearing the Heroic Symphony of Beethoven, how easily, during the Funeral March,—yes, even during the triumphant glories of the closing movement,—how easily, I say, may not the hearer wish himself back again in the midst of the striving life that the opening theme of the first movement introduces. Finite gain is also finite loss. This is the axiom of the temporal world, in so far as you view its events under the conditions of any finite span of conscious survey. Hence mere Progress, — Progress without any admixture of temporal decay and loss, — is not the law of the sequent events of the world.

On the other hand, in so far as any finite consciousness seeks, in its own future, a temporal goal that it has not yet won, and then approaches that goal, — for just this consciousness, in view of just this goal, there is indeed Progress. Now from our point of view, the general rationality of the world's temporal processes assures us that at all times there is, on the whole, and despite countless hindrances and evils, precisely this sort of attainment of significant goals occurring in the world. Hence Progress is, in one sense, but by no means in every sense, a fact always present in time. It is always present in the sense that at every moment of time some new and significant goal, that never before was attained, is approached by the finite agents whose will is just now in question. They seek new good, and, despite all evil, they always tend to win good, and always have some measure of success in striving intelligently for such good. On the other hand, Progress is not universal, if by universal Progress you mean a condition in which the temporal world should be in all essential respects better at any one moment than it ever was before. On the contrary, you can always say that in *some* respects the finite universe of any one temporal instant is worse than it ever was before, since it has irrevocably lost all those perfections that the past contained, and that now are sought for in vain, while with every new temporal instant of the world more and still more of such perfections become lost beyond recall in the past. For instance, Progress for mankind here on earth is not universal; for, remember, we have lost, beyond earthly human recall, the Greeks, and the constructive genius of a Shakespeare or of a Goethe; and these are, indeed, for us mortals, simply irreparable losses. Yet, on the other hand, Progress in a sense is universal for mankind; for daily civilization, retaining some of its ancient treasures, adds new ones; and, aiming at goods never yet won, attains them.

The one most essentially progressive aspect of the temporal order is that which is due to the appearance of new Ethical Individuals. For their perfections are additions to the world's stock of ideal goods; and they, as we shall see, do not pass away. Yet it has to be remembered that a new Ethical Individual, considered in any one temporal stage of his life, is not *merely* an added perfection, that the world never possessed before. He is *also* an added problem, — a new source of conflict and of often painful endeavor. Only from the eternal point of view is he finally viewed as a perfection. In time he may appear, for a long while, as a new evil.

Now, it is worth while to recall such considerations, simple as they are, whenever we are concerned to conceive the relation of Progress, or of that still more generally conceived realm of processes called Evolution, to the divine life. As a fact, all ages are present at once as elements in an infinite significant process to the divine insight. Every age therefore has, as the historian Ranke once said of the ages of human history, its "unmittelbare Beziehung auf die Gottheit." All things always work together for good from the divine point of view; and whoever can make this divine point of view in any sense his own, just in so far sees that they do so, despite the inevitable losses and sorrows of the temporal order.

III

So much, then, for some results of our general view of the divine Personality, and of the relation between the temporal and eternal aspects of its life. And now, in the next place, for our view of the human Person. Man, too, in our view, is a Person. He is not, indeed, an Absolute Person; for he needs his conscious contrast with his fellows, and with the whole of the rest of the universe, to constitute him what he is. He is, however, a conscious being, whose life, temporally viewed, seeks its completion through deeds. That from the eternal point of view this same life of the individual man, viewed as intentionally contrasted with the life of all the rest of the world, consciously attains its perfection by means of the knowledge of the whole of its temporal strivings, — this is, indeed, a corollary of our foregoing doctrine, a corollary which we have yet more precisely to develope. It is just this corollary which constitutes the basis of the philosophical theory of Immortality, — a theory which we have here briefly to characterize and to explain.

The human Self, as we earlier saw, is not a Thing, nor

yet a Substance, but a Life with a Meaning. I, the individual, am what I am by virtue of the fact that my intention, my meaning, my task, my desire, my hope, my life, stand in contrast to those of any other individual. If I am any Reality whatever, then I am doing something that nobody else can do, and meaning something that nobody else can mean; and I have my relatively free will that nobody else can possess. The uniqueness of my meaning is the one essential fact about me.

But when with this consideration in mind we turn to ask about the relation of the human Self to Time, our first impression is that our doctrine gives no positive decision as to how long a temporal process is needed for the complete expression of the whole life and the entire meaning of any one human Self. And as a fact, if we take the term "Self" with reference to those varieties of meaning that before engaged our attention when we discussed the empirical Ego, we see at once that there is a sense in which what can be called a particular finite Ego gets its temporal expression, so far as you view that expression apart from the rest of the universe, only within some very limited portion of time. The Self, as we said, can be arbitrarily limited, if you will, to this instant's passing selfhood, taken as in contrast to all the rest of the universe of Being. The Self of this finite idea, of this passing thrill of Internal Meaning, is, indeed, if you choose so to regard it, something that, from God's point of view, and in its relation to God, is seen as a genuine Self,—an Individual. For, as we have from the outset observed, the Self of this instant's longing has its true and conscious relations to all the rest of the infinite realm of Being. We men are, indeed, just now not wholly conscious of the true individual meaning of even this passing moment. But in God this meaning becomes conscious.

For this instant has its twofold aspect, the temporal and the eternal. Viewed temporally, it is just something that now occurs, and that, seen as God sees it, has its own unique contrast with every other event in the universe, and that also is in so far no other event, and no other Self. Nowhere else in time will its precise contents recur. Viewed eternally, it finds the complete and individual expression of its whole meaning in God's entire life. In so far as it is conscious of its true relations to the divine, it is this unique prayer for the coming of the kingdom of heaven. And in the eternal wholeness of the divine life, this prayer is answered. Browning's wonderful little poem, *The Boy and the Angel*, well expresses this aspect of the twofold meaning of every instant of finite individuality. Here and now, and not merely elsewhere and in the far-off future, this instant's song of praise, this moment's search after God, is the temporal expression of a value that is unique, and that would be missed as a lost perfection of the eternal world if it were not known to God as just this finite striving. The temporal brevity of the instant is here no barrier to its eternal significance. And in so far, the lesson of our whole theory is that, when you are viewed as just this momentary Self, working here in the darkness of your finitude upon the task of your earthly life, you have not to endure temporally, for a long time, in order to be linked to God. In him you are even now at home. For you here mean, by every least act of service, infinitely more than you find presented to your human form of consciousness; and in God this meaning of yours, just as the true meaning of this temporal instant's deed, wins its eternal and self-conscious expression.

But now, of course, as we have long since seen, the Self of the single temporal instant is far from being the whole human Self as we rightly come to contrast that Self of the Individual with all the rest of the world. The whole human Self, as we have seen, is the Self of the unique life-plan. And this Self needs a temporally extended expression, which no single instant of our human experience contains. The Self thus viewed has a meaning that seeks unity with God only through the temporal attainment of goals in a series of successive deeds. And of course the Self, taken in this sense, is a far truer expression of what we mean by our individuality than is the Self of any one temporal instant. Yet here again the length of temporal expression that is required for the embodiment of any one type of finite individuality varies with the temporal significance of the ideal that may be in question in defining the Self. A life-plan, in so far as it is conscious only of brief temporal purposes, needs only a brief life to accomplish its little task. The Self that merely reads this lecture to you, on the present occasion, is indeed, from the eternal point of view, an individual. But it is so far an individual of limited finite duration. The Self of the mere reader of this lecture has no endurance beyond to-day. It is defined by a contrast with the rest of the universe that is especially determined by the conditions of just this temporal academic appointment. Its particular social contrast is with your present Selfhood as hearers. Its work is done when the hour closes. Nowhere else, in time, has just that individuality its task, its duty, its deed, or its expression. On the other hand, the ethical continuity of just this selfhood with the selfhood of other tasks, of former lectures, of the writing of these lectures, and of my personal obligations to you and to the University, is so essential a fact in my life, as I *ought* to view my life, that here the sundering of one fragment of temporal processes from other processes seems especially arbitrary and useless. Yet, whenever we undertake any task, however transient its temporal expression, that view of the union of God and Man, of the Eternal and the Temporal, upon which our whole teaching here depends, requires us steadfastly to bear in mind that every fragment of life, however arbitrarily it may be selected, has indeed its twofold aspect. It is what it temporally is, in so far as it is this linked series of events, present in experience, and somehow contrasted with all other events in the universe. It is what it eternally is, by virtue of those relations which appear not now, in our human form of consciousness, but which do appear, from the divine point of view, as precisely the means of giving their whole meaning to these transient deeds of ours. To view even the selfhood that passes away, even the deeds of the hour, as a service of God, and to regard the life of our most fragmentary selfhood as the divine life taking on human form, — this is of the deepest essence of religion. From this point of view it is indeed true that now, even through these passing deeds, we are expressing what has at once its eternal and its uniquely individual Being. Here God's will shall be done as elsewhere in the temporal universe it can never again be done, and has never yet been done:—so to resolve is to view our daily duty as our duty, and this passing selfhood, even in its transiency, as possessing eternal meaning.

Yet not thus do we discover the adequate view of the relation of the Human Self to time. For the Ethical Self, as we have already seen, has its meaning defined in terms of an activity to which no temporal limits can be set without a confession of failure. When I aim to do my duty I aim to accomplish, not merely the unique, but such a service that I could never say, at any one temporal instant: "There is no more for me to accomplish; my work is done. I may rest forever." For that is of the very essence of Ethical Selfhood, namely, to press on to new tasks, to demand new opportunity for service, and to accept a new responsibility with every instant. It follows that the same considerations which imply the intimate union of every temporal instant's passing striving with the whole life of God, equally imply that an individual task which is ideal, which is unique, and which means the service of God in a series of deeds such as can never end without an essential failure of the task, can only be linked with God's life, and can only find its completion in this union with God, in an individual life which is the life of a conscious Self, and which is a deathless life. And thus at length we are led to the first formulation of our conception of human Immortality.

IV

As a fact, the sense in which the human Individual, taken in his wholeness, as one ethical Person amongst other Persons, is to be viewed as Immortal, may be more precisely defined, at the present stage of our inquiry, by means of three distinct yet closely linked considerations.

The first is a consideration founded upon our whole theory of the nature of Individuality, as we set forth that theory in defining the doctrine of Being.

We know Being from three sides. Whatever is, is something that in one aspect forms a content of experience. Nothing has a place in the realm of Reality which is not, in one aspect, something presented, found, verified, as a fact known to God, and given as a datum of the Absolute Experience. This is the first aspect of Reality. But secondly, nothing is real which is not also, in another aspect, an object conforming to a type, — an object possessing definable general characters, and embodying Thought, — an object expressive of the ideas that the Divine Wisdom contemplates. These two aspects of Being we studied at length in our foregoing series of lectures. But we found that these two aspects of Being are not the only ones. A third is not less essential, and is in fact the most significant of the three. What is real is not only a content of experience, and not only the embodiment of a type, but it is an individual content of experience, and the unique embodiment of a type. And we found, as the most essential result of our whole analysis of Being, that neither in terms of mere experience, which contains only contents immediately given, nor yet in terms of mere abstract thinking, which defines only general types, can the true nature of this third aspect of Being, viz. of the individuality of any given fact, be expressed or discovered. Individuality is a category of the satisfied Will. *This fact* is an individual fact only in so far as *no other* fact than this could meet the purpose that the world as a whole, and consequently every fact in the world, expresses. I can then never merely experience that *this fact* is unique, or that this individual is unique. Nor can I ever merely, by abstract thinking, define what there is about the type of *this fact* which demands that it should be unique, or should be an individual at all. In so far then as I merely feel the presence of contents of experience, I can postulate that they stand for or hint the existence of individuals. But as mere observer I never empirically find that this is so. In so far as, once having thus felt the presence of facts of experience, I proceed, as for instance in my study of science, to describe the types and the laws of these contents of my experience, I can once more postulate that I am indeed thinking about realities which, in themselves, are individual. But I can never discover, by my thinking process taken as such, what constitutes their individuality. When I become aware of the presence of one of my fellow-beings, I never either feel or abstractly conceive why this being is such that no other can take his place in Being. For if I observe how he looks and acts, I so far do not observe in him any reason why another might not look and act precisely as he does. And if I proceed abstractly to conceive the fashions and laws of his behavior, I expressly define only general types. It is precisely the *no other* character, the uniqueness, of this individual, the character whereby he is this man and nobody else, which neither my observation nor my description of my fellow can compass.

Hence, as we long since saw, for us, creatures of fragmentary consciousness, and of dissatisfied will, as we here in the temporal order are, the individuality of all things remains a postulate, constitutes for us the central mystery of Being, and is rather the object that our exclusive affections seek, that our ethical consciousness demands, that love presupposes, than any object which we in our finitude ever attain. Now this, our relation to the true individuality of the beings of our whole world, holds as well in case of the Self of each one of us, as of the remotest star or of God himself. The individual is real; but under our finite conditions of dissatisfied longing, the individual is never found.

Just here, however, lies the first of the three considerations whereby our general theory of Being has a bearing upon the doctrine of Immortality. The Self, however you take it, — whether as the Self of this instant's longing, or the Self of any temporal series of deeds and of experiences, is in itself real. It possesses individuality. And it possesses this individuality, as we have seen, in God and for God. In its relation, namely, to the whole universe of experiences and of deeds, this Self occupies its real and unique place as such that no other can take that place, or can accomplish that task, or can fulfil that aim. Now the consciousness which faces the true individuality of this Self is, by our whole hypothesis, continuous with, and directly one with, the finite and fragmentary consciousness that the Self possesses of its own present life. The Self can say: "As human Self, here and now in time, I know not consciously what my own individuality is, or what I really am. But God knows. And now God knows this not in so far as he is another than myself, *i.e.* another individual than the Self that I am. He knows me in so far as, in the eternal world, in my final union with him, I know myself as real. In him, namely, and as sharing in his perfect Will, my will comes consciously to find wherein lies precisely what satisfies my will, and so makes my life, this unique life, distinct from all other lives. Here, now, in the human form, my life so imperfectly expresses for my present consciousness, my will, that I indeed intend to stand in contrast to all other individuals, and to be unique; but still find, in my finite dissatisfaction, that I am not here aware *how* my will wins its unique expression. But in God's Will, and as united to him, my will does win this unique expression. What is, however, in the idealistic world, is somewhere known. The knowing, however, that my will wins unique expression in my life, and in my life as distinct from all other individual lives, is, *ipso facto*, my individual and conscious knowing. Hence in God, in the eternal world, and in unity, yet in contrast with all other individual lives, my own Self, whose consciousness is here so flickering, attains an insight into my own reality and uniqueness."

The inevitable consequence is that every Self, in the eternal world, wins a consciousness of its own individual meaning, by virtue of the very fact that it sees itself as this unique individual, at one with God's whole life, and fulfilling his Will through its own unique share in that Will. However mysterious our individuality is here, in our temporally present consciousness, we, in the eternal world, are aware of what our individuality is. We ourselves, and not merely other individuals, become, in God, conscious of what we are, because, in God, we become aware of how our wills are fulfilled through our union with him, and of how his Will wins its satisfaction only by virtue of our unique share in the whole. "I shall be satisfied," the finite and dissatisfied will may indeed say, "when I awake in thy likeness." And in our union with God, we are, in the eternal world, awake.[1]

So far, however, we make a statement of the conscious aspect of our union with God, — a statement that, in its reference to the temporal endurance of the Self, appears still ambiguous. What we so far assert is that, in God, every individual Self, however insignificant its temporal endurance may seem, eternally possesses a form of consciousness that is wholly other than this our present flickering form of mortal consciousness. And now, precisely such an assertion is indeed the beginning of a philosophical conception of Immortality. In brief, so far, we assert that individuality is real, and belongs to all our life, but that individuality does not appear to us as real individuality in our present human form of consciousness. We accordingly assert that our life, as hid from us now, in the life of God, has another form of consciousness than the one which we now possess ; so that while now we see through

[1] To the development of the aspect of the problem of Immortality that has here been summarized I have devoted my Ingersoll Lecture on the *Conception of Immortality*, published in 1900.

a glass darkly, in God we know even as we are known. This doctrine, as we shall soon find, implies far more regarding the temporal endurance of the Self than we have yet made wholly manifest.

V

But now this first consideration may be supplemented by a second. By the arbitrary selection, and isolation, of any one finite Internal Meaning, you can, as we have said, regard any temporally brief series of conscious finite ideas as a Self. And so regarded, this arbitrarily selected Self appears as implying, so far, no long continuance. It dies with its own moment, or hour, or year, or age, of the world's history. We have indeed just seen that in order to be at all, however transiently, such a Self has to be an individual fact in the realm of Being, and that, as an individual, it is inevitably linked in God with a form of self-consciousness in which its own life and meaning and place in the universe become manifest to it as its own. Even such a Self, then, possesses, in the eternal world, a form of consciousness far transcending that of our present human type of momentary insight. In your eternal union with God you see what even your present life and purposes mean; and they mean, even as they are, infinitely more than your human type of consciousness makes manifest to yourself. But there is, indeed, another aspect of even your most transient life as a changing and apparently passing Self. And this aspect comes to light when you ask in what way, and in what sense, any finite Self can come to a temporal end, can die, can cease to be.

A very neglected problem of applied metaphysics here awaits our treatment. In our seventh lecture of the present series we touched upon it briefly in speaking of the selective process in nature and in conscious life. It recurs here in another form.

This problem is the one of the very Possibility of Death. The statement of the problem in these terms may surprise. Yet what is our whole metaphysical inquiry but a seeking to comprehend the possibility of even the most commonplace facts? That death occurs, we know. What death is, common sense cannot tell us. I propose to take up the question here in its most general form, and as a question of metaphysics. The physical death of a man is but a special case of the law of the universal transiency of all temporal facts. We have studied that law, in former lectures, in several aspects. The most universal law of Nature we found to be that of the constant occurrence of events that, once past, are irrevocable. We found that the most general reason for this irrevocableness of every temporal event is simply the individual character of that event as a real fact. What once has occurred can never occur again, simply because whatever is real is individual, is unique, and therefore, in its individuality, is incapable of repetition elsewhere in the world than precisely where it occurs. The very reason that makes us often regard the past as dead beyond recall is then the fact, presupposed, but never experienced by us in our finite capacity, namely, the fact that the past is a realm where unique and individual occurrences have found their place. Because all temporal happenings, or real events, are incapable of being twice present in the world, therefore new times must always bring new happenings; and what has once taken place returns not. In this sense, in the temporal world, individuality and transiency are intimately linked aspects of the universe.

In dealing with the problem of time, we have therefore already dealt, in a sense, with the general problem that underlies this whole question about death. But here we indeed undertake this problem in a more concrete form. In a sense, indeed, the life of every temporal instant dies with that instant, yet what interests us at present is the fact of the temporal termination, not of any and every instant's life, but of certain significant series of life-processes, whose continuance from moment to moment, from year to year, from age to age, we indeed often desire, or regard even as necessary, if our human world is to win for us any adequate meaning, while nevertheless, as a fact, these processes prove to be, from our human point of view, of limited duration. Thus springtime dies, youth passes away, love loses its own; evolution, as we have just seen, goes hand in hand with decay; and above all, the lives of human individuals meet with a termination in physical death, — a termination which is, from our point of view, so meaningless and irrational that it stands as the one classic instance of the might of fate, and of the apparently hopeless bondage of our human form of existence.

And now, taking these concrete instances of death in our temporal world, and viewing them as peculiarly impressive and pathetic examples of temporal transiency, I once more ask, How, from our idealistic point of view, is such death possible at all as a real event? Here is a finite fragment of life, — I care not what it is, so long as it shall possess, for our present human purposes, some deep internal meaning. It may be the life of a mother's love for her infant; it may be the life of two lovers, dreaming of a supernatural happiness; it may be the enthusiasm that inspires a soldier's devotion for his flag, or an artist's longing for his ideal; or finally, it may be the whole personal human life of a hero, of a statesman, or of a saint. Now the law of our human realm of experience is that any such life some day, so far as we can see, comes to an end, and is lost beyond human recall. The mother's love for the present infant becomes a dear memory, while the infant, perhaps, grows into an evil and pain-inspiring maturity. The lovers part, or perhaps forget. Fate of all sorts cuts short, sooner or later, the soldier's, the artist's, the hero's, the saint's activities. Now in all such cases, whether or no what we call physical death intervenes, the same essential problem appears. This is the problem of death in a concrete, but still generalized form. Something with a meaning comes to an end *before* that meaning is worked out to its completion, or is expressed with its intended individual wholeness. The problem presented by such cases is not to be answered by the purely general statement, already made, — the statement that everything temporal is transient, and that only the eternal whole passes not away. That most general statement, by virtue of our theory of the temporal order, does indeed point out that the eternal perfection of the world of the divine Will can only be expressed in a realm of temporal deeds, each one of which, as temporal, is transient, and, as an individual deed, is irrevocable. But what now is our problem is furnished by those series of events in which something individual is attempted, but is, within our ken, never finished at all. We ask about the death which does not apparently result from the mere nature of the time-process, from the mere necessity that every finite and individual event should occupy its one place in the temporal realm. No, the death which here concerns us is the ending that seems to defeat all the higher types of individual striving known to us. And now, we state this problem, as idealists, thus, How can such death as this have any place at all in Being?

Our clew to the answer is, however, furnished to us by our whole Theory of Being. A realist would not venture to raise our question, if once he recognized the fact of death as a real fact at all. For him, death would be an independently real fact; and of no such fact could he consistently ask the reason. A mystic would indeed not leave unanswered our problem. He would reply, "Death is an illusion." But then, for the mystic, *all* is illusion. A critical rationalist would simply say: "It is the valid law of Being. All finite things pass away." But we, as idealists, have another task whenever we attribute Being to any object. For us, to be means to fulfil a purpose. If death is real at all, it is real only in so far as it fulfils a purpose. But now, what purpose can be fulfilled by the ending of a life whose purpose is so far unfulfilled? I answer at once, the purpose that can be fulfilled by the ending of such a life is necessarily a purpose that, in the eternal world, *is consciously known and seen as continuous with, yes, as inclusive of, the very purpose whose fulfilment the temporal death seems to cut short.* This larger purpose may indeed involve, as we have long since seen, the relative inhibition and defeat of the lesser purpose. But in our idealistic world it cannot involve the mere *ignoring* of that lesser purpose. The thwarting of the lesser purpose is always included within the fulfilment of the larger and more integral purpose. The possibility of death depends upon the transcending of death through a life that is richer and more conscious than is the life which death cuts short, and the richer life in question is, in meaning, if not in temporal sequence, continuous with the very life that death interrupts.

Or, to put the case otherwise: A conscious process, with a meaning, but with a meaning still imperfectly expressed, is cut short, and left with its purpose still disembodied. So far we have a fact, namely, the fact of death, but so characterized that its Being is stated in merely negative terms. We, as idealists, ask, What is this death? If real, it is a positive fact; it is not something merely negative. But what positive fact? For us, all facts are known facts, are facts of consciousness and ultimately of the consciousness of the Absolute. The defeated purpose is such only in so far as it is known, and then is known as terminated. But is known, I insist, by whom? In terms of what individual conscious life does even the Absolute know of the finite life that has ended? I answer, the defeated purpose is known by some conscious being who can say: "This was my purpose, but temporally I no longer seek its embodiment. I have abandoned it. It is no longer a purpose of my life." The life that is ended is thus viewed by the Absolute as followed, at some period of time, by another life that in its meaning is continuous with the first. This new life it is which says, "No longer is that terminated purpose pursued by me." But now, in our world, where only the fulfilment of purpose has any Being whatever, the new consciousness, in and for which the old life is terminated, must say, "That ceasing of my former purpose, that ending of my past life, has its meaning; and this meaning is continuous with my own larger meaning. My former Self is dead, only in so far as my new Self sees the meaning of that death." Or in other words, the new Self is really inclusive of and able to transcend the meaning of the old Self; or, in fact, the two Selves really form stages in the development of one Individual. Thus from our point of view, even the selective process which we before studied in Nature is a process involving survival as well as death.

Not otherwise, in our idealistic world, is death possible. I can temporally die; but I myself, as larger individual, in the eternal world, see *why* I die; and thus, in essence, my whole individuality is continuous in true meaning with the individuality that dies. The lovers may part, but in the eternal world, individuality that is temporally sequent to theirs, and continuous in meaning with theirs, is found as consciously knowing why they parted. Was it faithlessness? Then it was sin; and in the eternal world, this larger individuality is found viewing the parting as their fault, for which, as for all sin, atoning deeds are needed. Was it wisdom that they should part? Then, in the eternal world the sorrow of their parting is continuous with a willing bearing of this parting, as one of time's sorrows. It is so with the mother's loss of the infant, or with the hero's or artist's pursuit of his ideal. It is so too with physical death. How, and in what way, the deathless individuality sees itself as including and fulfilling the selfhood whose struggles death terminates, we do not in any detail at present know. That this larger selfhood is in the end in unity with the divine Selfhood we know; but we know too that it is not as something lost in God, that the dead Self of our human life wins its unity with the divine. For our theory implies that when I die, my death is possible as a real fact only in so far as, in the eternal world, at some time after death, an individual lives who consciously says: "It was my life that there temporally terminated unfinished, its meaning not embodied in its experience. But I now, in my higher Self-expression, see why and how this was so; and in God I attain, otherwise, my fulfilment and my peace."

The Possibility of Death, as a metaphysical fact, in a world where all facts are facts of consciousness, and where even the worst sorrows and defeats exist only as partial expressions of a divine meaning, depends, then, upon the deeper fact that whoever dies with his meanings unexpressed, lives, as individual, to see, in the eternal world, just his unique meaning finally expressed, in a life sequent to, although not necessarily temporally continuous with, the life that death terminated. I shall finally die, in time, only when I come to say of myself, "My work is consciously and absolutely accomplished."

VI

But this brings us to our third consideration, which, in fact, has been already expressed in our former words, both in this and in foregoing lectures. An ethical task is essentially one of which I can never say, "My work is finished." Special tasks come to an end. The work of offering my unique service, as this Individual, to God and to my fellows, can never be finished in any time, however great. For always, at any future moment, if I know my union with God, I shall know, whatever my form of consciousness, that there are my fellows beyond me, different from myself, and yet linked by the ties of the divine unity to my life and my destiny. I shall know then that I have not yet accomplished all of the relations to them which my ethical tasks involve. To be an ethical individual is to live a life with one goal, but contrasted with all other lives. Every deed emphasizes the contrast, and so gives opportunity for new deeds. A consciously last moral task is a contradiction in terms. For whenever I act, I create a new situation in the world's life, a situation that never before was, and that never can recur. It is of the essence of the moral law to demand, however, that whenever a new deed of service is possible, I should undertake to do it. But a new deed is possible whenever my world is in a new situation. My moral tasks spring afresh into life whenever I seek to terminate it. To serve God is to create new opportunities for service. My human form of consciousness is indeed doubtless a transient incident of my immortal life. Not thus haltingly, not thus blindly, not thus darkly and ignorantly, shall I always labor. But the service of the eternal is an essentially endless service. There can be no last moral deed.

And thus, in three ways, our union with God implies an immortal and individual life. For first, in God, we are real individuals, and really conscious Selves, — a fact which neither human thought nor human experience, nor yet any aspect of our present form of consciousness, can make present and obvious to our consciousness, as now it is. But since this very fact of our eternal and individual Selfhood is real as a conscious fact, in God, we too, in him, are conscious of our individuality in a form higher than that now accessible to us. And secondly, the death of an individual is a possible fact, in an idealistic world, only in case such death occurs as an incident in the life of a larger individual, whose existence as this Self and no other, in its individual contrast with the rest of the world, is continuous in meaning with the individuality that death cuts short. No Self, then, can end until itself consciously declares, "My work is done, here I cease." But, thirdly, no ethical Self, in its union with God, can ever view its task as accomplished, or its work as done, or its individuality as ceasing to seek, in God, a temporal future. In Eternity all is done, and we too rest from our labors. In Time there is no end to the individual ethical task.

VII

But now these considerations lead us, in our closing words, to dwell briefly upon an aspect of the life of the

Ethical Individual which has grown more and more obvious as we have proceeded.

We have often spoken of the Human Individual as a finite being. In the temporal order, he everywhere remains so; for he has a temporal beginning; and at any moment of time he has so far lived but for a finite period, has so far accomplished but a finite task, and seeks, as one whose life is unfinished, his own temporal future, which is not yet. The same can be said of any temporal being, of whatever degree of dignity or of wisdom, whose life is considered from any period of time onwards, and up to any point of time. But now what of the completed Self, of the Ethical Individual, as it comes consciously to distinguish itself from all others, in the eternal world, and as it finds itself fully expressed in its own unique aspect of the life of the Absolute? Is it still to be called a finite Self?

The plain answer of course is that, as the complete expression of a Self-representative System of purpose and fulfilment, it is there, viz. in the eternal world, no longer finite, but infinite. Yet it differs from the Absolute Self in being *partial*, in requiring the other individuals as its own supplement, and in distinguishing itself from them in such wise as to make their purposes not wholly and in every sense its own. It is, as Spinoza would have said of his divine attributes, "infinite in its own kind"; only that, to be sure, its existence is not independent of that of the other Individuals, as the Spinozistic attributes were independent of one another. For it is not related to these other selves *merely* through the common relation to God; on the contrary, it is just as truly related to God *by means of* its relation to them. Its life with them is an eternally fulfilled social life, and the completion of this eternal order also means the self-conscious expression of God, the Individual of Individuals, who dwells in all, as they in him.

There is needed a convenient term for expressing the nature of an individual being which, although "infinite in its own kind" (that is, infinite as a complete expression of its own self-representative purpose), is still essentially but a part of a larger system, involving still other purposes and beings. The word "finite" suggests, indeed, the character of *needing a relatively external Other*. In *this* sense, however, it remains certainly true that the Ethical Individual profoundly needs, in the eternal world, as its Other, without which it can neither be nor be conceived, the universe of the other Ethical Individuals. And it needs them not merely as parts of itself, but as its comrades. If then the term "finite" could be used without ambiguity in this special sense, one could indeed say that in contrast with the Absolute Individual, who is the sole *completely integrated* Self, the single Ethical Individual remains finite, since it is, even in the eternal world, essentially dependent, even for the expression of its own will, upon the other Individuals beyond itself, in contrast with whom it defines itself. But since the word "finite" is, with technical accuracy, used for systems that are *not* self-representative in type, the best way is not to attempt any unauthorized use of the term, but to characterize the eternal ethical Individual as *infinite but partial*. Its fellows, in the self-conscious organism of the Absolute, are, as we have seen, infinite in number, since the Absolute must possess an infinite wealth of self-representation. On the other hand, the various individual Selves may, and in an infinite number of cases *must*, as the various self-expressions of the same system, interpenetrate in the most manifold ways, sharing in countless instances the same immediate contents of experience, even while viewing these contents in different orders, and as the expressions of different, although interrelated, individual life-purposes. The possibility, and in fact the necessity, of some such structure, in the completed self-representative system, we discussed, in a very inadequate fashion, in our Supplementary Essay.[1] Had we time here to illustrate the complications which the recent investigations of self-representative systems have shown to be characteristic of their structure, we should see clearly that, although the world of the Absolute Individual is, from our point of view, an individual selection from an infinitely wealthy realm of unrealized possibilities, its internal structure, in order that it should be self-representative at all, must involve the sort of formal complexity here suggested, and must therefore make inevitable that interpenetration of the lives of countless and various Selves which our own theory of the origin and social nature of the ethical Self demands. It is this interpenetration, in various ways and degrees, of the lives of the completed Selves in the eternal world which, according to our hypothesis concerning Nature, would presumably be manifested, in a phenomenal way, in the temporal world, by the processes of intercommunication amongst the various members of any social order, or amongst what to us seem widely sundered regions of Nature. For according to our hypothesis, no actual rela-

[1] p. 517, *sqq*., p. 546, of the former series.

tions of various minds are merely external and mechanically determined; but all are due to the fact that every Self, representing in its own way the Absolute, represents also other Selves in a way and order that may, in the temporal world, appear to any extent as a process whose individual instances are determined by special physical conditions.

The *infinity* and the accompanying *partial* character of each Ethical Individual suggests, however, still one more consideration that older theological doctrines have very generally failed to recognize as a possibility. Yet the modern theory of Infinite Assemblages makes it almost a commonplace of exact thinking, when once any system has been recognized as infinitely complex in structure, to take note of this consideration in dealing with such a system.

To an infinite collection of objects, as we saw in the Supplementary Essay, *the axiom that the part cannot be equal to the whole does not apply.* There is a perfectly definite sense[1] in which a part of an infinitely complex system can remain, not only a part that excludes from itself *some* portion of the whole, but a part that is only one of an infinite number of mutually exclusive parts of this whole. Thus, to give a purely formal instance of what I here have in mind, let me ask you to consider the whole numbers. Amongst the whole

[1] See, concerning the mathematical considerations here in question, the recent report of Schönfliess: "Die Entwickelung der Lehre von den Punktmannigfaltigkeiten," in the *Jahresbericht der deutschen Mathematiker-Vereinigung*, Bd. VIII, Heft II, in particular, p. 4, *sq.*, p. 10, *sqq.*, and p. 18, *sqq.*

numbers you can select at pleasure a relatively very small sub-class, or *part;* viz., *those whole numbers which are powers of* 2, that is, 2 itself, as the *first* power, the *square* of 2, the *cube* of 2, and so on. You can then select *another* part; viz., *the whole numbers which are powers of* 3; and a third part; viz., *those which are powers of* 5. You can suppose this process of selection carried on so that each one of the demonstrably infinite collection of prime numbers, 2, 3, 5, 7, 11, 13, etc., shall form the basis of a selection of a partial collection of whole numbers, viz. its own powers. Thus the powers of 7, of 11, of 13, and so on, would form a system of collections of whole numbers. Now consider these resulting *partial collections of whole numbers.* Each collection is *precisely as infinite* as the entire series of whole numbers. For 2, or 3, or 5, or whatever other prime number you have taken, has a *first* power, a *second* power, a *third* power, and so on without end. For every whole number defines a new power of the prime numbers in question. Each of the partial collections of whole numbers thus defined has, in consequence, one number to correspond to *every whole number* without exception, namely, its first number, its second, its third, and so on without end. And yet no two of these partial collections contain *any* whole numbers in common; for no power of any prime number is equal to any power of another prime number. All of the partial collections contain nothing, however, *but* whole numbers; and there are an infinity of these infinite partial collections, although each of them is, in its own internal complication, precisely equal to the whole from which they are all alike selected. Nor do even they, if taken together, in the least exhaust the original collection of whole numbers; since there are countless equally infinite collections of whole numbers which are *not* powers of any prime number, but which are products of various powers of prime numbers. And so we can define an infinite system such that it contains an infinity of mutually exclusive parts, while each of these parts is equal to the whole in internal complexity of structure, and in the multitude of its own parts.

This instance, taken by itself, is formal and seemingly trivial. It assumes metaphysical importance, however, as soon as you remember that, from our point of view, the infinity of the real system of the Self, whether in case of the Ethical Individual, or in case of the Absolute, is an actual, and, in the eternal world, a completed infinity. We see then that, from our point of view, the Ethical Individual, however small a part of the infinite System of Individuals he may be, yet may be conceived as strictly equal in infinity of structure and of variety of content to the Absolute, having a series of experiences precisely as rich in its details, a knowledge precisely as multitudinous, a meaning precisely as complex, as the Absolute Self in its wholeness. Yet the Ethical Individual may be none the less *only* a part, — *only* one of an infinite number of equally partial Individuals, whose lives, to be sure, are not in every respect mutually exclusive, but who are not at all confounded either with one another or with the Absolute in its wholeness.

We therefore *need not conceive the eternal Ethical Individual, however partial he may be, as in any sense less in the grade of complication of his activity or in the multitude of his acts of will than is the Absolute.* And thus we see, in a new way, how the individual Self may recognize that in God it finds its own fulfilment, while still it clearly distinguishes other Selves, within the Absolute, as in one sense beyond it. It may be conceived then as a Part equal to the Whole, and finally united, as such equal, to the Whole wherein it dwells.

— But we must turn from the eternal back to our temporal world. The special, the very finite, and imperfect task of these lectures is indeed accomplished. We have dealt with the nature of God, with the origin and meaning of man's life, and with the union of God and Man. Our result is this : — Despite God's absolute unity, we, as individuals, preserve and attain our unique lives and meanings, and are not lost in the very life that sustains us, and that needs us as its own expression. This life is real through us all ; and we are real through our union with that life. Close is our touch with the eternal. Boundless is the meaning of our nature. Its mysteries baffle our present science, and escape our present experience ; but they need not blind our eyes to the central unity of Being, nor make us feel lost in a realm where all the wanderings of time mean the process whereby is discovered the homeland of Eternity.

INDEX TO THE FIRST AND SECOND SERIES

[The First Series, on the *Four Conceptions of Being*, is referred to in this index as I, the Second Series as II. The terms for the more fundamental conceptions are printed in SMALL CAPITALS. The names of authors cited appear in *italics*.]

world of Description with the final expression of the Will demanded by the Fourth Conception of Being, 95–104; this final expression is a World of Appreciation, 106. — Limitations of the World of Description: it is not a world of Individuals, I, 96; but of Validity, *id.;* its discovered series are not in the form of Well-Ordered series, 97, 101, 102; the endless search for the *between* meets limitations in experience, 97; it essentially implies the possibility of various descriptions of the same facts, 99, 100; hence never gives the truth its final and individual form, 100; it is justified mainly by the fact that discrimination itself is a type of action, 101–104. — The World of Description in concrete form as the world of our socially trained consciousness of Nature, 155, 156, 175–204. — Nature conceived by our common sense as the common object for various observers, 175–180; hence the contrast between the physical world and our fellows tends to grow sharper as we grow more civilized, 180, 181; consequent dualism, 184; and resort to discrimination, and to the search for the *between* in our dealings with Nature, *id.;* abstract notion of human experience in general, 185; search for law in nature, 187–189; invariants always discoverable in exactly describable series of facts, 188, 189; postulate of the further unchangeableness of these invariants through lapse of time, 189–192; social motives for this postulate, 192–195; the postulate not self-evident, 195; historical illustrations, 195–197; relative value and limitations of the postulate, 197–204. — The possibility of a process in Nature that is similar to our human search for the *between*, 319; relation to theory of evolution, 319–323.

Design, argument from, as topic of a possible study of Natural Religion, I, 1.

Determination, as a characteristic of Being, I, 39; relation of, to concept of Individual, 39, 40, 296–299, 335–339, 570–588, 455–460. [See INDIVIDUAL.]

Difference, Likenesses and differences in facts, as objects of knowledge, relation of these likenesses and differences to the Will, II, 46–53.

Dualism. Realism inevitably dualistic as to the relation of Idea and Object, I, 134; consequences of this dualism fatal to realism, 134–138. — Argument against the dualism of Matter and Mind, II, 207–242.

Eckhart, Meister, I, 42, 72, 78, 82, 176, 177, 547.

Ego, see SELF, and SELF, THE HUMAN SELF.

Eleatic doctrine of Being, I, 63; its One as an object of Thought, 64; its Realism, 98; permanence of the real according to, 105; mentioned, 109, 111, 163.

Empedocles, I, 63.

Empiricism, I, 360–374; II, 11–24.

Ens, I, 51 *note.*

Equal, In a self-representative or infinite system the part may be equal to the whole, I, 510–519, — this property used as definition of the infinite, 510, 511, 512 *note.* — Results as to the equality of the completed Ethical Individual and the Absolute, II, 449–452.

Equations, Theory of, the metaphysical aspect of the fundamental existence-theorem in this theory, I, 213–217.

Esse existentiæ, and *Esse essentiæ*, I, 51 *note.*

Essence, as contrasted with Existence in technical usage, 49, 50, 51 *note.*

ETERNITY and THE ETERNAL. — The concept of eternity founded upon that of time, II, 133; the temporal world, in its wholeness, an eternal world, *id.;* grounds for this conclusion, 138–142; the two senses of *present*, which are observable in our own consciousness of time [see TIME] enable us to define how the whole temporal order is *present at once* to the Absolute, 138; this presence the

CATALOG OF DOVER BOOKS

Philosophy, Religion

GUIDE TO PHILOSOPHY, C. E. M. Joad. A modern classic which examines many crucial problems which man has pondered through the ages: Does free will exist? Is there plan in the universe? How do we know and validate our knowledge? Such opposed solutions as subjective idealism and realism, chance and teleology, vitalism and logical positivism, are evaluated and the contributions of the great philosophers from the Greeks to moderns like Russell, Whitehead, and others, are considered in the context of each problem. "The finest introduction," BOSTON TRANSCRIPT. Index. Classified bibliography. 592pp. 5⅜ x 8.
T297 Paperbound **$2.00**

HISTORY OF ANCIENT PHILOSOPHY, W. Windelband. One of the clearest, most accurate comprehensive surveys of Greek and Roman philosophy. Discusses ancient philosophy in general, intellectual life in Greece in the 7th and 6th centuries B.C., Thales, Anaximander, Anaximenes, Heraclitus, the Eleatics, Empedocles, Anaxagoras, Leucippus, the Pythagoreans, the Sophists, Socrates, Democritus (20 pages), Plato (50 pages), Aristotle (70 pages), the Peripatetics, Stoics, Epicureans, Sceptics, Neo-platonists, Christian Apologists, etc. 2nd German edition translated by H. E. Cushman. xv + 393pp. 5⅜ x 8. T357 Paperbound **$1.85**

ILLUSTRATIONS OF THE HISTORY OF MEDIEVAL THOUGHT AND LEARNING, R. L. Poole. Basic analysis of the thought and lives of the leading philosophers and ecclesiastics from the 8th to the 14th century—Abailard, Ockham, Wycliffe, Marsiglio of Padua, and many other great thinkers who carried the torch of Western culture and learning through the "Dark Ages": political, religious, and metaphysical views. Long a standard work for scholars and one of the best introductions to medieval thought for beginners. Index. 10 Appendices. xiii + 327pp. 5⅜ x 8.
T674 Paperbound **$1.85**

PHILOSOPHY AND CIVILIZATION IN THE MIDDLE AGES, M. de Wulf. This semi-popular survey covers aspects of medieval intellectual life such as religion, philosophy, science, the arts, etc. It also covers feudalism vs. Catholicism, rise of the universities, mendicant orders, monastic centers, and similar topics. Unabridged. Bibliography. Index. viii + 320pp. 5⅜ x 8.
T284 Paperbound **$1.75**

AN INTRODUCTION TO SCHOLASTIC PHILOSOPHY, Prof. M. de Wulf. Formerly entitled SCHOLASTICISM OLD AND NEW, this volume examines the central scholastic tradition from St. Anselm, Albertus Magnus, Thomas Aquinas, up to Suarez in the 17th century. The relation of scholasticism to ancient and medieval philosophy and science in general is clear and easily followed. The second part of the book considers the modern revival of scholasticism, the Louvain position, relations with Kantianism and Positivism. Unabridged. xvi + 271pp. 5⅜ x 8.
T296 Clothbound **$3.50**
T283 Paperbound **$1.75**

A HISTORY OF MODERN PHILOSOPHY, H. Höffding. An exceptionally clear and detailed coverage of western philosophy from the Renaissance to the end of the 19th century. Major and minor men such as Pomponazzi, Bodin, Boehme, Telesius, Bruno, Copernicus, da Vinci, Kepler, Galileo, Bacon, Descartes, Hobbes, Spinoza, Leibniz, Wolff, Locke, Newton, Berkeley, Hume, Erasmus, Montesquieu, Voltaire, Diderot, Rousseau, Lessing, Kant, Herder, Fichte, Schelling, Hegel, Schopenhauer, Comte, Mill, Darwin, Spencer, Hartmann, Lange, and many others, are discussed in terms of theory of knowledge, logic, cosmology, and psychology. Index. 2 volumes, total of 1159pp. 5⅜ x 8. T117 Vol. 1, Paperbound **$2.00**
T118 Vol. 2, Paperbound **$2.00**

ARISTOTLE, A. E. Taylor. A brilliant, searching non-technical account of Aristotle and his thought written by a foremost Platonist. It covers the life and works of Aristotle; classification of the sciences; logic; first philosophy; matter and form; causes; motion and eternity; God; physics; metaphysics; and similar topics. Bibliography. New Index compiled for this edition. 128pp. 5⅜ x 8. T280 Paperbound **$1.00**

THE SYSTEM OF THOMAS AQUINAS, M. de Wulf. Leading Neo-Thomist, one of founders of University of Louvain, gives concise exposition to central doctrines of Aquinas, as a means toward determining his value to modern philosophy, religion. Formerly "Medieval Philosophy Illustrated from the System of Thomas Aquinas." Trans. by E. Messenger. Introduction. 151pp. 5⅜ x 8.
T568 Paperbound **$1.25**

LEIBNIZ, H. W. Carr. Most stimulating middle-level coverage of basic philosophical thought of Leibniz. Easily understood discussion, analysis of major works: "Theodicy," "Principles of Nature and Grace," "Monadology"; Leibniz's influence; intellectual growth; correspondence; disputes with Bayle, Malebranche, Newton; importance of his thought today, with reinterpretation in modern terminology. "Power and mastery," London Times. Bibliography. Index. 226pp. 5⅜ x 8.
T624 Paperbound **$1.35**

AN ESSAY CONCERNING HUMAN UNDERSTANDING, John Locke. Edited by A. C. Fraser. Unabridged reprinting of definitive edition; only complete edition of "Essay" in print. Marginal analyses of almost every paragraph; hundreds of footnotes; authoritative 140-page biographical, critical, historical prolegomena. Indexes. 1170pp. 5⅜ x 8.
T530 Vol. 1 (Books 1, 2) Paperbound **$2.25**
T531 Vol. 2 (Books 3, 4) Paperbound **$2.25**
2 volume set **$4.50**

THE PHILOSOPHY OF HISTORY, G. W. F. Hegel. One of the great classics of western thought which reveals Hegel's basic principle: that history is not chance but a rational process, the realization of the Spirit of Freedom. Ranges from the oriental cultures of subjective thought to the classical subjective cultures, to the modern absolute synthesis where spiritual and secular may be reconciled. Translation and introduction by J. Sibree. Introduction by C. Hegel. Special introduction for this edition by Prof. Carl Friedrich. xxxix + 447pp. 5⅜ x 8.
T112 Paperbound **$1.85**

THE PHILOSOPHY OF HEGEL, W. T. Stace. The first detailed analysis of Hegel's thought in English, this is especially valuable since so many of Hegel's works are out of print. Dr. Stace examines Hegel's debt to Greek idealists and the 18th century and then proceeds to a careful description and analysis of Hegel's first principles, categories, reason, dialectic method, his logic, philosophy of nature and spirit, etc. Index. Special 14 x 20 chart of Hegelian system. x + 526pp. 5⅜ x 8. T254 Paperbound **$2.25**

THE WILL TO BELIEVE and HUMAN IMMORTALITY, W. James. Two complete books bound as one. THE WILL TO BELIEVE discusses the interrelations of belief, will, and intellect in man; chance vs. determinism, free will vs. determinism, free will vs. fate, pluralism vs. monism; the philosophies of Hegel and Spencer, and more. HUMAN IMMORTALITY examines the question of survival after death and develops an unusual and powerful argument for immortality. Two prefaces. Index. Total of 429pp. 5⅜ x 8. T291 Paperbound **$1.75**

THE WORLD AND THE INDIVIDUAL, Josiah Royce. Only major effort by an American philosopher to interpret nature of things in systematic, comprehensive manner. Royce's formulation of an absolute voluntarism remains one of the original and profound solutions to the problems involved. Part One, Four Historical Conceptions of Being, inquires into first principles, true meaning and place of individuality. Part Two, Nature, Man, and the Moral Order, is application of first principles to problems concerning religion, evil, moral order. Introduction by J. E. Smith, Yale Univ. Index. 1070pp. 5⅜ x 8.
T561 Vol. 1 Paperbound **$2.25**
T562 Vol. 2 Paperbound **$2.25**
Two volume set **$4.50**

THE PHILOSOPHICAL WRITINGS OF PEIRCE, edited by J. Buchler. This book (formerly THE PHILOSOPHY OF PEIRCE) is a carefully integrated exposition of Peirce's complete system composed of selections from his own work. Symbolic logic, scientific method, theory of signs, pragmatism, epistemology, chance, cosmology, ethics, and many other topics are treated by one of the greatest philosophers of modern times. This is the only inexpensive compilation of his key ideas. xvi + 386pp. 5⅜ x 8. T217 Paperbound **$2.00**

EXPERIENCE AND NATURE, John Dewey. An enlarged, revised edition of the Paul Carus lectures which Dewey delivered in 1925. It covers Dewey's basic formulation of the problem of knowledge, with a full discussion of other systems, and a detailing of his own concepts of the relationship of external world, mind, and knowledge. Starts with a thorough examination of the philosophical method; examines the interrelationship of experience and nature; analyzes experience on basis of empirical naturalism, the formulation of law, role of language and social factors in knowledge; etc. Dewey's treatment of central problems in philosophy is profound but extremely easy to follow. ix + 448pp. 5⅜ x 8.
T471 Paperbound **$1.85**

THE PHILOSOPHICAL WORKS OF DESCARTES. The definitive English edition of all the major philosophical works and letters of René Descartes. All of his revolutionary insights, from his famous "Cogito ergo sum" to his detailed account of contemporary science and his astonishingly fruitful concept that all phenomena of the universe (except mind) could be reduced to clear laws by the use of mathematics. An excellent source for the thought of men like Hobbes, Arnauld, Gassendi, etc., who were Descarte's contemporaries. Translated by E. S. Haldane and G. Ross. Introductory notes. Index. Total of 842pp. 5⅜ x 8.
T71 Vol. 1, Paperbound **$2.00**
T72 Vol. 2, Paperbound **$2.00**

THE CHIEF WORKS OF SPINOZA. An unabridged reprint of the famous Bohn edition containing all of Spinoza's most important works: Vol. I: The Theologico-Political Treatise and the Political Treatise. Vol. II: On The Improvement Of Understanding, The Ethics, Selected Letters. Profound and enduring ideas on God, the universe, pantheism, society, religion, the state, democracy, the mind, emotions, freedom and the nature of man, which influenced Goethe, Hegel, Schelling, Coleridge, Whitehead, and many others. Introduction. 2 volumes. 826pp. 5⅜ x 8.
T249 Vol. I, Paperbound **$1.50**
T250 Vol. II, Paperbound **$1.50**

THE SENSE OF BEAUTY, G. Santayana. A revelation of the beauty of language as well as an important philosophic treatise, this work studies the "why, when, and how beauty appears, what conditions an object must fulfill to be beautiful, what elements of our nature make us sensible of beauty, and what the relation is between the constitution of the object and the excitement of our susceptibility." "It is doubtful if a better treatment of the subject has since been published," PEABODY JOURNAL. Index. ix + 275pp. 5⅜ x 8.
T238 Paperbound **$1.00**

PROBLEMS OF ETHICS, Moritz Schlick. The renowned leader of the "Vienna Circle" applies the logical positivist approach to a wide variety of ethical problems: the source and means of attaining knowledge, the formal and material characteristics of the good, moral norms and principles, absolute vs. relative values, free will and responsibility, comparative importance of pleasure and suffering as ethical values, etc. Disarmingly simple and straightforward despite complexity of subject. First English translation, authorized by author before his death, of a thirty-year old classic. Translated and with an introduction by David Rynin. Index. Foreword by Prof. George P. Adams. xxi + 209pp. 5⅜ x 8. T946 Paperbound **$1.45**

AN INTRODUCTION TO EXISTENTIALISM, Robert G. Olson. A new and indispensable guide to one of the major thought systems of our century, the movement that is central to the thinking of some of the most creative figures of the past hundred years. Stresses Heidegger and Sartre, with careful and objective examination of the existentialist position, values—freedom of choice, individual dignity, personal love, creative effort—and answers to the eternal questions of the human condition. Scholarly, unbiased, analytic, unlike most studies of this difficult subject, Prof. Olson's book is aimed at the student of philosophy as well as at the reader with no formal training who is looking for an absorbing, accessible, and thorough introduction to the basic texts. Index. xv + 21pp. 5⅜ x 8½. T55 Paperbound **$1.45**

SYMBOLIC LOGIC, C. I. Lewis and C. H. Langford. Since first publication in 1932, this has been among most frequently cited works on symbolic logic. Still one of the best introductions both for beginners and for mathematicians, philosophers. First part covers basic topics which easily lend themselves to beginning study. Second part is rigorous, thorough development of logistic method, examination of some of most difficult and abstract aspects of symbolic logic, including modal logic, logical paradoxes, many-valued logic, with Prof. Lewis' own contributions. 2nd revised (corrected) edition. 3 appendixes, one new to this edition. 524pp. 5⅜ x 8.
S170 Paperbound **$2.00**

WHITEHEAD'S PHILOSOPHY OF CIVILIZATION, A. H. Johnson. A leading authority on Alfred North Whitehead synthesizes the great philosopher's thought on civilization, scattered throughout various writings, into unified whole. Analysis of Whitehead's general definition of civilization, his reflections on history and influences on its development, his religion, including his analysis of Christianity, concept of solitariness as first requirement of personal religion, and so on. Other chapters cover views on minority groups, society, civil liberties, education. Also critical comments on Whitehead's philosophy. Written with general reader in mind. A perceptive introduction to important area of the thought of a leading philosopher of our century. Revised index and bibliography. xii + 211pp. 5⅜ x 8½.
T996 Paperbound **$1.50**

WHITEHEAD'S THEORY OF REALITY, A. H. Johnson. Introductory outline of Whitehead's theory of actual entities, the heart of his philosophy of reality, followed by his views on nature of God, philosophy of mind, theory of value (truth, beauty, goodness and their opposites), analyses of other philosophers, attitude toward science. A perspicacious lucid introduction by author of dissertation on Whitehead, written under the subject's supervision at Harvard. Good basic view for beginning students of philosophy and for those who are simply interested in important contemporary ideas. Revised index and bibliography. xiii + 267pp. 5⅜ x 8½.
T989 Paperbound **$1.50**

MIND AND THE WORLD-ORDER, C. I. Lewis. Building upon the work of Peirce, James, and Dewey, Professor Lewis outlines a theory of knowledge in terms of "conceptual pragmatism." Dividing truth into abstract mathematical certainty and empirical truth, the author demonstrates that the traditional understanding of the a priori must be abandoned. Detailed analyses of philosophy, metaphysics, method, the "given" in experience, knowledge of objects, nature of the a priori, experience and order, and many others. Appendices. xiv + 446pp. 5⅜ x 8.
T359 Paperbound **$1.95**

SCEPTICISM AND ANIMAL FAITH, G. Santayana. To eliminate difficulties in the traditional theory of knowledge, Santayana distinguishes between the independent existence of objects and the essence our mind attributes to them. Scepticism is thereby established as a form of belief, and animal faith is shown to be a necessary condition of knowledge. Belief, classical idealism, intuition, memory, symbols, literary psychology, and much more, discussed with unusual clarity and depth. Index. xii + 314pp. 5⅜ x 8. T235 Clothbound **$3.50**
T236 Paperbound **$1.50**

LANGUAGE AND MYTH, E. Cassirer. Analyzing the non-rational thought processes which go to make up culture, Cassirer demonstrates that beneath both language and myth there lies a dominant unconscious "grammar" of experience whose categories and canons are not those of logical thought. His analyses of seemingly diverse phenomena such as Indian metaphysics, the Melanesian "mana," the Naturphilosophie of Schelling, modern poetry, etc., are profound without being pedantic. Introduction and translation by Susanne Langer. Index. x + 103pp. 5⅜ x 8.
T51 Paperbound **$1.25**

***THE ANALYSIS OF MATTER, Bertrand Russell.** A classic which has retained its importance in understanding the relation between modern physical theory and human perception. Logical analysis of physics, prerelativity physics, causality, scientific inference, Weyl's theory, tensors, invariants and physical interpretations, periodicity, and much more is treated with Russell's usual brilliance. "Masterly piece of clear thinking and clear writing," NATION AND ATHENAEUM. "Most thorough treatment of the subject," THE NATION. Introduction. Index. 8 figures. viii + 408pp. 5⅜ x 8. S231 Paperbound **$1.95**

CONCEPTUAL THINKING (A LOGICAL INQUIRY), S. Körner. Discusses origin, use of general concepts on which language is based, and the light they shed on basic philosophical questions. Rigorously examines how different concepts are related; how they are linked to experience; problems in the field of contact between exact logical, mathematical, and scientific concepts, and the inexactness of everyday experience (studied at length). This work elaborates many new approaches to the traditional problems of philosophy—epistemology, value theories, metaphysics, aesthetics, morality. "Rare originality . . . brings a new rigour into philosophical argument," Philosophical Quarterly. New corrected second edition. Index. vii + 301pp. 5⅜ x 8. T516 Paperbound **$1.75**

INTRODUCTION TO SYMBOLIC LOGIC, S. Langer. No special knowledge of math required — probably the clearest book ever written on symbolic logic, suitable for the layman, general scientist, and philosopher. You start with simple symbols and advance to a knowledge of the Boole-Schroeder and Russell-Whitehead systems. Forms, logical structure, classes, the calculus of propositions, logic of the syllogism, etc., are all covered. "One of the clearest and simplest introductions," MATHEMATICS GAZETTE. Second enlarged, revised edition. 368pp. 5⅜ x 8. S164 Paperbound **$1.75**

LANGUAGE, TRUTH AND LOGIC, A. J. Ayer. A clear, careful analysis of the basic ideas of Logical Positivism. Building on the work of Schlick, Russell, Carnap, and the Viennese School, Mr. Ayer develops a detailed exposition of the nature of philosophy, science, and metaphysics; the Self and the World; logic and common sense, and other philosophic concepts. An aid to clarity of thought as well as the first full-length development of Logical Positivism in English. Introduction by Bertrand Russell. Index. 160pp. 5⅜ x 8. T10 Paperbound **$1.25**

ESSAYS IN EXPERIMENTAL LOGIC, J. Dewey. Based upon the theory that knowledge implies a judgment which in turn implies an inquiry, these papers consider the inquiry stage in terms of: the relationship of thought and subject matter, antecedents of thought, data and meanings. 3 papers examine Bertrand Russell's thought, while 2 others discuss pragmatism and a final essay presents a new theory of the logic of values. Index. viii + 444pp. 5⅜ x 8. T73 Paperbound **$1.95**

TRAGIC SENSE OF LIFE, M. de Unamuno. The acknowledged masterpiece of one of Spain's most influential thinkers. Between the despair at the inevitable death of man and all his works and the desire for something better, Unamuno finds that "saving incertitude" that alone can console us. This dynamic appraisal of man's faith in God and in himself has been called "a masterpiece" by the ENCYCLOPAEDIA BRITANNICA. xxx + 332pp. 5⅜ x 8. T257 Paperbound **$1.95**

HISTORY OF DOGMA, A. Harnack. Adolph Harnack, who died in 1930, was perhaps the greatest Church historian of all time. In this epoch-making history, which has never been surpassed in comprehensiveness and wealth of learning, he traces the development of the authoritative Christian doctrinal system from its first crystallization in the 4th century down through the Reformation, including also a brief survey of the later developments through the Infallibility decree of 1870. He reveals the enormous influence of Greek thought on the early Fathers, and discusses such topics as the Apologists, the great councils, Manichaeism, the historical position of Augustine, the medieval opposition to indulgences, the rise of Protestantism, the relations of Luther's doctrines with modern tendencies of thought, and much more. "Monumental work; still the most valuable history of dogma . . . luminous analysis of the problems . . . abounds in suggestion and stimulus and can be neglected by no one who desires to understand the history of thought in this most important field," Dutcher's Guide to Historical Literature. Translated by Neil Buchanan. Index. Unabridged reprint in 4 volumes. Vol I: Beginnings to the Gnostics and Marcion. Vol II & III: 2nd century to the 4th century Fathers. Vol IV & V: 4th century Councils to the Carlovingian Renaissance. Vol VI & VII: Period of Clugny (c. 1000) to the Reformation, and after. Total of cii + 2407pp. 5⅜ x 8.

T904 Vol I Paperbound **$2.50**
T905 Vol II & III Paperbound **$2.50**
T906 Vol IV & V Paperbound **$2.50**
T907 Vol VI & VII Paperbound **$2.50**
The set **$10.00**

THE GUIDE FOR THE PERPLEXED, Maimonides. One of the great philosophical works of all time and a necessity for everyone interested in the philosophy of the Middle Ages in the Jewish, Christian, and Moslem traditions. Maimonides develops a common meeting-point for the Old Testament and the Aristotelian thought which pervaded the medieval world. His ideas and methods predate such scholastics as Aquinas and Scotus and throw light on the entire problem of philosophy or science vs. religion. 2nd revised edition. Complete unabridged Friedländer translation. 55 page introduction to Maimonides's life, period, etc., with an important summary of the GUIDE. Index. lix + 414pp. 5⅜ x 8. T351 Paperbound **$2.00**

Orientalia

ORIENTAL RELIGIONS IN ROMAN PAGANISM, F. Cumont. A study of the cultural meeting of east and west in the Early Roman Empire. It covers the most important eastern religions of the time from their first appearance in Rome, 204 B.C., when the Great Mother of the Gods was first brought over from Syria. The ecstatic cults of Syria and Phrygia — Cybele, Attis, Adonis, their orgies and mutilatory rites; the mysteries of Egypt — Serapis, Isis, Osiris, the dualism of Persia, the elevation of cosmic evil to equal stature with the deity, Mithra; worship of Hermes Trismegistus; Ishtar, Astarte; the magic of the ancient Near East, etc. Introduction. 55pp. of notes; extensive bibliography. Index. xxiv + 298pp. 5⅜ x 8.
T321 Paperbound **$1.75**

THE MYSTERIES OF MITHRA, F. Cumont. The definitive coverage of a great ideological struggle between the west and the orient in the first centuries of the Christian era. The origin of Mithraism, a Persian mystery religion, and its association with the Roman army is discussed in detail. Then utilizing fragmentary monuments and texts, in one of the greatest feats of scholarly detection, Dr. Cumont reconstructs the mystery teachings and secret doctrines, the hidden organization and cult of Mithra. Mithraic art is discussed, analyzed, and depicted in 70 illustrations. 239pp. 5⅜ x 8. T323 Paperbound **$1.85**

CHRISTIAN AND ORIENTAL PHILOSOPHY OF ART, A. K. Coomaraswamy. A unique fusion of philosopher, orientalist, art historian, and linguist, the author discusses such matters as: the true function of aesthetics in art, the importance of symbolism, intellectual and philosophic backgrounds, the role of traditional culture in enriching art, common factors in all great art, the nature of medieval art, the nature of folklore, the beauty of mathematics, and similar topics. 2 illustrations. Bibliography. 148pp. 5⅜ x 8. T378 Paperbound **$1.25**

TRANSFORMATION OF NATURE IN ART, A. K. Coomaraswamy. Unabridged reissue of a basic work upon Asiatic religious art and philosophy of religion. The theory of religious art in Asia and Medieval Europe (exemplified by Meister Eckhart) is analyzed and developed. Detailed consideration is given to Indian medieval aesthetic manuals, symbolic language in philosophy, the origin and use of images in India, and many other fascinating and little known topics. Glossaries of Sanskrit and Chinese terms. Bibliography. 41pp. of notes. 245pp. 5⅜ x 8.
T368 Paperbound **$1.75**

BUDDHIST LOGIC, F.Th. Stcherbatsky. A study of an important part of Buddhism usually ignored by other books on the subject: the Mahayana buddhistic logic of the school of Dignaga and his followers. First vol. devoted to history of Indian logic with Central Asian continuations, detailed exposition of Dignaga system, including theory of knowledge, the sensible world (causation, perception, ultimate reality) and mental world (judgment, inference, logical fallacies, the syllogism), reality of external world, and negation (law of contradiction, universals, dialectic). Vol. II contains translation of Dharmakirti's Nyayabindu with Dharmamottara's commentary. Appendices cover translations of Tibetan treatises on logic, Hindu attacks on Buddhist logic, etc. The basic work, one of the products of the great St. Petersburg school of Indian studies. Written clearly and with an awareness of Western philosophy and logic; meant for the Asian specialist and for the general reader with only a minimum of background. Vol. I, xii + 559pp. Vol. II, viii + 468pp. 5⅜ x 8½.
T955 Vol. I Paperbound **$2.35**
T956 Vol. II Paperbound **$2.35**
The set **$4.70**

THE TEXTS OF TAOISM. The first inexpensive edition of the complete James Legge translations of the Tao Te King and the writings of Chinese mystic Chuang Tse. Also contains several shorter treatises: the T'ai Shang Tractate of Actions and Their Retributions; the King Kang King, or Classic of Purity; the Yin Fu King, or Classic of the Harmony of the Seen and Unseen; the Yu Shu King, or Classic of the Pivot of Jade; and the Hsia Yung King, or Classic of the Directory for a Day. While there are other translations of the Tao Te King, this is the only translation of Chuang Tse and much of other material. Extensive introduction discusses differences between Taoism, Buddhism, Confucianism; authenticity and arrangement of Tao Te King and writings of Chuang Tse; the meaning of the Tao and basic tenets of Taoism; historical accounts of Lao-tse and followers; other pertinent matters. Clarifying notes incorporated into text. Originally published as Volumes 39, 40 of SACRED BOOKS OF THE EAST series, this has long been recognized as an indispensible collection. Sinologists, philosophers, historians of religion will of course be interested and anyone with an elementary course in Oriental religion or philosophy will understand and profit from these writings. Index. Appendix analyzing thought of Chuang Tse. Vol. I, xxiii + 396pp. Vol. II, viii + 340pp. 5⅜ x 8½.
T990 Vol. I Paperbound **$2.00**
T991 Vol. II Paperbound **$2.00**

EPOCHS OF CHINESE AND JAPANESE ART, Ernest T. Fenollosa. Although this classic of art history was written before the archeological discovery of Shang and Chou civilizations, it is still in many respects the finest detailed study of Chinese and Japanese art available in English. It is very wide in range, covering sculpture, carving, painting, metal work, ceramics, textiles, graphic arts and other areas, and it considers both religious and secular art, including the Japanese woodcut. Its greatest strength, however, lies in its extremely full, detailed, insight-laden discussion of historical and cultural background, and in its analysis of the religious and philosophical implications of art works. It is also a brilliant stylistic achievement, written with enthusiasm and verve, which can be enjoyed and read with profit by both the Orientalist and the general reader who is interested in art. Index. Glossary of proper names. 242 illustrations. Total of 704 pages. 5⅜ x 8½.

T364-5 Two vol. set, paperbound **$5.00**

THE VEDANTA SUTRAS OF BADARAYANA WITH COMMENTARY BY SANKARACHARYA. The definitive translation of the consummation, foremost interpretation of Upanishads. Originally part of SACRED BOOKS OF THE EAST, this two-volume translation includes exhaustive commentary and exegesis by Sankara; 128-page introduction by translator, Prof. Thibaut, that discusses background, scope and purpose of the sutras, value and importance of Sankara's interpretation; copious footnotes providing further explanations. Every serious student of Indian religion or thought, philosophers, historians of religion should read these clear, accurate translations of documents central to development of important thought systems in the East. Unabridged republication of Volumes 34, 38 of the Sacred Books of the East. Translated by George Thibault. General index, index of quotations and of Sanskrit. Vol. I, cxxv + 448pp. Vol. II, iv + 506pp. 5⅜ x 8½.

T994 Vol. I Paperbound **$2.00**
T995 Vol. II Paperbound **$2.00**

THE UPANISHADS. The Max Müller translation of the twelve classical Upanishads available for the first time in an inexpensive format: Chandogya, Kena, Aitareya aranyaka and upanishad, Kaushitaki, Isa, Katha, Mundaka, Taittiriyaka Brhadaranyaka, Svetarasvatara. Prasna — all of the classical Upanishads of the Vedanta school—and the Maitriyana Upanishad. Originally volumes 1, 15 of SACRED BOOKS OF THE EAST series, this is still the most scholarly translation. Prof. Müller, probably most important Sanskritologist of nineteenth century, provided invaluable introduction that acquaints readers with history of Upanishad translations, age and chronology of texts, etc. and a preface that discusses their value to Western readers. Heavily annotated. Stimulating reading for anyone with even only a basic course background in Oriental philosophy, religion, necessary to all Indologists, philosophers, religious historians. Transliteration and pronunciation guide. Vol. I, ciii + 320pp. Vol. II, liii + 350pp.

T992 Vol. I Paperbound **$2.00**
T993 Vol. II Paperbound **$2.00**
The set **$4.00**